OPEN PAPERS

Odysseas Elytis

OPEN PAPERS

TRANSLATED BY
Olga Broumas
& T Begley

COPPER CANYON PRESS

Publication of this book is supported by a grant from the National Endowment for the Arts and a grant from the Lannan Foundation. Additional support to Copper Canyon Press has been provided by the Andrew W. Mellon Foundation, the Lila Wallace–Reader's Digest Fund, and the Washington State Arts Commission. Copper Canyon Press is in residence with Centrum at Fort Worden State Park.

Translation of this book was funded in part by the Witter Bynner Foundation for Poetry, Inc.

Library of Congress Cataloging-in-Publication Data
Elytēs, Odysseas, 1911–
[Anoichto chartia. English]
Open papers / selected essays of Odysseas Elytis ;
translated by Olga Broumas & T. Begley.
p. cm.
ISBN 1-55659-070-9
1. European poetry – 20th century – History and criticism.
2. Elytēs, Odysseas, 1911– – Biography.   3. Poets – 20th century – Biography.
1. Title.
PN1271.A4913 1994
889'.132 – DC20
[B]
94-31307

COPPER CANYON PRESS
P.O. BOX 271, PORT TOWNSEND, WASHINGTON 98368

THE TRANSLATORS thank Odysseas Elytis for his faith and encouragement.

They thank the editors of *The American Poetry Review*, *Ploughshares*, and *Shambhala Sun*, where versions of these essays were first published.

They thank the Witter Bynner Foundation for a grant that supported this work in a difficult time.

They thank Maria Moschoni, Georgia Stathopoulou and Anita A. Williams.

Olga Broumas thanks her collaborator, T Begley, for her immeasurable contribution to rendering this joyous and complex text audible in the key of English.

Contents

Introduction

SETTING ASIDE the manuscript of *Open Papers*, I have stepped out of my office to walk in the garden. My eye follows a newly placed river of stones leading to a headwaters of stone in the valleys beneath three stone mountains. To the east, a sea of grass. To the west, plains of moss. And I think not of the ch'an and zen gardens of China and Japan, but of Odysseas Elytis and the poetry of correspondence, a poetics that stretches back in an unbroken line over twenty-six centuries of western culture; I think of Sappho's

> *Eros seizes and shakes my very soul*
> *like the wind on the mountain*
> *shaking ancient oaks*

From Sappho's fragment *ca.* 600 B.C.E. to the contemporary Elytis, Greek poets have sought a lyric rooted in a language of correspondence rather than abstract emotion. The surrealism of Elytis is a stimulant to the senses, a hyper-awareness that apprehends a world *of* the senses. The vision itself may have changed, but the experience of information derived through the senses is a poetics of correspondence not the least at odds with the poetics of Sappho as she developed the Mixolydian mode, working by *ear*, her *melos* (music) inseparable from her *logos* (meaning). Sappho's impassioned songs of self become Whitman's songs of self and Elytis's ecology of the psyche.

In an interview with Ivar Ivask in 1975, Elytis responded to a frequent categorization of himself as a poet of ecstasy or joy: "This is fundamentally wrong. I believe that poetry on a certain level of accomplishment is neither optimistic nor pessimistic. It represents rather a third state of the spirit where opposites cease to exist. There are no more opposites beyond a certain level of elevation. Such poetry is like nature itself, which is neither good nor bad, beautiful nor ugly; it simply *is*. Such poetry is no longer subject to habitual everyday distinctions.... The final goal of every exploration is inescapably nature. This, obviously, is very much part of the Hellenic tradition." And yet Elytis has never used ancient myth in any way resembling a traditional manner. "Since my chief interest was to find the *sources* of the neo-Hellenic world, I kept the mechanisms of myth-making but not the figures of mythology." And, finally, "There is a search for paradise in my poetry. When I say 'paradise,' I do not conceive of it in the Christian sense. It is another world which is incorporated into our own, and it is our fault that we are unable to grasp it." The "neo-Hellenic" world of Elytis is stripped of the romanticized idyllic countrysides of daydreams, but illuminated by the same intense blue and yellow transparencies of the Mediterranean of antiquity nevertheless. In short, he has not merely conceived of Hell and Paradise made of the same exact elements, but has experienced firsthand the extremes of that truth, binding as it does the cry of horror and death to the cry of ecstasy, the Janus mask of the terrible and the sublime.

In "Équivalences chez Picasso," Elytis notes that the severe lines of a bare mountain ("*les lignes sévères d'une montagne nue*") suggest simplicity and evoke actions on a moral plane that in turn teach us a world of enchantment and demand that we achieve such a realization of poetic potential "beyond all preconceived ideas" ("*dehors de tout préjugé*"), beyond any notion of prejudgment. In "First Things First," he observes, "And yet from *what is* to *what could be* you cross a bridge that takes you, no more, no less, from Hell to Paradise. Even more strange: a Paradise made of the very elements of Hell. The only difference lies in our perception of the arrangement of these elements, which is easy to understand if you imagine it applied to the architecture of ethics and emotions... The common characteristic of all poets is their dissent from current reality." In the United States, Odysseas Elytis, recipient of the 1979 Nobel Prize for Literature, is not yet a household name. Even in Greece, where his work is a topic for passionate discussion, one must occasionally defend Elytis's use of archaic words and regional figures of speech, explaining that precision in language will not be limited to the parlance of the streetcorner, especially when the terrain of the poem is the dreamscape of the subconscious. How can one entirely abandon the old "pure" *katharevousa* or the profound accuracy and intimacy of regional dialect?

In a suite of poems based upon an imaginary conversation between an older man, "the Antiphonist," and a rebellious young woman, *Maria Nephele*, the poet utilizes a mathematical structure drawn from Pythagorean theories of harmony, the voices echoing the strophic/anti-strophic composition of ancient tragedies and liturgies. Perhaps this complex limpidity has contributed to his reputation as a poet of the cognoscenti and literati as opposed to, say, the more blue collar Yannis Ritsos. All agree, however, that he is one of the three great mountains of Greek modernism, along with George Seferis and Ritsos.

"Poetic metaphor," Elytis insists, "instantaneously transcending terrible distances, renders the spiritual physiognomy of objects at their birth." Objects and ideas exist in locality, he suggests, and it is through understanding such a context for objects and ideas that correspondences and resonances can be revealed. His work, then, becomes an ecology of the psyche, as in this declaration, from the poem "Sun the First":

I give my hand to justice
Transparent fountain source at the peak
My sky is deep and unaltered
What I love is always being born
What I love is beginning always

When a great artist gives over his or her life to the process of art, to the demonic magical practice of her or his art, and when that commitment is articulated as an act of devotion, a world is transformed. It doesn't matter that Picasso professed socialist ethics while indulging in unspeakably crass rites of the bourgeois nouveau riche; what does matter is the line and the architecture that reveal another world. "Picasso," Elytis points out, "has never searched for Greece, but Greece has found him." The "Greekness" of which Elytis speaks is not a metaphor or merely a matter of nationality, but of psychic energy and apprehension of a world defined by particular light, as by a handful of ideas that have come to dominate western civilization. Just as I, walking in my garden, see how these deep rich greens, these gray skies, distant blue mountains and cold hard sea have come to shape my own psyche and provide my own points of analogy, correspondence, and metaphor. The "Greekness" of which Elytis speaks is born of an inner light, and comes to be understood only as it is lived.

"I'd like, in presenting these texts," Elytis writes, "to confess at once: I am not a critic or a prose writer. Psychological analysis does nothing for me; my powers of observation are largely absent, and every attempt at description bores me to death. I have no way to exhaust a subject except to live it...writing." Then what *are* these "open papers"? Reflections on the life of poetry.

Elytis, born in 1911 in Iráklion, Crete, of parents from Lesbos, left Crete for Athens at the age of three, his parents concerned about the beginning of World War I. Born Odysseas Alepoudélis, in choosing Elytis as a nom de plume the poet recalls such classically Greek ideals as *Ellas* (Hellas), *elpídha* (hope), *eleuthería* (freedom), and of course *Eléni* (Helen). "Contrary to those who strive an entire life to 'fix' their literary likeness, I'm intent every hour and each moment on destroying mine, my face turned to prototype alone, whose nature is to be endlessly created, ready to begin again precisely on account of life and art's oneness, which exists far before or after the sashaying of salons and of cafes."

And thus Elytis, "the most Greek of Greek poets," a poet who consciously resisted learning the English language perhaps because of its influence on his friend and fellow Nobel Laureate George Seferis, poet and translator of Eliot and Pound; Elytis the poet who resists conventional autobiography; Elytis the translator of Éluard, Rimbaud, Jouve, Lautréamont, Brecht and Lorca; Elytis the poet of the Greek Resistance, of the famous Albanian Campaign, and of the cultural revolution of 1935; Elytis the young poet prepared to risk it all for his solitary art can be found in these essays, is revealed among his *Anihtá Hartiá*, his *Open Papers*.

Writing fifty years ago, in 1945, with the end of World War II in sight, Seferis posed a question that remains absolutely current: "What should an intellectual do in the face of the religious fanaticisms unleashed by the political orthodoxies of the time?" He divides artists into two camps: "those who devote themselves to their work," believing the work itself will provide the best answer; and those who opt for one of the existing camps of social struggle. "My belief," Seferis wrote, "is that the solid artist is one of the most responsible beings on earth. He carries the burden of the responsibility for the struggle between life and death." And it is precisely such a mantle of responsibility that Elytis assumes.

xii

A dozen years ago, during my visit to his apartment in Athens, he told me, "A real poet needs an audience of three. Since any poet worth his salt has two intelligent friends, he spends his whole life searching for the third reader." This from a poet whose poems are recited by cabbies and in tavernas all over Greece. Elytis's name has been associated since publication of his first book, *Orientations*, in 1939, with a poetry of deep moral awareness, passionate openness, and a distinctly personal mythology. Most of our visit was spent exploring correspondences between Greek and classical Chinese poetics, especially *ch'an* (zen) poetry. And indeed his insights, both in the poetry and in the prose, turn on his comprehension of what Buddhists call "co-dependent origination." In the poetry of Elytis, this is most clearly seen in what he has called a struggle to achieve limpidity – so that one sees through a surface image into an image within, finding yet another, deeper correspondence. His keeping of "the mechanisms of myth-making but not the figures of mythology" is a poetic equivalent of Confucius telling his followers, "Worship the virtue of ancestors, not ancestors themselves."

Walking among the deep and varying shadows of my garden in the woods of the Pacific Northwest, in a single shaft of yellow sunlight, I find the sleepy Arab gardens of Seferis and the expansive, exquisitely intense lyrical poetry of Elytis, both writing – quite differently – a poetry of light and passion. "One's Paradise," Confucius observed, "is one's own inner nature." As is one's Hell. *Open Papers* chronicles the life of poetry in modern Greece while identifying the allegiances and passionate particulars of one of the supreme poets of an age. It opens a world that is palpably within this one.

– SAM HAMILL

OPEN PAPERS

First Things First

A

...I'D LIKE, in presenting these texts, to confess at once: I am not a critic or a prose writer. Psychological analysis does nothing for me, my powers of observation are largely absent, and every attempt at description bores me to death. I have no way to exhaust a subject except to live it...writing. Which means I dive in a long way before clarifying what I want to say, I let myself drift, here and there, preferring the darkest corners, trying to *see* or, if not, at least to *touch* and *recognize*.

As much as I can. Because, unfortunately, currents often take me, I lose myself near something I like and – as my pen runs away with its own charm, arousing in me other instincts – I notice, as soon as I exit this strange swim, that I have drifted far, sometimes not even having touched what I was after. To be more precise, only then do I know what I must say. But it is already late. You don't step in the same river twice, to honor in my turn the great Ephesian.

There are, of course, poets endowed with admirable critical talent. There are also those who never overstep the limits Poetry sets them. My own sin – and stubbornness – is that, not belonging to the former, I refused to conform to the latter, believing that what is generally forbidden a law-abiding essayist as bad taste can not only be forgiven a poet who wants to remain really himself wherever he goes, but perhaps even be ascribed to his credit. I'd go so far as to say that even in a field such as criticism or essays, surveyed by the precise instruments of thought, it is a poet's duty to risk sudden and uncontrolled *coups d'esprit*, to provoke new oscillations by syntactical intervention and to acquire, in style and speech, something of a young organism's shimmer or the carriage of a bird toward the heights.

Naturally, such a thing is not without danger. My ideal may have always been transparence, and, at least in Poetry, the psychic clarity an expression encompassed could make me believe I had achieved it. Yet the transparence of meanings was a different matter, and I had to travel

3

far and arrive at hyperboles that marked my first texts deeply before I found its analog. Rereading them today I feel that they revive in me, along with the enchantment of the "heroic age," also a strong revulsion. Inexcusable, sometimes even repugnant enthusiasms, phrases of improbable if not forced length, unredeemable lyric exaltations, glottal acrobatics and pyrotechnics of phrase, taken all together, compose an excess of speech that, on top of everything else, never let me speak directly about the motives and justifications of my life.

It's all right; I neither disown these texts nor seek to correct their basic structure. To my eyes they represent the time when, at least for one adolescent, writing could only be a conscious, uncompromising and constant enactment of unorthodoxy. That's the point. When I picked up the pen I wanted to feel, I remember, above all else free, as though I were in the mountains, scratched by wild branches, crushing now and then a musky pea, fording ditches and drinking handfuls of clear water. I wanted more than anything to sing differently than the others, even if that meant off-key. I mean that the weight of enchantment fell on violation. I came to see, slowly over the years, that it was less a simple willfulness than it was a foretaste of the deeper truth that youth unconsciously carries, so judge it kindly and pass it by. Even if it caused the sins I listed, my inexperience was to blame and not the principle itself that made me suspect and systematically defy the already established.

My red cloth – my reddest – was, and is, the facile. I suspected it everywhere: in the sermons on simplicity, order and restraint. I sniffed it out in the recipes for prose whose duty, so they said, was to restrict itself to small succinct phrases and avoid the devils of *iconoplastic* analogies and emotional associations. Besides, I was becoming increasingly disgusted by the fact that everyone seemed to lean, through some kind of neo-intellectualism, toward abstract expression, willful ellipses – that ultimate fear, lest we tell all – studied innuendo, and indirect references to older educational strata: a true feast for all species of contemporary hydrocephalics!

In reaction, I reached for the other extreme. I wanted to make it clear that our language was ready and able to render the most elaborate rhetorical schema, follow the most explosive delirium, be endowed with the brightest luxury, and fill two or three pages, if need be, with a single phrase whose orbit inscribes its trajectory with the largest possible leisure and grace, like a comet ambling in slow curves and losing itself in the night sky, sparkling. Granted, I may not have been the one to put this into practice, but I believed that, sooner or later, someone simply had to liberate our language from its inferiority complex, detach it from its voluntary invalidism and help it find its strength by activating its secret abilities – all those juices whose vivid circulation warms even the most theoretical expression – to rid it of the stench of the office, the jaundice of parchment, the terrible curds of constipation.

I KNOW how ultimately difficult simplicity can be and do not need to be referred, again, to the Ancients. Simplicity was different for the Ancients. Their hands had not yet met the wrinkle; that is, they had not yet come across the need to efface it. But as soon as every cheek is no longer fresh, your longing to caress makes you invent a newer, tighter skin. Here's something that needs you to be man and thinker, both, to take it seriously! When this celebrated simplicity is achieved at all in contemporary texts, it is clearly at the unfortunate expense of a host of other elements – the fever of the well-imagined, the joy of having all your limbs and vigor – which our theoreticians, turning the bitter into sweet, eagerly proclaimed useless but which I believe are still as necessary to an uncompromised reader as salt on food.

Of course, to be honest, such a reader becomes more rare with time. We rush to call our famous epoch "risky" while deep down it swarms with all kinds of "abdicators," strange as that may seem. Never before have there been so many collective retreats from freedom's most elementary meaning, so many mass attempts to reduce ideal simplicity to simplified practice. Surely some average American, having understood he has conquered us, is taking revenge. We throw out our ideas as soon as they start to bother us, as if they were paper napkins. As for the new ones, we "open" them like cans of food and rush to consume them lest they spoil. Ask us to transmit our thoughts, no problem: we resort to the nearest dialect, even foreign ones, since the result is about the same either way.

Unless, of course, we cling to tradition, in which case we run to any school manual for some ideal demotic, and the more intact we transfer it to our writing, nicely starched and ironed, the more we bask in the praise of our critics who, by a tragic alienation from reality of which they are unaware, run the risk of preserving Noumas' grammarian era. In literature, and especially modern poetry, such a mentality – so elementary it discerns only black and white – has achieved a plethora of replicas, as if from a mold: if you don't whine, it means you're a hedonist, or worse, in nirvana; if you don't recount your blues, you have none, you're carefree; if you speak of Greece, you're a provincial, without ecumenical spirit; if you care for your language, you're backward, outside the beat of your time; and finally, if you seek to create something solid, you are a formalist and an esthete.

The literary cafes of the entire world, from St. Germain-des-Prés to Greenwich Village, obey an unwritten law expressly forbidding the poet – in our licentious era, no less – from taking up meanings fundamental to his art, simply because our time has made them empty, instead of insisting, as in fact it should, on their return to, and original function in, current reality. One does not renew oneself in love by abolishing women: one simply becomes a masturbator. I personally believe that a virgin eye fresh from familiar surroundings can tell us more than a common eye that visited some virgin region. We need only remember how Aragon spoke of the legendary city the day after the First World War in *Paysan de Paris* and how the cosmonaut Leonov spoke of the unknown void the day after his space excursion, to feel the difference.

It is the absence of imagination that turns humans into invalids of reality – and let the practical-minded, who will one day leave their life without having sounded it, twice illiterate, talk. *La seule imagination me rend compte de ce qui peut être, et c'est assez pour lever un peu le terrible interdit.*

AND YET from *what is* to *what could be* you cross a bridge that takes you, no more, no less, from Hell to Paradise. And more bizarre: a Paradise composed of the exact same material as Hell. The only difference is our perception of the material's arrangement – more easily understood by imagining it applied to ethical and emotional architectures – yet it's enough to pinpoint the immeasurable difference. If the reality created by people whose half-mast emotions and sensations disallow, now and perhaps forever, the *other architecture* or, in other words, the *revolutionary re-synthesis*, then, to my thinking, only the spirit is free and able to take it on. This is the common qualifying trait characterizing the genus *poet*: dissent from current reality. From there on, the specifics of each poet's reaction, while inevitably categorizing him, cannot possibly be construed as the essential qualifying trait.

Many people (most in fact, since Christianity formulated a specific and homogenous psychic world) seek to express their profound distress at such dissent and to represent the conditions of the Hellbound by an increasing hyperbole of shrillness and drama. Then there are others who are closer, in my opinion, to imagination than thought, who are by their nature bound to a constant "reparation" of life, who feel the overwhelming need to "directly" express their tropism toward the vision of a Paradise. This phenomenon has nothing to do with optimism or pessimism, as a majority of young people like to think, aided and abetted as they unfortunately are by our critics, who should have enlightened them instead.

As if half our poets had no ideals and the other half no griefs, and did not share a common fate of needing to, at some point, divorce their responsibilities from a condemned and desensitized world! But the poetic state – one must repeat this though it seems self-evident – is a *third state* not subject to daily life's contradictions and distinctions. It is a para-signifier, notated in words but interpreted in the soul by reverberations so far-reaching that they sometimes arrive (and it is then that they are closest to their ultimate aim) at something totally unrelated to the words' original meaning. The sun is unrelated to sunniness, the sea to boating, death to zero and the firmament to infinity or, in other words, nature to *naturolatry* and rebellion to revolution, as a constant, permanent and incurable mentality of our times would have us think – the same mentality that measures poetic seriousness in direct proportion to its darkness (light has always been considered painless in Greece, how strange!), to raise a most typical example.

But if you catch birds with woven reeds, you never catch their song. For that you need another kind of reed, a magic reed, and who can manufacture it if not given it from the beginning? Bless its existence! Where it touches words and their marriages, the true night falls and the actual sun rises and all violations lose their simple – as the simple see it – arbitrariness, assuming instead the same position in contemporary texts that orthodoxies once had in the classics. Revirgining is their justification. Or, in other words: the splendor of youth and of error.

7

B

THE SPLENDOR of youth is, to a point, the splendor of error. Jealous the old, who have everything previewed! The nightingale will never come sing over your wisdom. It won't, darlin', it won't.

—Who speaks?

—Noman! Noman!

O voices, reaching from the unknown, half-questions and half-tyrannical oracles, meteorites of inner space, fragments of conscience calcified on sirens' lips angered by wind, bellows brazened in a demonic sound chamber, *ou-ou, ou-ouou*, large invisible surface under the forest while over it peaks the need to pierce the sky like a nightingale!

—But who speaks? Nothing is audible in the dark. The words, where are they? Not these, the others, the way they were before losing their edge, before gathering hair from one mouth to the next? When first they shivered and the Greek spoke?

—In the water... In the water...on a night my mother lay awake, a piece of moon in her hands. It was red, huge, pointed like a saw on its cutting edge, and smoking. Sitting on a boulder, she did not speak, just looked away toward Smallwater. A harmonica wept the whole length of the shore and you saw shadows lengthen. Then wind came up. I heard, one by one, the leaves talk in my sleep. "Child, small child." The water rocked me, and the land as well, and the windows shining in the distance, and the white suspended chambers.

—It was a pitch black night. The waves lowed wildly. An old woman with unbraided white hair and a silver paisley on her shoulders held him by the hand and walked on – in the uproar.

—She was beautiful! Beautiful! Right angel fragrant all over from rosemary. In a few hours she drank all my darkness, down to the last drop. At dawn, when I opened my eyes, she stood turned to the East, a wet, transparent shell raised in two fingers. She studied it like a prophet, I remember, and said:

Νάγ' ἰωδόσσα ἠνὶς μυριόλεον ἐνιπέσσα
'Ιτόεν οὐ κιλδάνα. Συμβιδὶ δ' άς. Παμφώετις.

—Crazy, she was delirious, you couldn't make out a word. Nothing.

—I'll give you a skin people can see through. You'll have no secret. You'll belong to everyone. All light.

Ἀλλότερος ἢ θὶν παρὰ σαλτὸς ἰαῖος. Κιδάναν φερ᾽ ἄλκαν
Ὑμμήταον, ἰμίπαμπον
Παμβωετὶ νικώτερον
Σχὰς ὀλλεπίων λύκτωρ κὺν θαλτὸς οὐ ἰατὸς
Παιδόεν ἰρισίμας. Θόης, θόη. Θμώς.

Only so does surf or foliage talk.

—Just like a curse: a curse the wind speaks night and day, unstable syllables that trick the nightingales to delirium.

—FROM CHILDHOOD he took to letters wrong, he asked for "a script of sun's seaweed." Who else understands it? Only he kept the command.

—It couldn't happen otherwise, impossible. Someone had to be found. I started training on a smile; a difficult thing, my lips hurt me. I had to regurgitate years of childhood diseases, family mourning and neuroses to reach the place where I could give them a proud mountain's carriage, the habits of the sunset and the east. But people, doubting, brooded in their souls. Some even asked me to account for that tear I didn't shed.

—Who, really, betrayed the nightingales? People went, others came. They territorialized, they legalized. "Leave," they shouted to the poet, "Judas the traitor too wouldn't conform!"

—For no reason did I want to give in. It was enough the women were weeping. I envied only their tenderness. I took the sun in my apron like a flower and opened its petals one by one. What *had* the wise been saying? It was blue with a shiny patch in the middle. A funeral passed in the distance. I didn't feel like crossing myself. I felt a different serenity, something like a great distilled intoxication. In fact, someone cursed me. I thought of Christ and the Romans.

—With two kinds of ears at night each hears death, which walks directly at us. A charm, a betrayal and, if you lift the hem, a sob; each victory cast from a thousand small defeats!

—Things started to come closer, trustful, like birds. The most difficult I domesticated with a smile. I made a whole world my familiar and started training it, shaping it and charging it with what sleep, in the bitter hours, had taught me.

A small sick child made me try to plant shells for the first time. I drew courage and began with seawater and a small church. It smelled like a cave and there, close to the altar, lilies suddenly blazed. From weeds I made names, and from names women I embraced, their fresh waists trembling like running water. At last, I only had to think of something to see it scored in capitals on stone. A large weight left me, as if the jails and hospitals had emptied in one stroke.

Winds came; I catechized and dispersed them. They beat the boys' shutters, making them turn the other rib, then girls flew in, naked, unfolding hair gilded by a thousand gleaming drops. Eons had longed for this uprising. I took pleasure and revenge.

—He too lived in a cell and stared at the same wall. A luminous stain reached now and then from the small high window, trembling; that was all.

—It can't be, I kept saying, it can't be. For such a bright stain to exist, somewhere there must be a sun. I shaped it, like the hungry knead bread in their sleep.

—Doors slammed every so often, then a commotion of horses and bodies dragging on the tiles. A creature full of ugliness, a fat human with a whip, sat in the saddle and gave orders. Priests, Judges and Policemen in brilliant uniforms surrounded him. And the people tried to speak but couldn't, as in nightmares. They only moaned mmm... mmm... mmm...

—Strange, no one made an effort to extract anything from Paradise. Only a few tried to deserve it, as if they'd done something wrong. They tormented their flesh too, as if God had created it for that purpose. I revolted. Such hubris I could fight only with flowers, rain them on mourning's willful persistence like stones – I, alone, wearing a small green leaf for my own loss.

—On death's eve, tell me, how is a body suffered?

—On death's eve, tell me, how is a *white* voice written?

—We walked on some shore, not feeling each other. Someone's walking "was bothered by angel's wings." Until suddenly everything turned dark, and it seemed to him the far neck of the cove groaned deeply.

—It's that I couldn't bear to be half in this world; I went after Poetry as after a woman, to give me child, as though from one to the other I might not die. I never thought to cry that everything was dim. If it were possible to save a palmful of clear water! I cried in front of waves and saw in poems the sky clear.

—Goddesses of the *pelago*, remember? He was a child, a small child. "Don't cry," they told him, "don't cry." He turned then and opened his eyes. And true, from the beginning, a great sun began to dawn new in his tears.

—A gift, nothing else, something to give to the others. I put flowers in the Virgin's arms and in the Saints' too, girls and birds. I remember the yelling all around me. What could I do? For a small bright moment, literally, I was sold; I gave back even the wrinkles; I slept on something green, unsullied. Already my blood throbbed high in the sun.

IT HAPPENS occasionally that, on some inspiration, one reveals a different version of the world's cause and causality. And if one happens to be what's called "minimally poetic"?

Oh yes, especially then!

C

BEING MINIMALLY poetic, I loved Poetry the most, just as being minimally "patriotic," I loved Greece to the maximum. In any case, it's not from clumsiness that I become *other* when I pick up the pen. Truth emerges only from solitude's clear waters, smooth as a new statue, and the pen's solitude is among the greatest. Contrary to those who strive an entire life to "fix" their literary likeness, I'm intent every hour and each moment on destroying mine, my face turned to the prototype alone, whose nature is to be endlessly created, ready to begin again precisely on account of life and art's oneness, which exists far before or after the sashaying of salons and of cafes.

If this is called severity then I am severe and I recommend it to others, at least to those I love.

I don't know, but it seems that when ideas boil in a common pot, the steam billows so high you see nothing. And I have often noticed the strange dimensions of what I allowed to pass through me when I found it again at the end of my pen. There, at the end of the pen, fish writhe like truths, excuse me, I mean truths writhe like fish and a good thing too, as I'd never want a frozen truth in the world. A frozen truth for Greece, for instance, is its history as the official Greeks interpret it. Another is its history according to the Europeans. Live truth, I believe, is also its history, as you discover it rising like Aphrodite from your personal experience, so that events or monuments of art simply annotate and illustrate it.

Greece is, I have believed for some time, a concrete sensation worth finding a linear symbol for, whose analysis and discovery of analogs in all fields reproduces its history, its nature and physiognomy, automatically and at every moment.

From the time I was small I read, as much as a "child fanatic for letters" can read, the chronicles of this country (coldly, as if it weren't mine), and I traveled its regions and later took part in its adventures, those that coincided with my years. But I only came to truly know and love it by writing – writing those imperfect poems I wrote and, most importantly, *with no relation whatsoever to their content*. It was the discipline of poetry that was important. An unexpected School of reverse, relative to other Schools, *patriognosis*. And from then on I felt I was a Greek as another comes to feel he is a junkie or homosexual: organically, psychologically, sensationally and invincibly!

I knew how badly this might sound to the young who were impatient, and justly so, to appear independent and hip, and what risk I ran of seeming superficial, at least as superficial as our politicians' campaign speeches. Besides, I agreed completely with my more enlightened colleagues who lamented, in writing and in interviews, the off-handedness that plagued us, the inexcusable arrogance and hollowness that made us consider foreigners "dumb Franks" and invoke the "demon of our race," when often we couldn't even separate two donkeys' hay. I knew our national character flaws because, above all, I found them in myself. This kind of realism found its place in me next to my friends' voices crying, "We're just a Mideast principality," and "We're fit to be tied."

And yet the next day, at the end of my pen, I too was almost ready to shout "those dumb Franks!" Of course, it wasn't exactly that. It was rather the profound intuition that in their place we would have done better, or, more seriously, that in our place they might have vanished forever from history's proscenium. In their behavior and evaluation of reality, foreigners had always seemed more accurate, more impeccable than us. Still, I felt a terrifying awkwardness in my friendships with them, or worse: an inexplicable revulsion which I tried to check, lest it be a remnant of old prejudice. No. One day I understood there was no mystery. Simply, these people had everything, that is, much more than us *minus one*, which was for us a *plus* but as untranslated, untransmitted and inexplicable as the radiance of an eye or of a smile. So subtle and yet so huge that I was ultimately unable to recognize the image of the world in their art or the religion of Christ in their cathedrals.

It seems madness to say this in the twentieth century, when mother and child can lose each other in the shuffling of nations, after two cannibal wars, on the eve of a United Europe. The madness is lessened though and ultimately overturned when you consider the metals being assimilated in the crucible of the present, yielding a sensation so potent it seems to strike the first spark.

This sensation allowed me – without ever becoming servant to my poet – to perceive life by its poetic aspect deeply, throughout my *physical being*. Does one work of art appeal to me and not another, one human behavior agree with me and not another, the landscape, the house, the love affair – in this I was never ambivalent or felt the slightest unease. I know how the bread is baked, how the fishing boat prow is painted, and I know the psychic motions of a Halepás shaping clay, or of a Venizélos shaping the events of the First World War. It is a "key" which, along with everything else, much more than science unlocks our understanding of how the Parthenon arose or how the Greek language was preserved through four hundred years of slavery, not to mention that it gives you the wherewithal to support – realists, please excuse me – the notion that this small nation is not one and the same as other small nations.

It's not a limiting notion but rather a sensation as large as the world, a world with North and South poles charted already from either side by Kavafis and Solomós. Unfortunately, we live in this century of ideological taxonomy and get plastered with labels like a suitcase door to door, hotel to hotel, before even reaching the station. I never thought of myself as a nationalist, as I don't believe nationalists are the only ones who love – reduced by self-interest – Greece, as I never believed that only the Left is entitled to invoke social justice. How naïve I must be (because immoral I'm not, I insist) to believe I've found my own way to stand between these contradictions with a quiet conscience. What can we do? There's a dark sky up there, and while its physical properties never reach us, its metaphorical ones increasingly shroud the hearts and souls under Attica's stunned mountains that no longer know what to do with their lavender flares or the other-worldly message of their fragrant grasses. What good are they now that we're all homogenized, a grounded Boeing with the entire human sampler aboard? Logic has rid us of the absurdity of our clothes. That's progress, no irony, only now we are cold. Hale and ill trade bodies with unusual willingness, while in midair souls tangle. The young start out disgusted and Poetry is left to the memo-writers. The spirit of novelty substitutes for the *idiorhythmic* spirit. Our natural tendency towards what surpasses the human has moved from religion to marijuana. In a few years, potential Great Alexanders are turned into Constantini Paleológi. And there are many Kerko-gates. How will they get to them all?

Oh yes, I think the age of the literature of independent countries is over; we're entering the age of the *illiterature* of European provinces: something readable but not exactly language, concerning thought but not occupying it, and proffering imagination in a package, prefab as in the movies, requiring no alliance with our own. Fine. It's just that if no one asks for razor blades, like it or not, no one produces razor blades.

The entire mechanism that once collaborated in the composition of an impeccable and original page whose every nuance, verbal precision, comma, dash, parenthesis and pause produced a unique physiognomy, a mechanism in whose service lives were sacrificed, no kidding, is gone in one stroke. No customer exists for this page, no worshiper for these life-giving texts of written speech. Everyone wants the great truths and, beyond that, could care less how you tell them. It has never occurred to them that, in literature, the existence of truths is, at least to a point, inseparable from how they're told. I heard many young people admire André Breton, and even more so Albert Camus, but just as I started to rejoice I realized my mistake: what attracted them was the theory, the problems, this or that confirmation of the absurd in life, not a word about the one event that made their words irrefutable: that one of them

14

had achieved the most eloquent and the other the most diaphanous and unmarred prose in contemporary French letters. *Peste*, not *Noces* or *Été*. Automatic writing and not *Point du jour* or *Amour fou*. *Voilà où nous en sommes*, as they themselves would have said.

Nevertheless, I speak without melancholy; I know it's a mistake to prejudge the future's offspring while they're still in the womb. As a rule, progenitors are not smarter than posterity, and I believe that a society where our criteria will have absolutely no solvency is quite possible. Still it is our right, while the bridge planks still creak, to consider the danger and look with awe on the ravine. The celebrated global unification, which from one perspective we all want and work for, encompasses, on today's stage at least, oxymoronic situations, I should say phantasmagoric, whose meanings we have yet to make conscious.

Small young nations, brimming with juice and propulsive power, are forced to align with large and mighty ones that have lost their sap and are preserved only by these intravenous solutions of culture-serum. Their mutual spiritual introduction, through the skew of translation, ensures a *strabismus of values* which is immediately seized by a perfect technical organization that consolidates, establishes and presents it with all the external appearances of truth. Their passport is, inevitably, a good translation, which is much easier to achieve when the original text has been the least kneaded and transubstantiated in its mother tongue.

Dionysios Solomós, one of the five or ten greatest poets of the world and the centuries, remains unknown and will remain so while any number of fifth- and tenth-raters circulate in multiple editions.

Faced with so illogical a situation, I neither mourn nor revolt but simply lose my logic too, and let my irrationality be the final consequence of an uncontested logic. Let us pray. Let us do anything to one day have five or ten Solomí, so that the world is forced to come to Modern Greek as it was once forced to Ancient Greek by the Pindars and Sapphos.

D

LOVE FOR POETRY reached me from afar and, if one may say, outside literature. I became aware of it one day when, wandering the halls of the

British Museum, I found myself before a green papyrus with, if memory serves, a Sapphic fragment inscribed on it, clearly enough. After the piles of Latin manuscripts I'd swallowed in those years, I felt true relief; it seemed the world righted itself and took its proper place. These slender-bodied, compact capitals composed a graphic representation, luminous and mysterious at once, that made a friendly gesture through the centuries. As if I stood again on a Lesbian shore and heard our gardener's daughter sing. And suddenly, just as a sound or odor resurrects a long-buried impression before we even realize it, I saw myself again as a grade-school boy poking at the adult books, perplexed by a Pindar ode. I'm not mistaken; I'm sure the classic *ariston men hydor* has stayed with me since then. I wasn't so much drawn by the writing's essence as by its different arrangement. What came over people to make them combine words that didn't speak as we did every day? And why didn't they go to the edge of the page but stopped and started on the next line?

It never occurred to me to ask this of the songs I heard each day or of the poems we learned in school. Perhaps the simple meanings, perhaps the end-rhyme above all, gave me sufficient reason. But here, in the solid German edition in my hand, there were no such things. There was something else, which I didn't understand, because of course I didn't understand Ancient Greek. This, I thought, would surely explain the special manner of the writing.

I'm trying to express with today's words the emotion I had then; I found it again only in the spells which I observed, with fear and unrestrained admiration, being cast by our old Cretan cook. There was of course the ritual aspect, the repeated crossings, the drops of oil shaken in water, the sizzling, burning hairs, and the icons sprinkled with basil buds. But above all were the words, strange, "madtrap" mother would call them, entirely unrelated to anything else I heard and incoherent, "a transposition of dream into verbal idiom," as I might define it today. If I might speak of old impressions unintentionally gathered and corrected by later experience, I could assure you that a wave of mystery rose from the material body of the poem and, in it, the heretic use of speech corresponded to the heretic manner of the script. The older I got the more this correspondence deepened and reached the common root where the phenomenon of language and its symbolic representation meet.

* * *

THE WAVE of mystery radiated by each head-on collision and repulsion of the poet by his very means of expression was always latent in me and, when a chance encounter with a text that breached so-called convention allowed it to, it revived to strike back with equal force. I offer two specific examples: "Ishtar's Descent to Hades," the familiar Assyro-Babylonian poetic-religious text I first read in Dr. Pierre Mabille's book, *Le Miroir du Merveilleux*, in 1940, and a popularized work on Chinese script by Charles Leplay based on "River Song" by Li Po, which I came across in France in the spring of 1949.

The first reached to the depths of time. It showed how the human psyche was, from its inception, of one root with paralogical expression and its subjugation to liturgical tones throughout the most diverse civilizations, the most contradictory temperaments, the most acute sensory deviations, toward what we might call, how strange, "miracle-work." It contained the mechanism of fairy tale replicating the mechanism of dream, the tropism toward superhuman powers and the irreversible magic influence of numbers, a whole millennium before the cycle of our own civilization.

The second example reached to the depths of human imagination and the way it functions when it first feels the need to *broadcast*. Indeed I don't know of a more poetic imprint of the human spirit's inventiveness than the Chinese ideogram, especially in its first, its archaic, form. It is a literal x-ray taken just as the human mind equally grasps the world of matter and abstract thought in its net of schemata. Everything we have to date admired in the noblest of poems – analogical power, instant transformation of thought to image, the compound risks of imagination and its endless associative coherence – is simply the analytical phase of the same phenomenon which appears to us, after a mental dramatization, locked in a final stenograph.

The phenomenon of birth is, in speech and script as in human life, perhaps less impressive but definitely more powerful than the phenomenon of death. This is the sense in which I considered the birth and formation of Greek language – to return to the subject – not only as a poet who naturally seeks to waken objects from their slumber within words – to restore, I mean, their newborn condition – but also as a human being, whose sensitivity over time acquired the discipline of hearing, despite what we might call "the echo of phenomena." This too is a way of perception and right now I don't care if it threatens to drag me into irrationalities or outmoded theories.

I am getting ready to say: all the mouths that spoke this way and no other, articulating words of such phonetic perfection, so aligned to their grammatical one and never left behind, surpassed or altered by it – their lips unconsciously obeyed the specific radiance that physical phenomena assume in the Greek geography. Syllable by syllable they ferried meanings, embodying them in symbols of the same clean outline, the same lack of instability or musical confusion or shadow play, as the objects that birthed them: a mountain in the good weather of morning, a sun exploding from the sea, a pebble on the luminous seafloor.

The day I understood that Greek *has no chiaroscuro* I saw the logic of our inability to accept the Renaissance, and the last block to my grasp of the fundamental unity of Ancient, Byzantine and Modern Greek art took its leave. The phenomenon of Greek assumed for me the level of the inevitability of natural phenomena, and I came to fervently believe that the dimmest, most elusive foreign tongue would, after a millennium of life in this region, see its nature change, its sounds rise from the larynx and descend from the nose into the oral cavity, its words lose their useless syllables and be bathed and smoothed in light, their essence cleansed, if not exactly in the same way as Greek, at least parallel to it.

I'm not evaluating now; I'm ascertaining; it's something precious to me. Because today it helped me discern that even my small code of social behavior, my personal ethics, shall we say, are only a visible transcription of my esthetics, which are, in turn, a transcription of the natural conditions defining my human circumstance. But such a road, from its high side, leads finally to Metaphysics. As each wave of Poetry, having first crashed against my youth, returns to me, I feel closer to the light. Inside me, the meaning of Resurrection is inseparably bound to the meaning of Death, and very early on, in the secret region that is the antechamber of Birth. I rediscover my utter frugality in my peaceful symbiosis with such an enigma, for instance my intimacy with the coherence of secret meanings or the ritual that adds two angel wings to man; finally, in my fierce, characteristic emotion of pride, I come to find the words that make me an enemy of the grimace in Art (and in Life, of course), and make me obey the secret voice dictating without pause: *That which disempowers you is unfit for your song.*

So then yes, no doubt, my native tendency to sanctify sensation opens directly into the vision of Paradise. And grasping the abstract through sensation of the concrete makes me return, remorselessly, myself a victim of the eternal, to the absolute brilliance of a sea in the sun:

Elle est retrouvée
Quoi? L'éternité
C'est la mer mêlée au soleil...

E

FULL NOON, July, my eyes dazzled by the infinite lacerations of sun on surf, so much so that if the olive groves didn't exist I would have invented them in just such a moment, like a cricket. This is how I imagine the world was once created. And if not created better, human fear is at fault and should look at itself and admit what it is before it speaks. I speak. I want to descend, to fall into this blossoming fire and be taken up like an angel of the Lord...

Lightness, absence of weight, winging it in the heights as idea and experience of my sleep's free hours was always for me an ineffable hedonism. And perhaps it's not accidental that psychoanalysis, from its perspective, gave that phenomenon a specific sexual interpretation. We meet it often in fairy tales, songs and folk traditions. Whenever a human explodes and lets his instincts speak, he flies. I mean he defies the natural laws that nail him down. He protests against another near-adventure denied him. He wants to conquer, rape, ejaculate and extend his somatic powers the length of his mental functions. Those helmets and swords he struggles with from childhood, the disemboweled dolls and ruined clocks, what else could they mean? Reading history, particularly its anecdotal and cultural aspects, one is horrified at the lack of security humans have known. Still, if these people could return to life and read our history they would be horrified in turn, I believe, at the lack of insecurity we have achieved, living literally with both feet in one shoe. I have no nostalgia for the primitive but, on the other hand, I oppose every sadomasochistic deviation and, even more so, every cultivation of artificial bliss. I also feel obliged to seriously consider some typical symptoms of "rage," "rebellion" and "anarchy" characteristic of today's youth in order to understand them and applaud them as they deserve while they are still in their disinterested phase, that is, not yet channeled into camps seeking advantage.

How thick-skinned one must be to not understand that one suffers the same distress as they, and that only one's age is to blame if one's reactions differ from theirs. If I were a pantomime director, I'd choose an actor with the somatic abilities of an acrobat and set him on stage for half an hour trying to figure out how best to perch on his seat, one foot ending up over his head, the other under his ass, hands upside down behind his back, neck choked, mouth gagged, breath labored, and eyes half-closed. Another actor, a creature supposedly arrived from a distant planet, would wonder at this superhuman and futile effort, until, noticing something, he'd strike his forehead. He'd understand that this pained contortionist only sought to fulfill the posture needed by a complex machine for its function – a machine full of tubes, hoses, buttons, funnels, and aspirators – the fruit of years of research, which allowed him, by its incredibly mechanical perfection, albeit only in this posture, to maintain his life, breathe, eat, defecate, have sex and watch TV all without moving.

Forgive my facile symbolism, but our age is exactly commensurate with this truth: a stunning technical progress strives to heal humankind of ills caused by a stunning technical progress. How long since a man dreamt of a bird! When the first airplane flew, he lost his wings. Wings that very often distanced him, it's true, from a finale in a peaceful bed. So what? In the meantime he ejaculated. I mean he had the largesse to spend not only a percentage of that white sperm that is given him, and which, one way or another even without a partner, there are ways to expel, but also a large percentage of the other, black sperm enclosed – now's not the time to ask "why" – in the depths of his soul, and which, if not also spent by means of the unexpected (I should say the miraculous) or by some adventure, threatens to lead him to discord.

All those people and their historical migrations, their near permanent unpoliced existence, the virgin ground they first stepped on, their robberies, kidnappings and seizures, their explorations of the unknown despite a myriad natural dangers or unfamiliar habits and mores, their hand-to-hand combat, their sacking of mythic cities, their duels and their love affairs, all correspond to whole rivers of black sperm that repulsed any notion of satiety or boredom and loosened the reins of a nervous system that endures everything but disuse.

Among intellectually developed nations, the pressure of psychic powers found outlet in various forms of art, dance, music and drama. Only to a point, because not all citizens of a nation are equally developed, nor are the more developed always satisfied, unfortunately, by this type of sublimation, and especially as the mathematical induction of individuals into a whole that is constantly ranked, graded and controlled had not, as of yesterday at least, been completed – nor had its final muzzling. The problem is clearly visible in the mirror of art. Even before the end of the First World War we see it trembling, that is, protesting its asphyxiation. The unattainable perpendiculars, which a life parched for fulfillment has every right to know, are now transformed into the lines and colors, the cries and sounds of intellectual creation. How could it be otherwise when every aspiring Achilles had survived the war, having deigned to endure entire months in the few muddy feet of a trench? And when, as soon as peace was declared, an Arch-accountant God stubbornly set out to and, in a few decades, succeeded in crowding hundreds of thousands of people into microscopic hives, indexing their myriads under an invisible Authority and forcing them to comply with the regulations of an oversized stupidity of universal proportion?

The asynchronicity between nature and humanity caused the asynchronicity between body and soul. Where the nightingale isn't heard the Molotov cocktail is. The birds avenge; they never went to Sunday school. From Sweden to Hungary, from Czechoslovakia to France, young people demand the black sperm's rights by overturning cars and setting fires. Life can't be made to go backwards; people need to keep advancing to catch it, one might say, by the tail.

The invisible, thus more essential, more stunning miracle work continues in the form of a simple flower opening its petals, or a sea cut by the lightning of the sun; therefore we have the right to hope that one day, between the terrible cyclotrons and electronic intelligences as between two flintstones, Poetry will spring again like the purple poppy. I don't mean the ability to compose verses but the ability to recompose the world, literally and metaphorically, so that the more its desires are actualized the more they contribute to the materialization of a Good acceptable to all humans. For a dreamtaken and chimeric Greek, which

I confess I am, the meaning of such a good, ultimately, can only lead to some ideal point, albeit fashioned of earth and water, an "Island of the Enlightened," hardly suffused by natural or other wealth but as modest and as demanding as the Parthenon, nude and in harmony with the golden rule of winds and the whitewashed little wall of a church above the most resplendent sea.

F

I HAVE CONCEIVED my form somewhere between a sea emerging from the whitewashed little wall of a church and a barefoot girl whose garment is lifted by the wind; a lucky moment I strive to capture and trap with Greek words.

Here is the smallest canvas where my life's ideogram can be embroidered; if you think it worth examining, it would be enough to yield a space whose meaning lies not in the natural elements that compose it but in their extensions and correlations inside us to our farthest limits, so that, in order to become easily read and understood, the entire significance of the vision is finally concentrated in the psychic clarity it presupposes and needs. To understand me one must be convinced *a priori* that the psychic work necessary to conceive of an angel is more painful and frightening than the one that manages to midwife demons and monsters.

I spoke of a clarity whose metaphysical meaning is precisely superimposed on the ethical, and it, in turn, on the esthetic, so that we recognize it and have inherited it almost as a simple *gesture of the hands* ever familiar to Greeks whether they are called Pheidias and Iktinos or Anthemios and Isidoros, or are the anonymous sailors and carpenters of centuries of Ottoman enslavement. Its weave is so broad it reaches from sensation to idea or, more precisely, from faith in the material world to faith in the *divine*: the *Theophany* of Dionysios or Maximos as seen through a *heliolatric* lens entirely outside the facile solutions of pantheism.

But our concern here is of a different order: the more we advance to the North and the more we approach our own time, what increases is not clarity but the threat of clarity. But then, what secret in our tradition prevented the poet's or artist's hand from blaspheming or vilifying life or even attempting the superlative unless toward good and beauty? When another life's brilliance is allowed to pass through this one, what prevents it from causing a metamorphosis of the kilometric surface of things, as it has done elsewhere, but does achieve a transformation in kilometric depth? No one can be sure.

Many spoke of the light, but did anyone ever tell us what "light" might mean in the elevated plane of critical thought? It is wiser to reach for the essential and the large by way of a humble scale's proportions.

Ever since the fate of intellectual and spiritual affairs slipped from the hands of Hellenism, the artist's personality has been aggrandized under the guise of some inflated individual exception while, simultaneously, its force as the interpreter of an ideal, even an individual one since the communal had long ceased to exist, weakened into extinction. This fact has always impressed me, just as, conversely, I have been amazed at how the difference between emotions in life and emotions in art has been rendered incomprehensible, so that we seem to believe it enough to write that one hurts or rejoices in life, for one to hurt or rejoice also in art. I suspect that the differentiating secret between Western and Greek concepts of artistic creation lies precisely on the invisible and ill-defined juncture of these two seemingly unrelated themes.

Of course, our amputation from divine myth had been complete even for Sappho or Archilochos, just as for Dylan Thomas and Pablo Neruda, and, clearly, only the poet's Ego had remained to be called Protagonist. The problem is that in entering this lunar, so to speak, phase of the Western world, the Ego acquired a tone so shrill it overwhelmed what it should have accentuated. Nevertheless, the poet's Ego – I insist on this and we must face it – is not the Poet as he is formed in the world, it is the world as it is formed in the Poet, which means that if the Poet constitutes an exception, the exception itself is of no interest. What is of interest is in how the exception conceives of the rule.

I don't know if I make myself understood. To walk the straight path in Poetry you must often take detours. I have a thousand discontents about the poems I wrote – not one exists that I can stand with – yet I bless the hour and the moment they moved my hand to write them, indeed to write them *as I did and not otherwise*. I speak in truth and not irreverence. Had I thought I would be just another griever for this futile world, I don't believe I'd ever have lifted the pen. Contrariety drew me. It was my fingerprint. At least, so I believed. Today something else makes me believe that the concentric lines of that print are less the fibers of a singularity than of a community, fibers drawn from who knows what depths to coil at the place where the pen is held. I respect and obey biographical circumstances, that is, the catalysts of each materialization of the self and each highlighting of one of its aspects, but only insofar as they can verify, often in the least expected way, the clarity the world ceaselessly tends to take in my almost completely detached Ego.

If I spoke in the beginning of *girl* and *small church* at the risk of appearing foolish, I had my reasons. I would like to draw the former into the latter and make it mine, not to scandalize but to confess that eros is indivisible, to further condense the poem I want to constitute with the days of my life.

Pomegranate branches would then sprout from the temple and, through the little window, wind and wave would harmonize psalms when the stronger sirocco helped it mount the ledge. Once, naked, I touched on such a ledge and felt my entrails cleansed, as if the whitewash with its disinfecting properties had, leaf by leaf, penetrated my heart. That's why I never shrank from the fierce gaze of the Saints, as fierce as anything that reaches the Unreachable. I knew it reached just far enough to decode the Laws of my imaginary *polis* and reveal it as the seat of innocence. Don't think me exalted; I'm not referring to myself; I speak for whoever feels as I do and is not naïve enough to confess it.

If a separate personal Paradise exists for each of us, I reckon mine must be irreparably planted with trees of words the wind silvers like poplars, by people who see their confiscated justice given back, and by birds that even in the midst of the truth of death insist on singing in Greek and saying, "eros," "eros," "eros."

G

DEATH IS the first truth. The last remains to be known. The sensation of "things turning" is familiar to me, just like the wave of Poetry I mentioned earlier, crashing against my first youth and returning, here where

I wait, smaller each time but still standing, as I had wished, unrepentantly in love, arriving at the secret meeting place early, always with the same longing, the same tightening throat, the same pacing up and down, waiting... For what? Perhaps for what thickens and presses on the chest if not allowed to rise and fall as tears, and then the whole world seems suddenly so sweet and bitter. Sometimes it is a girl, sometimes two or three verses, often simply summer itself.

The way a bird leans to one side, or the yogurt vendor calls a little louder on the downhill at dusk, or the way an odor of burnt grass billows through the open window (from where?), the subtlest, most invisible marks assume their entire meaning, as though their only mission was to convince me that at any moment the beloved arrives. *This is why I write. Because poetry begins where death is robbed of the last word.* It is the end of one life and the beginning of another, the same as the first but deeper, as deep as the soul can scout, at the border of opposites where Sun and Hades touch, the endless turn toward the Natural light which is Logos and the Unbuilt light which is God. This is why I write. Because I am enraptured by obeying whom I don't recognize, who is my whole self, not the partial one wandering the streets and "listed in the draft registers of the *Polis*."

It is correct to give the unknown its due; that's why we must write. Because Poetry unlearns us from the world, such as we find it; the world of decay we come to see as the only path over decay, just as Death is the only path to resurrection. I know I speak as if I had no right, as if I were almost ashamed to love life. It's true, once they forced me even to this. No one knows; no one has ever discovered where our passionate hatred toward the possibility of our salvation comes from. Perhaps we'd rather not know – but do know – that it exists, and that we are the reason we can neither know nor surpass it. Willing or not, *we are all hostages of the joy of which we deprive ourselves.* Here springs love's pre-eternal sadness.

So no, I didn't paint the sky gold from ignorance, like the iconographers; it wasn't hearing I lacked while others shouted. While they shouted I heard and saw and smelled and felt and tasted and caressed the infant whose conception never graced me. I feel responsible only to this, never to a camp filled with idiots and the self-satisfied. Each time I touch the pen, I consider, bitterly, the futility of speaking on behalf of a world saturated with hints of an ideal perfection, when it is our imperfection, for which we suffer and weep, that keeps us from recognizing them and, with their help, moving on.

Surely in the chapter on the art of the soul we have not yet come to synthesis. We stutter; we spell; at best we emit cries which we admire and are moved to tears by, because we need to feel that they are the most we are capable of. Still, on reflection, how much of life's true value do they cover? I confess, this is why I aspire to the maturation of speech, as a conspirator aspires to the supremacy of his ideals, full of machinations and dreams. I'm not, I never was, in the majority, I know. We must be so naïve, those of us who discern some pattern between the stars and our entrails, between the birds' flight and our soul, and say so. Still, our naïveté is not enough to lead us to speak the crux. You have to grab the sea by its odor if you want it to give you ship, and ship to give you Mermaid, and Mermaid give Alexander the Great and all the passions of Hellenism.

And so, at the fulfillment of time, our senses, drawn one through the other, will compose the second and third history Poetry seeks. But its very motion is to immortalize our senses, which, unlike our emotions, have no history (how strange), which, not subject to change, provoke it and assist it more effectively, and which, not subject to the blackmail of succumbing to an epoch's spirit, express it more fluently. This is why I believe that the most current, the most modern poetic speech must prove that it can be reduced, like them, to a "first inscription." This seems so simple, yet realizing it I felt a truly infinite freedom.

A metaphoric summer awaited me, inalienable, eternal, with the creaking wood, the wild grass aroma, the figs of Archilochos, and Sappho's moon. I traveled as on a transparent seafloor, my body luminous, traversed by green and azure currents; I touched the speechless female statues and heard, by the thousands, their birdsong gaze in underwater light; an endless procession of ancestors, fierce, tortured and proud, moved my every muscle. Oh yes, it's no small thing to have the centuries on your side, I kept saying as I walked.

This is how I passed between the "indifferent public" and the "enemy Powers," as between Scylla and Charybdis. The golden fleece exists; accept no lie. Each of us is the golden fleece of our being. Death doesn't keep us from seeing and recognizing it; that is a hoax. We must empty death of all it's been stuffed with and bring it to absolute clarity, so that the real mountains and real grass are seen in it, the maligned world brimming with dew more luminous than any precious tears.

This is what I await each year, one more wrinkle on my brow, one less on my soul: complete reversal, absolute transparence....

The Girls

A

I NEVER FOUND SORROW in the flesh and, it seems, I've yet to read all the books: I am immature. The sky I sought in the distance is above my head, the names of the sailors known to me one by one. Only the Sirens remain. They are close by; I hear them taunting:

οὐ γάρ πώ τις τῇδε παρήλασε νηὶ μελαίνῃ,
πρὶν γ᾽ ἡμέων μελίγηρυν ἀπὸ στομάτων ὄπ᾽ ἀκοῦσαι,
αλλ᾽ ὅ γε τερψάμενος νεῖται καὶ πλείονα εἰδώς.

My tongue itches to say it: was Homer immature? We know him as an old man but what about those tales of boulders shifting in space, witches and princesses, and rose-gold dawns? Could it be that what settles in the mind with age and experience is what had pre-existed in immaturity and youth? Could it be that only then can the living cells and hemoglobin shift things more easily in the imagination, that its virginity can only be preserved by the true poet, while the rest of us must wait for it to wrinkle like a prune before we accept it? Why this enmity?

No, no. As for myself, I say: I fear that we unduly fear the harshness with which young organisms remind us that life goes on among all our despairs. But we don't live – here is the proper place for *alas* – only by what we like, and the mature first and foremost should know this.

Once, in the final months of the Occupation, returning home at dusk through sniper-fire, out of breath, my soul in my teeth, I heard a suspicious sound from the sheltered entrance of the house I lived in. "Who's there?" I shouted with false bravado and flicked on my flashlight. A pale girl looked me evenly in the eye. She wasn't pretty. She was calm, decisive; she exuded something that brooked no argument. By her side, the young man dropped his gaze. Love was shameful to him in times like these. "Excuse me," I mumbled and went to my room. That whole night, the whole day after and its night as well, I remember her face before me with the strength of a Medusa no obstacle can stop, attended by a mysterious music that drowned out the warmongering clatter, saying, "We must, we must, we must live."

Strange! It was the same command, the same siren's song in my head each time I sat, as if punished, in front of my writings.

A world, contradictory and illogical on the surface but solid and hard at its core, flashed me, strobe-like, the grimace of a martyr next to the beauty of a naked breast. Duty (necessity?) and grace (truth?) formed a mouth asking to speak. "Well, speak," I finally shouted, "and let the idiots protest." It was then that I began, surrounded by execution and torture, to compose a text with the monolectic title "The Girls."

Like the Lautréamont of "Fourth Song" but from the other end of the wire, I exorcized natural elements, mobilized them, shook them even, hoping for a few white flowers on the scorched grass. And further: by distorting and exaggerating reality, I anticipated a teaching that was also a game. I plucked at the sacrilegious like a hangnail. Blake and Novalis aphorisms encouraged me. If a magician could pull only one smile out of his hat, it would, at that moment, prove to humanity its purpose was not yet over.

"I like to begin where winds shake the first branch," I wrote provocatively, spreading myself on an awkwardly staged vernal expanse where *temptation* had anything but a Solomonic meaning. "Soon the wide creek is heard again, fences are newly whitewashed, a dog's bark reminds us that men with rolled-up sleeves are sawing their cypresses nearby. How the saw comes and goes, how blood comes and goes, how the sun's flint comes and goes behind deep-breathing pines!... Now is the time to lie in wait, to secretly view the mistral's body nude and adrift on its small fresh archipelago at dawn or to light a fire where the hot breath of a heaving dune crowns the earth's impatience."

Essentially, I wrote of my own impatience; I wrote of something deprived me and I wrote, most importantly, without remorse.

"Smoke still rises left and right. People look as if they just emerged from the dark inexplicable epicenter of a terrible earthquake. Why do I feel I am already among embryos of another world? When, but when will we all feel the deep, serious, enchanting thing life is? I mean when will we see it, be constantly seeing it, different every second, virginal, passionate, displacing the eternal from the features of some immaterial concept, such as its form, to the features of its very *becoming*?

"Whenever we part the spiderweb of ideas that stops us from facing life free of influence, we diagnose in its folds what lies in ours, a tangled cohabitation of what we have polarized, vainly emphasizing oppositions out of weakness or habit. Joy, sorrow, passion, ecstasy, dream, action, fear, hope, heat, coolness, yes, no – everything flows through these folds, composing a myriad annihilations of partial contradiction by their repetitive intersections, as well as a final point where even the contradictions of those annihilations vanish. This final point, at peace now with death, is simply the moving statue of life, advancing by our steps, seeing itself with our eyes, offering itself through our breasts, witnessing the Poet approach by a primeval rhythm to lay wildflowers devoutly at its feet..."

COINCIDENCE, when raised to a symbol, occurs with mathematical precision at the most crucial moment, even for the squarest of minds. A moment the rest of us call higher will, Fate's gesture, something like that. I suspected it even as a child; it stirred behind my curtains, in street scenes, I watched it with the light anxiety of wondering whether the unknown taps your shoulder for good or ill. I was right. By the third or fourth page of the text I was so bent on writing, I froze: impossible! I flung my pencil, along with all the imaginary gardens, and went to the window.

There, a young girl had hung two ropes from the mulberry of the inner courtyard; she was swinging!

Each forward swing struck me like the raw March wind already hiding the subtle velvet of white petals, each backward swing extracted from my breast the fragment intended for my private Paradise which, by all indications, I'd never find. I was not, never had been, a sentimentalist. I'd never before even imagined I might direct words of worship to those curls. What then? What was it? *Sensation, self-isolated and assigned to an eternal moment.* That's what it was. I see it today. Perfection achieved only as lightning, the briefest duration necessary to negate our daily misery! Beauty is harsh, as they say: there's a cliché not yet worn out. And, confidentially, the only.

I returned to my writings. Immediacy, objectivity, legitimization of the hyper-real, exploitation of memory, morphological empowerment, diffusion into the world, and youth's mythos, all together assumed the dimension and significance of autonomous capitals spoken by that ideal unit embracing contradictions without a trace; the same one I found in the meaning of "girl" or "island," the exact autonomy and coincidence of a host of *heteroclite* elements:

> *Sus muslos me escapaban*
> *Como peces sorprendidos*
> *La mitad llenos de lumbre*
> *La mitad llenos de frío...*

Some such verse, coupled with the old but always relevant Baudelaire sonnet "Correspondences," cleared my way. My Freudian studies had already brought me to "Interpretation of Dreams." How natural! My ambition was to extract a poetic theory from a biological phenomenon, more specifically, to formulate rules equally governing matter and spirit, something Gaston Bachelard later achieved. I failed, not from immaturity as you might think, but because I lacked the strength to transport my immaturity intact to the level of theory.

The *latent* content of dream alongside the *overt*, the mechanism of *control*, the so-called *condensing* and *dematerialization* lulled more than convinced me, for a while, that my interpretation was achievable. Still, the simple vision of some essayist, scalpel in hand, exterminating what he loves just to dissect it, was enough to stop me. No, and no again. It was still winter; no heat other than poetry. Phrases from beloved books, regardless of their geographic or chronologic distances, inhabited me as easily as the four seasons inhabit the face of a girl and, impeded only by my naïve enthusiasm, refashioned the seamless prototype of the author who *writes by unwriting his ephemeral part*. These were enough, at the time, to reconstitute for me the vernal which the fallen from grace construe as sin.

"Ever since the beautifully-sandaled, golden-haired Iris mated with Zephyr and birthed Eros, and hungry earth opened her arms to its large meaning, grass grew fragrant and memories paused in their usual path to fly *vers l'avenir, cette fenêtre nue*. The day named Today leapt on the sand, green-leaved and yellow-rosed, red-nailed; the wind set out for the sea's inaugurals, brimming with white birds; the young Siren who once sang softly by licking summer's body with the surf, this *sirenita de la mar, montada en bicicleta de corales y conchas*, now runs astonished, scattering lightning bolts. They are the lightning bolts that claim the young: each corresponds to a desire; desires are girls, their names as fresh as if they'd been raised on the pelago or had once lived with Azure April in their breasts; they come out to kiss the boys they love, to leave on the lips *un raro gusto de hiel, de menta y de albahaca*.

"*Du vent qui prend le goût de la jeunesse* to the distant seacaves with their capacious dreams, one flame burns, dances and sings – their flame!

"How clearly the childhood of this world appears then. Here, the ragamuffin cloud chased fireflies! There, the boat with red smokestacks passed at three in the afternoon. Here is the boulder where Marina wept for no reason. The song 'Youth, youth how lovely your hair' echoes now as it did then, the ripe earth boldly bolsters trees, and a nude body, *un corps simple sans nuages*, turns like a huge plant to the sun. It is she, who shapes all others in her likeness and image. They arrive from afar, *parées de calme et de fraîcheur, parées de sel d'eau de soleil*, they arrive, as purple-winged Penelopes tear their smallest cloud, to imprint the seal of their great desire on our lips. The boulders spark; afternoon slowly advances; the distant city windows iridesce.

"Nothing is heard for a few minutes. But soon, scattered church roofs are lit again by the evening star's passion; a rusty well moans; a tuft of blue smoke stirs the rose horizon *y un horizonte de perros ladra muy lejos del río*... No bird, no fish, no shadow between sparse elongated trees! Only later, when dark is tight in its silk leaves and all the cypresses say midnight, do souls pour out *par un escalier de frissons et de lune au galop* and strike, strike, strike their golden sword on the stars' small bells. A new voice, a metamorphosis of their sound, rips the waters of the celestial *Guadalquivir* and signals again the upper world's ecstasy: *las estrellas de la noche se volvieron siemprevivas!*"

THE SEIZURE of childhood is, in the realm of sensitivity, a demonic machine whose unplugging, when the moment tolls, leaves us awestruck. We are then slowly reduced to disbelieving ourselves for the sake of those unwilling to believe in themselves. Then why write? Why make poetry? I ask as in: Why make love? From sender to receiver, nothing mediates the cheeks of a girl, the lines of a poem. The translation occurs without interpreter, the gold dust on our fingers seems enough. And if the wind should blow again? Then all of nature will be inhabited by a million secret signs, and the demon of the insatiable lying in wait inside us will open its maw for more and more.

"I am a classicist," I went on, as soon as poetic compression ushered me to an imaginary springtime, "who occasionally happens to drink so deeply of the world's spectacle, he no longer knows what's going on. I also have *idées fixes*. One is to use, in place of theory's traditional directives, the correlations I suspect exist between life and organic thought as analytic tools of Lyric phenomena, convinced they will be better servants for an activity outside prejudice and convention. Poetry eludes definition *a priori* by successfully linking circumstances the world's materiality has separated, circumstances the spirit lusts after without humility. This led me to the inkling that even a simple detail of life could achieve something analogous, which might have served once as our original prototype, though we don't perceive it.

"Stone, plant, girl: if their existence extends beyond their surface calm or agitation, then Poetry, and art in general, falsely create the impression that they add to, transform or surpass life, while all they do is reveal a part of its deeper essence or render its wondrous function by an instinctual mimetics. Stone, plant, girl: one girl or many – let's be straight, I don't mean the trendy beauty they might aspire to and might be flattered to possess, but the unknown beauty that transforms them into instruments of an orchestra of global music, makes them the juncture of contradictory charms, transfigures them into the locus of the human occasion to express its tenderness, its compassion for the smallest thing, as well as its terrible harshness, its implacable advancing, always young and strong, assimilating death in its blood.

"Stone, plant, girl: one must overcome their acquired and superficial vanity to notice what fluency of life speaks through their changes, their surprises, the life that taunts us as we fill pages with complaints against its silence, the fluent life chattering its myriad, polyglot reflections beyond endurance through these beings, who are ignorant of their true role, incognizant of their allure's huge responsibility, which they carry night and day, dangerously and casually, from place to place.

"Long before I was aware of the ideal of a Poetry that could record the smallest transformative idiosyncrasies of emotion, I was proud of the generous human freedom that believes not only the *extant* but also the *possibly extant*, and so passes into a dimension of divine theory where *eros, a simple tree in a storm, or a song* are now equivalent.

"Democritus maintained that whatever appears to our senses as existing, does; William Blake wrote that what is self-evident today was once only imagination's mere offspring; Shelley called imagination an instrument of Good, in its ethical sense; all three were simply referring to its function to potentiate memory toward the future. The creative imagination is synthetic, both in its core nature and its spiral trajectory; it compels the phenomenal world's elements to refuse the role forced on them by conventional and ephemeral valuation and to obey only its voice, exactly as that voice has just obeyed emotion. Established as the Lyric continent's most powerful state, creative imagination now must find an expressive instrument generously endowed with similar capabilities and indisputable virtues. It must find an instrument that scales the higher synthesis of contradictions and creates – by its agile, dynamic images of distinct chromatic moods – results accessible according to people's emotional receptivity rather than encyclopedic knowledge. It must find an instrument capable of something more (I'm thinking here of the phenomenon of a simple human cry), something attuned to the most basic biological urges; responsive to the multiform shades of emotion from bliss to despair; accentuating wonder, admiration, surprise, disapprobation, enjoyment, agony, and passion; and accomplishing all these by the lightest, subtlest tonal displacements."

Here, now as then, exhausted perhaps by our peregrinations, we need a little silence before hearing again with a virgin ear the huge, susurrating poplar of our thoughts.

B

EVEN WHEN an idea seduces us without sufficient reason and threatens to expose us to serious accusation we must never, I believe, abandon it. The fact that we lack the arguments to defend ourselves is insignificant next to our obligation to track the mysterious attraction that we may one day discover was not accidental. Not to mention that no one has decreed that we must defend ourselves, for anything. It's time to reclaim this part of our writer's flesh from servitude – to let the sun see it.

I don't even want to imagine the gossip when Archilochos spoke as he did about his shield or when he monikered his girlfriend's father (whom he couldn't stomach) *Flatusidis*, in precisely today's sense of the word. He certainly reduced some of that ancient servility scourging the human race. I think it symbolic that he is, chronologically, the first Greek lyric poet we know. Our A-B-C's had a good start. It was we who failed along the way. Our downfall was that other scourge of literature: solemnity. As it becomes more cultivated and developed, the beauty of the "imagined universe" is further limited and narrowed, policed by regiments of literati with thick myopic lenses and neurotic fountain pens. From early youth, this awareness made me value, above all else, the inventive factor in every artistic creation, which is always part debt to nature, part unconditional gift.

"As we understand it today, a poem," I noted even then, "surpasses knowledge and approaches the meaning *nature*; it exhibits, that is, many more analogies to natural phenomena. Such analogies, luminous in the shocking beauty of their fate, are created from the same powerful impetus by which life welcomes the infinite possibilities of the future. The ideal poet begins from the faith that he can and must provoke physical phenomena in the spirit." And further on, "He would use his very soul for a body, but with so many more senses or agilities than his own body."

It is significant, if not oxymoronic, that one can communicate better with a self of thirty years ago than with one's contemporaries.

My insistence on achieving the largest possible transparence in all I undertake originates in the understandable longing to read my thoughts deep in the thoughts of others. Alas, it rarely occurs. More likely I offer a glass of water and hear, "What great liqueur – where did you find it?" Meanings not even *in* my vocabulary…optimism, say, or joy (except if it's the other joy) or the picturesque (what's that?)…occur again and again to my critics. "Clear view" becomes carefree; "penetrating natural *being*" becomes sightseeing; "innocence," well-being. It's all so easy. If they only suspected what bitter roots must stir, what darkness must be counterbalanced, for innocence to endure our days… Bah! We understand coffins, we already gaze protectively at our immature interlocutor, as if only we possess the secret that humans die. "But that's just why," the poor one whispers, but the daily papers are due any minute with their screaming headlines. Who has the time?

That's why I like to imagine in such moments that somewhere a girl takes revenge for me. She closes her eyes and dreams. She is insignificant and larger than life. Aztecs discover Greeks! Hölderlin bellows, "Ein Rätsel ist Reinentsprungenes!" Venizélos unfolds the map of two continents and five seas! Santorini erupts!

We have far to go. Embeirikos is right, "Pulp turns solid on scorched earth; the echo of some battle turns to crystal. Thrust into soil's flesh, the spear marks the end of a completed epoch and the beginning of a history just starting to flower. The girls' baskets are full of legends. Many are beautiful. Many will be remembered forever in the way the breasts of women or girls are caressed. Therefore I cup the breasts of girls and, brimming with victory, with *hedone*, I shout through the century: 'No deceit digested! Woe, to the defeated, woe!'"

Where then are the concentration camps, the gas chambers, the dead of Stalingrad, the gallows? Where the Security interrogations, the outskirt hovels, the Negroes, Vietnam?

DESPITE THEIR great differences and occasionally because of them, poets, musicians, and artists, throughout the centuries, do nothing but constitute the second condition of the world. This condition is available to everyone, and to this day no military demon has been found to head us off at the pass. It's just that obese human stupidity narrows our access now and again. No one is obliged to care about Poetry. But if one does, one is obliged to "recognize and travel to" that second condition, to walk on air and water both.

We think it natural that, in painting, "grey" tones might guide us to limestone, and from limestone to the core structure of the pliable truth that is Greece. The same is impossible in Poetry. The intervention of language, which also happens to be our daily medium of communication, confuses the two levels so much that we come to believe that our finger bleeding on a knife bleeds also in the poem. No way! Before it bleeds, the knife must first be in the poem – not to mention that the pain of human presence is not always measured in blood. We are all searching for a human landscape to set against the "natural," how awkward. In Poetry, the human is not Ethnic or Christian, heretic or orthodox, communist or fascist, to list just a few of those who – justly or unjustly, it makes no difference – cannibalized each other this side of Necessity. In Poetry the human is the one whose true characteristics "eternity renders final"; you can already find them in a stone, a cloud, a casual glance, a human cry not even aimed toward you.

We don't eavesdrop enough on the secret conversation among things. That's the problem. So that even when a realistic phrase about the sky strays to our lips we think it fantastic and, upside down, feet in the air, we beg the ghost of reality to turn us right side up. When the sun rises in our imagination it's always dusk in our mind, but death has no night or day.

Terrified even then by the threatening cloud of this growing delusion, I wrote, "I pass through despair, agony and pain with a seductive smile and an inscrutable mien, then see a group of macho thinkers mocking my serene face. I am no demagogue of pain or passion. I am a human among humans and like them suffer the ancient and renowned antagonisms between desire and the means of its actualization; a human, I must add, who prefers to measure the future through art's decisive speech instead of a sterile lament; a stubborn human who intends to claim infinite natural wealth as eternal companion to the lightest stirrings of his heart." *Cela revient au même*, as the French would say.

A few verses and a place remain from each poet. When you focus on them, you see what you thought were mountains, trees and rivers start to move, transform, dissolve and become what they always were: simple, condensed sensations. This cove is a shiver, that shadow a lump in the throat, the running water a legend. Emotion is quick to substitute for sensation. Then, if the devotion persists, associative analogs – with their imagistic wealth in which individual life unwittingly enacts the life of others – substitute for emotion. The metamorphosis of "natural landscape" to "human landscape" is thus verified, as in a theorem. Walking this road in reverse is enough to reveal to what percent and in what ways the poet counterweighs death's minus. As for the senses...

One of our hierarchs, Gregorios of Thessaloniki, wrote, "The soul's fantastic, being of the senses, appropriates not the senses themselves but, as we have said, the images in them, quickly separating bodies from their specificities, rendering everything *visible* to itself: the heard, the tasted, the touched and the smelled." I'd found this quote by chance in that strange book *On Guarding the Five Senses* by Nikodemos of Athos, a

38

monk self-exiled to Skyros; it served, I recall, as a bridge to the much more interesting but at the time sharply contested chapter on the surreal image.

"How FAR we are already," I wrote in 1944, "from the *iconoplastic* tastes of mythology (Ariadne hands the thread to Theseas), allegory (justice: blindfolded woman with a scale), symbolism (a moth flies into lamplight and burns up), and academic simile (lover's teeth like strands of white pearls). We reject these icons. We see no Theseas, no Ariadne, no justice, no lover's lips. We still see only a man and a woman in tunics, a blindfolded woman, a scale, a moth, a lamp, and a few white pearls... White pearls! For years, poets' insistence on showing what the most idiotic reader already knows has made them comic. Of course, pearls are white. And in the spring, leaves are green. What else? Honey is sweet? Thanks for the information.

"The true poet scorns overstatement, illustration and documentation. He makes the invisible visible, the noetic sensate, and the irreal real. He replaces a poor strand of words with one more suited to inspiring unknown visions than to recalling the known. The typical simile, based on analogy and 'like' (this is like that), annoyingly reminds him that someone is speaking and underscores a collusion between poet and listener by which the latter undertakes to believe whatever the former fancies to tell him. By contrast, in contemporary poems the world explodes triumphantly and is whatever it wants, each time, to be. Analogy yields to *identification*. This is that. Surprise, small or large, leaves no time to consider whether something is possible or not; it does not brook debate; what the poet says *occurs*.

> "*Ma faim c'est les bouts d'air noir*
> *Cette famille est une nichée de chiens*   RIMBAUD
>
> *Ma tête est une coupe de vin sombre*   LAUTRÉAMONT
>
> *Venus es una blanca naturaleza muerta*   LORCA
>
> *And the whole sky was a dove's large wing*   SEFERIS

39

Her belly is the story of Belthander and Crysanza   ENGONOPOULOS

The forest is the shiver of bayoneted legions   EMBEIRIKOS

"Forced relations between two things that superficially appear foreign create a new, instantaneous state. Authentic poetry asks nothing more. A kinship completely nonexistent moments ago was created by the poet's authority, just as it might have been created in life by the authority of chance. The endless metamorphosis continues; in it, the battle-scarred human sees, feels, hurts. There are no more prisons, handcuffs, pigeonholes, taxonomies, divisions or classes. The same omnipotence scores, erases and rescores the boundaries of earthly adventure. Until now, the sun lit the sky; thoughts invaded the mind; ships tore the sea; green fruit shone on its branch; the distant bell sounded vespers; the washerwoman put blueing in her wash. Now:

"The passing thoughts are ships   EMBEIRIKOS

Le matin allume un fruit vert   ÉLUARD

A distant bell stains the sky with blueing   GATSOS

"The poet's eye confirms the presence of a different world. It dissolves the solitude of elements in the known world, pacifies enemy populations, and raises all flags as high as humankind's one and only flag.

"When just being moved takes so much more, only imagination's violent gesture can hope for real tears.

"Simile, even when it fails at complete identification, continues to reflect the hyperbole of this longing, even when using 'like'; it continues, by great intellectual strides, to parallel the unparalleled, endanger experience, and cause the very meaning of unattainable to despair.

"Le vautour des agneaux beau comme la loi de l'arrêt de developpement de la poitrine chez les adultes dont la propension à la croissance n'est pas en rapport avec la quantité des molécules que leur organisme s'assimile, se perdit dans les hautes couches de l'atmosphère.   LAUTRÉAMONT

40

L'ombra s'addensava negli occhi delle vergini come sera appie degli ulivi.

UNGARETTI

L'écho du soleil comme la soude melée au sable.   BRETON

And a red horse like a flag!   ERGONOPOULOS

"The surreal image can *equally* have and not have a clearly esthetic character. Inspiration and its varied moments determine this:

"*Le bocal de ta voix*   APOLLINAIRE

Dehors l'air essaye les gants de gui   BRETON

La noche negra estatua de la prudentia   LORCA

Heel of strength   SEFERIS

"Language needed distance from daily speech; it needed an entirely new course. Each word had to earn such a foothold in the poem's small universe, that it could proclaim all the secret powers it had shouldered for thousands of years, in thousands of mouths. Each word had to marry, so that together they might convince the most ill-tempered sensitivity, first by causing it unknown reverberations, then by causing the most complex associations to train their strength as if one body on this aspiration: to track, verify and restore our endless internal transformations, usually dependent on the assimilation or interchange of impressions guided to our senses by deep emotion. We need words. And they must be more than a handful of letters or sounds when they reach the end of the pen, they must be a stem of images, an armful of objects, a sheaf of memory's peculiarities and, also, butterfly words, rocket words, or grenade words.

"Once the poet had listened at the psychic receiver, he knew he could re-articulate the secret message he had received only by hefting the weight of language in other, virgin palms. He saw a world existing behind every word, subjectively bound to him and hungry to surface. If he could take that world and couple it tightly to another word's world, as

41

life conjoins its events, but *in a direction untried by life*, wouldn't this signify the dawn of a new mental and spiritual attitude, a new order's projection in objective space?"

Gregorios, who had set me off, now concluded, "Who looks at another's beauty has a prostitute, not a pupil, for an eye." Fine. Note that he refers to a prostitute as demanding as Magdalene; she too was ultimately interested in Perfection. Has perfection no ethical meaning then? Or don't we care? "It is the concept and not the pursuit of perfection that has changed from the old poetry to the new," I wrote, "an essential difference." The success of authentic art still depends, as it always has, on the difficult balance, assimilation, and superimposition of a host of undisciplined elements that are contradictory by their very nature. Today it wants to exact something more. It no longer wants to represent the state of serenity, which can be rendered by successive curves that have been crossed or projected on each other's dead points in some compositional attempt. Instead, it wants to represent the pulse of their motion, the corresponding and final *dynamic line* symbolic of the partial excursions catalyzed by this singular purpose: to solidify a small and perfect Universe.

"It seems oxymoronic to uphold the concept of motion at the moment of balance. This might be more easily conceptualized by running from micro to macrocosm, to stand before a modern physics maintaining that a stable, immobile universe contradicts a universe in constant motion only phenomenologically: two meanings which prove equivalent under insistent examination. One may also run backwards, from macro to microcosm, and stand without prejudice before the phenomenon of a young living organism, to see just how awful the natural mechanism is that can present so many enemy elements inside an incontestable and fully formed unit of beauty, elements of superb innocence and repulsive baseness, elements which – if anyone tries to arrest them – constantly project their strobe-like motions and constantly escape to incarnate singular Beauty.

"The transformative adventure that *the Spirit assumes for itself* when matter cannot, as well as the expressive experiments begun at lyric poetry's birth – which have reached a zenith of freedom in our days – share a central cause and aim: imagination must instantaneously re-experience the successive series of forms that compose its *becoming* before it can assume, each time, a concrete form. Having done so, it passes into expression and seeks to maintain the verve, flexibility and vigor of its intense spiritual training.

"In this way, a dynamic imaginative line exists and passes, deeply rooted in living matter, through the world of actual forms to the world of possible forms (as in dreams) with an increasingly luminous consciousness of the spirit's omnipotence. The poet must be willing not only to follow this line, but also to etch it in his work, translating its secret teachings through the language of technique (metaphor, simile, transposition of meanings, rhythmic unfolding, emotional coherence, etc.)."

Enough. It's time to disperse the fumes of theory, time for a Caliban to enter with his somersaults and shrieks.

IN OUR PARTS, we call Caliban *Panayis*. It's short for Panaghiotis [*from* PANAGHIA, *all holy, name of the Virgin Mary*] and, in its familiar form of Panayis or Panaeis, comprises *pan* and *aei*: *all* and *eternity*, body and soul. His head is shaved; his huge eyes stunned; his right knee bloody. He's only visible in summer, as if he couldn't move without the fig trees' aroma, without the sea's particular blues. If the cicadas stopped for an instant he'd vanish – he is that nourished by what for us is a piece of fallen time, a Monday or Tuesday insignificant to us and our future. Naturally, Panayis has just returned from the future; tomorrow he'll hang flower wreaths on doors, singing the first of May mid-August:

> *Come swallow, swallow*
> *bring good hours,*
> *good years,*
> *on your white breast,*
> *on your black tail.*
> *Roll us a fruitcake*
> *from the wealthy house,*
> *a goblet for wine*
> *a container for cheese;*
> *. . . . .*
> *swallow, swallow, break our door;*
> *we are not old, but children.*

"Children" always have their way. The point is that Panayis, lacking dark forests and lily ponds – "oh joy!" – acts in an absolute light he restores even to night, casting luminous meanings on our pillow, which heavenly bodies abandoned. He speaks his mind in his own tongue, often without his lip even stirring, like this: suspended over the pelago whose waves join his screams, especially when the sirocco gathers, until everyone bows and obeys the ventriloquist. His vowels are made audible by a bare fragrance. If you pause by an open gate and the hour is suitable, you'll hear them, sonorant, round as balls, by the sweet william and basil. In each alpha, omicron and epsilon a smile flickers on and off in time to a little curtain rising and falling in the window.

I don't want to reveal what goes on in deserted places at high noon, terrible things requiring at least five lives concentrated on one thought, silently and exclusively, to yield meaning. Presently we recognize only some flaring monsters, embodied in wild olive trees or, at best, some signals trembling in the wind, hinting that somewhere, maybe, a continuous *Oresteia* is being written, backwards.

How easily a specter takes us from one end of existence to the other and reveals the slight difference between our serious and not-serious acts, as we perceive them; it teaches us to use our emotions in dreams. Not even Technocracy can reach a different conclusion, even if it progresses as fast as it would like. In the meantime it's crucial to unretire our liveliest self.

Panayi, Panayi, I call you back to active duty, and let the cops be suspicious! Didn't you stay with me while others slept, midafternoons? Didn't we eat melon seeds awaiting the ship to round the cove of Hermione? Didn't you pretend to chase me so we could run through my cousin's legs as she ironed in her short pink slip, bare-armed, her hair wet? It's not what you think; that's not what I want from you; I want the first glimpse of the world. May I never lose Columbus' emotion. There are so many little things no one has managed to explore.

Remember going to the fields to pray at the small chapel and eat our pasta afterwards under the pines? I marveled at how softly you caressed a donkey's neck, your boundless respect for its superiority. That's why I believed you, loved you, cherished you. Who knows, maybe something told me that I'd need you, twenty or thirty years later, the front doors closed, the wide-eyed girls in their diaphanous nightgowns gone. Oh how you knew to light my lights when they passed my window at night, holding one arm aloft, their trembling shadow on the wall. Come, you who knows, let's do it one more time! In this horrid, frigid city, can we show people their immortal side once more?

Look, look: the dead – I do not fear the dead, I do not pity them – *Death shall have no dominion*. It "is in our future." "We are all in our future!" Let's go! Music! Horses! Lights!

C

"WHAT WIND! As much as necessary to blow the little cloud so long at play with the sun," I wrote, as if continuing a current text on the other side of time. "The walls, the tall houses I see from my open window, are lit again. Slowly, majestically, a cat walks on the ledge, pauses, stretches its front then hind legs, curls up and regards me calmly. Two young girls on a balcony speak with someone I can't see. One of them holds up a little mirror now and then, intently. Children kick a ball in the street and their shrieks rise through the atmosphere mixed with the off-key song of a servant in a basement laundry. The air is fragrant with food cooking downstairs. The postman knocks. A bicycle disappears in the distance. An old woman (I imagine her old) is grinding something, I can't tell what. I just hear the grrr, grrr, then a pause, then grrr again, as if eternity's gears were slowly turning.

"Life, life, how strange, how beautiful you are! Surely one day the war will stop. Surely a tree crazy with birds will always exist; so will a girl in love, swearing wholeheartedly – what miracle – on her love. Where could Poetry swear but on this oath: the ultimate oath that raises life to the dignity of emotional self-determination, that raises action to the free function of thought and eros to the infinite ethics of touching bodies? It is the sun that will preserve the flame of youth's mythos…"

The sun…even I marvel that I dared invoke it, while most still considered it a distant celestial body, indifferent to our miserable fate. Communication is so difficult. Of course back then, as today, the raw and cannibal events favored the hoarse. The illusion that you become terrible by simply mentioning the horrific raged. Always the last to know, like toddlers or cuckolds, our writers took a number and lined up,

45

armed with all-purpose ancient Tragedy. Mr. Mitsos and Mrs. Anna, who in my humble opinion far better represented the Greek spirit, were left out, on their boat or doorstep, thoughtful and calm. They probably needed less explaining than the others. Of what? Of the fact that the revolution ongoing on a tree continues even when the hero and his works come to naught. So what if this can't be proved, if it's yet to come? On the unprovable and still-to-come true Poetry is inscribed. As for the rest, there are accountants (ourselves aside) who, on hearing "sea," rush to assign it to the "Debit" side of International affairs or the "Profit" side of our national Tourism. Alas.

THE FIRST TIME I stood on the deck of a ship, sailing south of Santorini, I felt like a farmer surveying his patrimony in light of a pending inheritance. Those curly, wavy fields were cultivatable; only the cypresses remained to be planted at the perimeter. I counted my flocks, my granaries, my winepresses; I held dominion over shack roofs. Not even the boats were missing. There stood Monastiraki on the hill, the cottages by the boulder, the dovecotes and mills. An infinite familiarity allowed me to interchange the characteristics and properties of things with great ease; I felt it pre-exist in me, beautifying everything not dragged to the seafloor by the Atlantis of others. Of course, even among them I'd fit in, glued as I was to the notion of "hidden treasure" or, to use the current idiom, to the "potentialized improbable." Everything is possible when what we see and what we imagine not only continues to interact but ends up being true. Because that's where I wanted to end up, in that truth. If one could transcribe into visual symbols the kinetic phenomena I felt in that blinding-gold expanse, could one then follow, orbit-like, its course from sun to plant-root and plant-root to sun, its analogy between herbal properties and human urges, between our urges and artifacts, our houses, boats, tools... All achieved with such energy, such consequence and simplicity of means, that the moment they occupied would become convinced it was a singular, ideal justice; because justice *is* a precise moment, nothing more.

If, on the other hand, I were asked, "Why only Greece? Why not everywhere?" I'd reply, "Because nowhere else does the triangle of mountains descend so naturally into architecture, nowhere else do the mythic creatures of marine legends so convincingly assume two wings of wind."

46

The basket these wings bring us – flying, thigh nude and transparent before the small cloud of space – is filled with fruits of a wisdom that ranges from mathematics to intoxication; the beauty that connects them is unflawed, like those nineteen-year-old faces, startled by stirring love, knowing something is about to happen and pretending otherwise, perhaps to trap their very anticipation.

A virgin disrobes in the half-dark of an isolated room as July sets its moon on fire; suddenly she turns – the entire birdsong of a Mozart concerto transcribed for fountains and jasmined cupolas of sky!

Speaking this way, I sketch a difficult figure, I know; especially as it occupies two levels: one geometrically clean, the other still sand, sea and loose hair. Freedom is constituted for me here, not in the seemingly straight-edged delirium of monomaniacs and traitors, not at all.

They pursue the thankless role of the old Humanists: black-clad, copying copies, praying at the Acropolis, appending syntactical notations to texts with such absence of emotion that the real Greece was literally repulsed to its antipode. Is this maturity – this willingness to serve calculation, this preaching where the heart is absent and self-interest reigns? Were our fingers not numb from centuries of enslavement (and not only the Turkish one – some Kolokotronis could always be found to abort that kind with simple soapy water) we might still feel the secret intercourse of natural elements and not judge the Aegean *picturesque* or one's concern with girls *young superficiality* like any anesthetized fool.

The poet mimics the lightest stirrings of the yet-to-be-mummified, he studies them as astrologers study rivers of sky. He returns its weight, its isotope in human pain, to an ecstatic night that can quell it with the basil's dark dew. Thank God, in Greek expression – except for Tragedy, which always aimed elsewhere but whose pleats were always straightened with architectural care by the chorus – the grimace is quieted by grace. This is one of the secrets that console us, whispering "power is more than multitudes and swords."

THE CLOUD PASSES through the girl. Three degrees above "Hello, how are you?" your life, about to reach the point of no return, is stopped as though by cemetery gates. The iron-grinder in the street throws off sparks. The lumbering bus soon arrives. Progress! Humanity! National salvation! Omnipresent, impeccably dressed generals issue commands.

What about? Anything, as long as they are commands: love, cry, dream, today or tomorrow, morning or afternoon, spring or summer. Submission is essential, and lately that means submission to the interests of the sum. In the name of that sum, which we constitute, a million small deaths occur inside the large one before it even happens. We become the murderers, each moment, by degrees.

If we could only notice it, we'd walk on our knees to worship at the unbuilt Temple, the Holy Kore nude and adorned with pomegranate boughs before the sanctum. Only her smile can still resist iron; only her gaze can illuminate a length of centuries where freedom is finally not givable, where justice ripens and falls like the fig. Who, on death's eve, would dare suspect that only during such a sense of time do real poems ripen, only during a meaning of time such as hers?

> *Hearing the swallow   trill for me at dawn*
> *death-equal sleep*

As for me, I understood. The God-child, inexplicably, inhabited me:

> *by night She dispersed the smileless*
> *high noon She showed the all.*

Truthfully. Though I never reckoned on her eyes, she helped me through the hardest moments, simply, throwing a pebble at my window. Not out of kindness or love or self-interest, just because. Poetry is made *just because*. The rest is words. I know I didn't avoid them. Still, wanting fish, you cast nets. You wait, bent over the water, for hours. Suddenly what you waited for arrives by air. What? *Not all fish dwell in the sea.* I understood, as I abandoned the pen for the third and, as I imagined, final time. Early March. The God-child made her third appearance. She took the form of a carpenter's daughter with the body of a small Aphrodite, as only the most demanding fifth century sculptor might have dreamt her. This time it was more than a benevolent sign, a lowered eyelid, a smile; it was a signal, a summons. I swear she gestured with intent. She seemed to answer the uneasy "What?" I made, opening my palms from afar, by writing in the air with an insistent finger, "Write! You must write!" She was, of course, motioning about us meeting, let's not pretend. But if some of our acts have a second significance it is that they occur the very moment they can acquire it.

My encounter with the Carpenter's Daughter stands among the most meaningful of my life; it convinced me of the exceptional seriousness of the ephemeral. I felt I was discovering new units of weight where re-inforced iron hardly tipped the scale, and my last trace of inferiority to-ward the collectors of the sadomasochistic tariff rose from me as lightly as down. My room – its narrow bed, its ascetic little desk, its Oscar Dominguez painting, something between a bird and a plane – hung in the balance for a moment and then, by the rattle of automatic fire, set out to meet Spring halfway.

When I glanced at my watch it was "A quarter to Spring," exactly.

A QUARTER TO SPRING

A quarter to spring! A young couple stares eye-to-eye; no eyelid lowers. Blood changes direction in the veins; the boys' voices drop; the girls' breasts harden; the distant impassioned song of love, led astray by the azure radiance of a half-woken horizon, trembles... A quarter to spring! Soon, the nettle and the prick-ly bush pound their fists on the muddy stones behind hedgerows in empty lots and, through the broken glass and upended basins, victorious against garbage trucks, luck's aster dawns naked on the spear of its ray. Sideways, defying the wind that carried it elsewhere, the fanatic poppy explodes in the spark of two flints, to wave its red coat of arms under winter's nostrils. And girls, little girls, bending to tie their new sandals, suddenly see the world lean into take-off and rise up to vanish in the untrembling ether.

Their belts, always sky-blue, tighten around their high waists. Their hair, behind the ear or loose in the wind, is the caress, materialized and playing the game of enthusiastic flags. Flame, black flame, gold flame: how often I said I wouldn't live without my right hand surrendered to your fire! How often swore I wouldn't pass the clamor of nightingales perched on the leaning masts of their floating gardens at dawn, unless as God inside you, girls!

Around the well and its crank, around the huge cisterns, where a clean firmament of water, shimmering, reflects creation upside down, I catch for a moment your fleeting idol waving from the bottom of earth's first looking-glass. And when the prow of day, half-black from evening fires and laden with grandeur, touches the forest depths, it is you again, traversing the suspended rooms in your strawberry nightgowns, singing so passionately that rosemary honey drips from the masculine blissfulness of stars.

Let no kerchief dampen, let no branch creak before the dew, lest suddenly the sun rear up to blind me with that enigmatic lightning bolt attending Nature when you lower your eyes. The branch creaks, the sun rears, I see your transparent voices paved with endless gardens, roses, brimming with slingshots of birds and the roar of bride bees.

Yes, yes, the world thirsts and you, who hear by heart and smell by eye, know what it thirsts for; you throw a word into the air, one only, but it means all things we adore on this earth and swear to never abandon. This word – love! love! – pelts light, through a myriad prisms, on the joyous moment luck embodies each time as a gift to two people who are always new; strong as the Sirocco it throws itself above rooftops and clouds. The mountains take it then and throw its endless charm one to the other, until church bells are its greeting, flying cranes and young storks its eternal ally, ferns shivering on tiptoe waiting for the commotion to pass and hearts to still.

In all countries people emerge, whether from terrace, belfry or high fork of tree, to salute and celebrate the incredible journey. Love! Love! Old people, children – those familiar with its moods, those yet to be – emerge, right hand shading their eyes as if chasing kites or seeing their own life, sick with regrets and dreams, tear through the ether... Love! Love! And the impatient creatures stamp their feet, their bodies shake, a tuning fork struck over endless cisterns of lilies and dew. A voice – love! love! – flies above the rippled, disappearing fields, the cypresses plunging into earth, the oleanders drowning in the rivers, over people stretching their arms out to embrace you, girls, the minute you stretch from your invisible stalk, waist yielding, the gold dust of your naked body closer to the pestle.

I didn't want to arrive without trembling to where flesh gathers blood and thrusts a hasty clock into the heart. Tick-tock, the same tick-tock since childhood, the ceaseless tick-tock pushing me with fists of wrathful roses to your feet, breathing into my breath the notion to stroll slowly and in awe through the June of your most secret pleat. I crush the petals surreptitiously wetting my palms and seem, from afar, a small hero who can bear to see you in your peachskin only. I still don't know when you will enter your destiny; when, sprinkled with drops of an unsullied spring, you'll groan like splendid beasts? Your breasts, untried, defy the future. I am not ashamed to name them nude, proud, impatient. As long as they tremble life also will, as will my hand and every

50

poppy of every field. As long as their nipples regard the world, it will continue to float, proudly, amidst its fiery satellites.

Often, when the sunburnt boys, sated with solitude, sleep on a pillow of foaming sea at noon, a shadow I fear is my own lies in wait behind the geraniums for your step across the dark verandas. You pause a moment thoughtfully under a large stone arch, as if far away crystal castles had developed a silent crack. You vaguely raise your hand and, a cold glimmer turning your pupils emerald, you surrender to the hedonic shiver measuring you from neck-root to soles. What awe, moistened by rapture, rises to the ceiling then, ricochets off the walls, reflects the sea all the way to your internal hillsides, girls! My hour to stand on your lips has arrived, my hour to take communion – body and blood of life eternally new – from your lips; my hour to be new as often as nature can place the world's essence newly on your lips; my hour to conceive a kiss of as ceaseless a metamorphosis, endowed with as many hues as the swift metamorphosis and myriad hues of the savor our earth's young body assumes on the lips of every one of you, girls – sanctity of our world!

1944 & 1972.

Chronicle of a Decade

WHETHER YOU HAVE *written poems or not is less important than whether you have suffered, been impassioned or longed for what leads, by hook or by crook, to Poetry. The wind of life hits you before its material body, as the aroma of a woman before her actual presence. What remains is the embrace, and love.*

When the wind of Greek poetic texts first struck me, the weather vanes rasped and the barometer promised change. In barely a decade, a state of expression would have been transformed, and for a country (I'd say for a language) whose greatest honor is the high poetic tradition, such deep, radical reversal could not but have special meaning.

I believe that what we usually call ephemeral, itself unsalvageable, can salvage an epoch's spirit. Therefore, I want to take in my hands again events of seemingly secondary importance and texts written in the margins of a main effort, hoping these, more than larger accomplishments, will sketch the features of its physiognomy.

I set out today with such a feeling: to traverse my memories rather than write my memoirs and to concern myself at last with myself, without the charge of narcissism. After all, a kind of life where the smallest personal detail takes on a public meaning, and all things public become the personal concern of all, is not, one day, improbable. Meanwhile, let those who can, set an example.

This story begins the day I looked my fate in the face and accepted it. I mean the day I separated my responsibilities from family tradition, university niceties and ambitions for a social career, the day I abandoned my rationalizations and said: A thousand times better to be tested and fail than stay this side of danger and be comfortable in obscurity. And yet, this story is as little mine as the smallness of our soul before the unknown powers that steer it.

A

IT IS 1934, in the east courtyard of the university. As if on an ungoverned ship, a possessed and discombobulated crowd of students comes and goes. They have wild hair, threadbare overcoats and briefcases in hand. They circle, they discuss, gesticulate and shout. Some impromptu speaker, who has mounted a bench, draws attention, and soon foes and allies form around him, bellicose, glaring, threatening and marching against each other,

The signal comes quickly. Someone always makes the first move. Fist fights erupt, books scatter, buttons rip, caps hit the flagstones, and one sees occasional drops of blood. The cowardly run away. A "marked one" tries to escape, doesn't make it and doubles up shouting, "brothers!" while blows fall harder on his back. The countless councils call an assembly that afternoon. Proclamations will be passed; some will bring clubs or brass knuckles; heads will crack. Oh yes, the world must be improved. But no, aren't Greek values the most important? The whole world's attention is focused here; here, perhaps, its fate is being decided. Youth, having the least, has basically the most, but doesn't know it.

"Youth, youth, how lovely your hair," as the poet would later say. I couldn't, of course, see then how the struggle to make a living would, like a huge cesspool, suck this beautiful crowd with its flushed cheeks and exhaust it on a clerk's chair. I could see from afar, between the bars of the fence I had climbed, these fighters and their problems form the shape of a wide belt. And on this belt, as if superimposed, another belt, as wide but with different problems, eternal ones, that no armed hand or anything could change, except perhaps the human mind.

What held me back? Was I a coward or did I have the intellectual's virus? Their vision undid my knees. I was jealous. I certainly preferred to be one of them, to believe, defend and be beaten for my ideas. I was, in my fashion, a communist anyway; the leadership was convinced of it. Secretly, I translated Trotsky for a Marxist newspaper. But when everything calmed down and I returned home to my books, I felt this enthusiasm suddenly turn to an easily crushed material in my hands, a measure of power deflated by the infinite power of the simple joinery of language, a rare expression or a perfect verse. Then I'd go back to the University yard, which was now totally different, deserted, as if a magic hand at dusk had changed its visage. It was more reminiscent of the courtyard of an island monastery with its sparse, flitting shadows and half-dark archways in back. There I joined three or four friends belonging to a different tribe.

Pale, dreamtaken, they all wrote similar poems confessing faith in one god only, Karyotakis:

A dry bay leaf this hour will fall
the pretense of your life denuded
alluded to a leafless tree
caught up by winter in mid-street.

It was, without doubt, a new language. Still, something about it bothered me. I'm not sure but perhaps it's this: I found no relation between the poem's tone and the tone our life was taking then, no relation between the poet's vision and our daily vision of our classmates being beaten or our nightly encounters with our girlfriends on Lycabettos Hill. I don't mean of course that the poems had to be combative or erotic, not at all. The problem was clearly tonal and esthetic:

I see the ceiling plaster.
Meanders draw me to their dance.
My happiness I think will be
A matter of stature.

The boldness of expression attracted me. The content left me indifferent, as did Tellos Agras' neo-tropic revelations, which were extremely popular then in the journals but were prevented by end-rhyme from reaching their just brilliance, at least in my opinion:

Salt moon like water moon.

Still, the human psyche was a strange thing. I took example from my own, which, if asked, was full of despair but didn't want to find it in what it read. To explain my character, I will push what I'm saying further. It struck me strangely that everyone writing poems then, good or bad it makes no difference, was trying to express in verse their emotional situation, that is, to begin with their circumstance and, in other words, recount their blues. Though this had always been the purpose of lyric poetry, it interested me the least. To be emotionally moved was somehow secondary. Not that I wasn't moved by a simple scene of life, a song or a film.

Perhaps my absurdity lay in the fact that I wanted to use a glass not to drink from but for anything else, for instance, to note and enjoy the transparence of crystal, since transparence was more meaningful to me than any drink. So perhaps it was this, or else surely my reaction to the erosion of some basic meanings precisely defining the human soul. With painting as my prototype, I wanted to replace them. Poetry could give substance to many fluid meanings. There was a worthy goal! As for the poem, meeting place of a myriad elements all answering to a different name, it could, past a point of fusion, amalgamate all of them into a meaning which reality, as we knew it, did not permit: a Paradise beyond our capabilities whose absence caused each of us our distress.

Surrealism touched me, I think, from this side, as a protest against our slavery which instead of lamenting, as it had done, is now the exalted and infinite mistress of the recombinant imagination, proposing intellectual and spiritual solutions in accord with eternal human desires. This seemed more in harmony with the open white shirts the boldest of us had already donned in those years. Agras and Karyotakis wore double vests and stiff collars. I'm not kidding.

MY FIRST EXCURSIONS to the Greek outdoors happened to start that year. I'm still grateful to the luck that sent me a friend at a critical moment in my development. Perhaps he was not an intellectual, but he was definitely a conscientious lover of Greece and one of the first motorists in the land. I insist to this day on the symbolic meaning of our friendship, fate's favor. At a time when going from Athens to Delphi was still an improbable expedition requiring a whole day (and you never knew if you would get there in one piece), we literally roamed all over Greece. True pioneers, we went on for days – starved, unshaven, hanging onto the carriage of a dying Chevy, up and down dunes, traversing lakes, in clouds of dust or merciless rainstorms, climbing obstacles and eating miles with an insatiability that only our twenty years and our love for this small land we were discovering could excuse.

It was as if lying for the first time with a woman, whose body until then you had only imagined. Different, but better than expected. Solid matter slowly filled the mental schema in my head – like clay or architecture's concrete – sometimes so precisely it made me wonder at reality's force. Other times not. But what I want to note is that my native tendency (to recompose an ideal prototype from elements I judged to be most worthy) was relentless, causing me, after a series of subtractions and additions, to finally retain a "synoptic landscape," clearly oneiric, yet one which felt more real to me than the one available to my senses at any given moment.

Of course, my senses were still the organs receiving and rebroadcasting the vision. Except that by being placed in untried relationships, they had acquired extensions (until now asleep in human beings) that sounded the chords of their most secret areas and commandeered, by a word, the whole dynamic of the soul: as if music, painting, mind and speech were instantly compressed, as physical elements compress through the millennia, into jewels of uncatalyzed splendor. This was the miracle. What loftier goal for a human than to be a producer of miracles, what more miraculous than that he, death's subject, forever cast the death-bound from what he loves and so become the owner of another immortality's mirror and, possibly, also his own.

The subject is nature, yes. European sensibility, as I saw it in her poets, had pushed it aside some time ago and had stored it on lower levels, like a mass of matter no longer able to resonate the soul. Among us too the more naïve called it "landscape," "folklore," "impressionistic painting." Their loss! The sun too is, for some, metaphysics, for others, a walk in Zappeion Park. But here, on the road, the way I saw Nature ended up not being Nature. Vision led to sensation and sensation again to vision. The motion was essential – I mean the parallel motion of the soul – or else the constant motion between the Immobile and the Eternal.

A ceaseless penetration of sea into mountain that was also mountain penetrating sea, the luminosity of water when seafloor is also ceiling over our heads, the bamboo aroma both clearing the sky and erasing our mistakes, the stone fountain on the public road a small daily Parthenon...! Is all that, I ask, *a landscape?* Or merely *nature?* This ultimate reduction drawn so as to be indelible, an order at last whose number is as real and inconceivable as water leaping and shouting like an infant or the moon, co-conspirator of breezes, the embrace in which only a lover's vow remains, these palmfuls of wet pebbles I can smell as though my eyes are cleansed by most immaculate meaning... All these, I ask and ask, are *landscape, nature?* Or maybe not. Maybe they are the world's end and beginning, the human alpha and omega, God himself – just as I started to plead Lord have mercy!

No, no, Poetry is a mechanism that demechanizes humans and their relationship to things. The poet beds his contradiction. Linguistically, the temptation to test one's endurance for abnegation often leads to another kind of admission: *this* is a human; what poet dare define him? The truth remains to be invented. Meanwhile, let's speak of simpler things.

For my young self, Greece was dazzling. Neither patriot nor nature-lover, I was perplexed to have both attributes ascribed to me; what one might feel if, in some earlier time, one had suspected electricity in storms and been called an autumnal romantic by one's contemporaries. So much had I, apparently, failed to separate sensation from its object and show its derivatives to the spirit!

But, to return to the subject, my first contact with the material body of Greece: either it was something other than merely *nature* or then... then Greek nature is so charged with secret messages – as some had told us but we were reluctant to believe – as to rightly assume inside us the meaning and weight of a secret mission.

This perception leads far, and now is not the time to traverse the distance. It does however constitute a metaphysics where language is not just the sum of a few words or symbols – as landscape is not the sum of trees and mountains – but a complex signifier, an ethical power mobilized by the human mind, precursing things, to create them in this and only in this manner. From then on, the analogy between the phonetic composition of words and the material content they give to phenomena presents the qualities of the inevitable character of Fate or of primary physical elements.

The point is not to evaluate the different languages now, though Greek, which twice in history took on a global mission, has virtues its contemporary neurotic carriers appear to ignore, lacking a long-term critical grasp. The point is that the correlation between Greek and at least some of what we might call "first meanings" is astonishing and more, circumscribing and also privileged. So that even if you didn't want to accept it logically, you'd nonetheless be forced to concede that, in practice, *this instrument directs the meanings it expresses more often than it is directed by them.*

Here's something that, though illogical, explains the idiomatic tropism of Greek thought in its expression, particularly when the spiritual element is chief, either during the times when it has carried all the weight of civilization or, by contrast, when it has been compressed by the entire weight of a civilization foreign to its nature. From there issues the right, or whatever you want to call it, the demand or delusion that "Greece be the exception." I mean this is why, for example, nature can't fail to have a place in our poetic expression, as has happened in other western countries. I believe it is the reason why "angst" or "demonism" can't take hold on the tree of our language. The reason Greek poets, regardless of what generation or period they belong to, always concern themselves with their land. A phenomenon that provokes perplexity in foreign scholars and unreflective Greeks.

I speak, I repeat, from today's perspective. Still, even in my early travels to the ends of Greece, I felt what I would now call *the ethic of language* as fanatically and absurdly as idealists and lovers feel their passions. And I'm naive enough to think that, had I been foreign, I would have lacked the slightest interest in writing poems, so deeply rooted was my conviction that the elements I wanted to rouse and subject to the omnipotence of the associative imagination (even though I'd taken example from foreigners) could not possibly obey a birdsong other than the one first learned millennia ago in this same place with these same phonemes. Don't laugh. Exaggeration and childishness, in the realm of art, sometimes prove wiser than the oracles of science. And, confidentially, I'd like to shout, "woe to Greece from the Universities of the West, whose rodents already gnaw at its foundation," if I weren't scared they'd put me away.

Because the justice of might acquires finally a logic all its own, dispatching to prisons and asylums those who still cherish the small of their pride.

I had gained so much momentum toward clarity. And in the marine horizons I was discovering, I found a natural clarity that *gave body* to the spiritual one I longed for. So it was natural to seek a poetic method that could, by the opposite road and through my own soul's intervention, embody the corresponding sensations that enchanted me: the "brilliant," the "transparent," the "watery," the "fresh," the "leafy," the "immaculate."

But could these goals excite an emotional peasant? My sentence to solitude was absolute. I would live only by the mistakes that escaped me. Could I have turned myself into an actor of foreign emotions? It's lucky that poetry was never a lucrative undertaking. Who knows, I might then have run the risk of bowing under and becoming a carpenter who makes horrible furniture just because it sells in the market. My university friends loved horrible furniture, I thought, not because they loved Karyotakis, but because they, although Greek, cultivated a spirit unsuited to the ethos of the Greek language. And suddenly I felt nothing tied me to them.

I felt them drift away, become one with common opinion, and I became the foreigner, as foreign as Kavafis confesses himself to be in Myre's poem. The same poem let me go on. Already, a doubt approached. Had I been tricked by my passion to write? Was I perhaps not a poet? Other suspicions fueled this doubt. I began, as if with many years behind me, to scratch at my memories.

B

As A CHILD, I remember, poetry barely touched me. The *Modern Greek Reader* left me with the vague impression that it was nothing but a garrulous and boring metronome. One used poems to make mountains or rivers speak, saying the commonplace. Besides, our professors bypassed them, demanding them only at June finals. Yet while my brother, almost my age, spent all his pocket money on sweets and footballs, I, with an almost pathological love for printed paper, filled my closets with magazines and books. What was I looking for? What did I adore?

The *idea of a book*, nothing else. I was no longer a child. A few years before, an issue of *Children's Formation* had helped me break from Jules Verne and the fat gilded volumes of *Bibliothèque Rose* and had put me in contact with the first modern Greek literary book. It was *Poppies and Hay* by Gregorios Xenopoulos, which I had won in a competition. Of course, this is not about content. It was the very fact that a contemporary, live person (not distant and foreign like the others) could transform himself into this small rectangular object that hit me squarely on the head. To suffer in this life, as I heard from the adults, to be humiliated and, despite it all, be able to save your cleanest part once and for all in a six-by-nine shape, well, that was not just any occupation, it approached magic. It was candidacy for some vague victory worth any sacrifice in the pursuit.

I don't know if I correct my memories now as we unwillingly correct the dreams we narrate. But, inseparable from that fascination and inexplicably tied to it, a totally opposite sensation mastered me, a sensation of almost metaphysical fear. It was as though my fate sat across from me. An instinct (descended from what ancestral mountains) made me recoil in defense. Was I born to serve letters? I made a beeline for the opposite shore. I quickly excelled in track. I became the most fanatic member of the school touring team, which every Sunday climbed the peaks of Pendeli and Hymettos. I was about to start regular training at the national track. Perhaps a psychoanalyst can shed some light on why I wanted to be admired for excelling in what I didn't admire at all.

In any case, I remember, some reconciliation took place. Now the books I bought had to have some relation to nature. Kambouroglou, Pasayannis, Granitsas, and even a three-volume *Guide to Greece* from Eleutheroudakis could literally have me hanging by a thread. This thread was cut (precisely when I least expected it) by an unknown enemy already pregnant with a minuscule friend: illness. I was diagnosed with the classic overexertion of adolescence: adenoids and fever. In other words, I had to spend at least two months in bed and postpone my examinations to September.

Despairingly, I said goodbye to my athletic dreams, took a deep breath, and set off straight for the opposite shore. In my first round against fate, I had been roundly beaten. Now, along with fresh butter and steak, I gobbled up enormous quantities of Greek and foreign literature. Day and night, a small train passed over my bed loaded with books and journals: *New Hestia, Elysia, Breath, Logos, Innovation, Greek Letters, Philotechnic,* and *Alexandrian Art.* Bent patiently for hours, I caught many fish. Only Poetry didn't bite. I needed Kavafis to feel the pull – something very strong, my god, what was this? Strange. A deep curiosity overtook me that later became deep interest and later still deep admiration. Charm, never.

I want to be truthful or the game is worthless. Nine-tenths of the poetry I read repulsed me by something that I would call, politely, *absence of pride* and also a false progressiveness, stinginess, small-mindedness, and, finally, facile philosophy. Of course, the Asia Minor tragedy was still fresh. So what? Defeat may tie your hands, but it also loosens the soul and aims it high, eager for revenge. While the intellectuals lamented, the popular soul was won by propulsive forces, and in twenty years the valve would burst with an explosion that made even them wonder.

What could Tragedy's form share with this pettiness around us? A horrid misunderstanding! Under the Sun's terrifying machine, we stood naked before our enigma – toys in the hands of chance, life a few seconds between ruins, a handful of clichés comprising the gratuitous philosopher's bible – well, at that point, the thinking man is *obliged* to say something. But those nurtured on the lakes and lilies of impoverished translations never faced the sun. And Asia Minor was distant.

I know that these are preposterous expressions, but they correspond exactly to my emotion at the time. You have my word. My sixteen-year-old mind, as I see it now, yearned for an expression more difficult than despair, which I'd gone through in a few months, synoptically, as one goes through measles. I also yearned for my own, completely personal *analog* to express what I had stored as a child wandering the shores of an island barefoot in moments of exaltation and solitude: smoothness, mica spark, thrill of young organisms, daze of the nude. Now does any of this relate to Kavafis, who, as I said, had given me this sudden jolt toward poetry? *Not at all.* And precisely so. This is precisely why my reaction was so large.

I felt poetry could be something else. And yet, how lovely for this *difference* to be different. All of life with its daily associations could fit in the smallest space. How lovely then if life could proceed in this space by an order that we had yet to encounter, but which our spirit could freely impose. And, more seriously: in Kavafis I also encountered the *wrinkle*, whereas my innate disposition was to exorcize the world's old age by every means. And then…a large void, as in dreams. The last year of high school, the exams, the diploma, detoxified me from such *philologitis*.

Finally the day came when, a free academic citizen, cigarette on my lips and a seriously reinforced wallet, I began to make the rounds of the bookstores. I've recounted elsewhere how I came upon a book by Paul Éluard, entirely by luck. It's true. Now, of course, it occurs to me that such an event does not escape an indisputable symbolism. It was under these zodiacs that I was meant to find a theory giving so much weight to chance (specifically the so-called *hasard objectif*), a theory aspiring to inoculate life with the serum of magic. Still, some idiot did criticize my purposeful confession, saying I had arrived by cheap roads to my craft. *Passons:*

> *Toi la seule et j'entends les herbes de ton rire*
> *Toi c'est la tête qui t'enlève*
> *Et du haut des dangers de mort*
> *Tu enfantes la chute.*

"So plausible the Incomprehensible!" I could explain nothing then, nor can I today. Yet I couldn't wait until the house was empty so I could take these verses one by one and let them live in my oral cavity, and not because they were musical. What then? I don't know, a different engulfment, a loss of habit of the tongue and lips (which were losing the habit of the entire world), an oversaturation of syntax to the benefit of the instantaneous soul, brevity at the service of dream... And above all, revirgining. New vocalizations mobilized; blood circulated more; cheeks glowed. I recognized the thrill of young organisms, which, by an irony of fate, I had vainly sought in the innovative but aged Alexandrian.

It is not only difficult, it is impossible for a youth to stand in my place today and feel the same emotion, the same invincible pull, now that authentic speech has been around for thirty years. He would have to erase everything behind him and stand with one leg in "Step aside boulder, let me pass." My other leg was already in Surrealism without knowing it. Who might talk to me about these things? Taking pen and paper, I sat down to write to the publisher José Corti. Was Éluard, as I had read somewhere, a Surrealist? Were there many Surrealists? Who were they? What did they believe in? I was not satisfied. I received an advertising brochure with photos of poets and as many titles of books, nothing else.

A second collusion of fate was needed before help could arrive, from an unexpected quarter, in the person of an unknown Greek, D.

Menjelos. Unknown to us, as far as I could tell, but well-read and sensitive, as he would later show. He contracted severe tuberculosis and was hospitalized at *Hôpital Source* in Lausanne during the time that René Crevel, one of the first Surrealists and its most distinguished prose writer, was there for the same reason. It was their common fate, alas, not to survive, one from the illness that smote him, the other by his own hand. But there, in the interminable hours of thermometers and open windows, the French initiated the Greek in the secrets of his theory, and the Greek had time to write a study, with a rare insight and precision for the period, which *Logos* published. I no longer have the issue and don't know what I'd say if I read the study today. I remember it as an honorable, inspired, brief but complete exposition of a view of life – above all, of life as well as poetic craft. From then on, plausibility was less important.

So, AT EIGHTEEN, tentative about my future and my studies, in a house where mourning hadn't left one window open, I read that everything around me was the least substantial. That perhaps even the life we lived was real life's sleep, continuing each night from dream to dream. And that if we couldn't conceive of and decode it, our logic was to blame, or our upbringing based on a bad tradition. A tradition excluding our genuine parts. It was our business to revolt, say no and stretch our hand over the Mysteries. How beautiful. My bed was already lighter and Karyotakis grew distant, miniaturized, as if from the wrong side of a lens.

A remnant of age-old superstition and habit coated the entire surface of the earth, depriving us of the joy of true contact and free association with things, as our secret desires longed for but dared not confess. Surely another road, parallel to logic and courageously taken, would lead far into the unsuspected, where everything was possible, realizable. Who knows? We might even laugh at what we once thought inscrutable and angst-ridden. Then, even death might take its other, its true meaning. This mass cancellation of the properties we had learned to ascribe to things would enable us to put reality on the bench. Eros, Poetry, Eros and Poetry, indivisible: their duty was to set examples and overcome the barriers erected by false modesty, language and syntax, the shackles of a mediocre, stupid society. A secret voice moved within and beyond rea-

sonable order, above and independent from time, and in constant dura-
tion. To render its presence sensible even for a moment was the poet's
mission. The eons' sharpest spirits, from Heracleitos to Sade to Rim-
baud, had already, unwittingly, achieved it. They had conceived the Sur-
real voice in moments of exquisite disarmament from esthetic concern
and in absolute obeisance to the Mysteries. And this voice will exist and
resound for all.

FORGIVE ME for changing Menjelos' writings. After so many years, it is
natural to alter, silence, or complete. This is not as significant as the
then absolute inability of people of letters to become initiates of a spirit
that all but evicted them from letters. Their reaction, either out of inad-
equacy or self-preservation, was to cut and refashion the Surrealist flags
to their stature. The oneiric became – O horror – "the dreamy," and
Surrealism, a tendency to the immaterial.

And I was looking for co-conspirators! Everyday, with a secret heart-
beat, I tended the pages of periodicals, the bookstore windows. If a title
just slightly escaped the usual, I'd leap to take the bounty home. Soon,
the first crop of modern poetic texts piled up on my student desk, refut-
ing the old *Introductions to Roman Justice*. Caesar Emmanuel's *Off-key
Flute*, Theodore Dorros' *At Rescue's Awe*, Niketas Randos' *Poems*, and
George Seferis' *Strophe*.

I adored them. I dressed them in tissue paper. I opened and closed
them ten times a day. Even I wondered at my naïveté. Perhaps having
the virus meant just that. Also, I needed their help. Unequal as they
seemed in quality, and as different in direction, these books besieged
and tightened the noose around the great "favorite," K.G. Karyotakis:

> *And since it will be late by then*
> *to roll between your hands the new chimeras*
> *or even a conventional and superficial pleasure,*
> *you'll part the window one last time*
> *and seeing all of life you'll laugh serenely.*

Yes and no. As long as I stayed in bed, face down for hours and hours,
with teary eyes and a bitter taste in my mouth on account of something
terrible that had yet to happen but which, I later understood, my youth

imposed on me like a romantic need to reach orgasm by pain, at one with my Christian origins – as long as I stayed in bed then yes, indeed, a genuine emotion could be found there. But if I swung from the iron fence of the University or, higher, from those ramparts from which I could see land and sea burnt in the sun of solitude, amidst the thousand secret voices of birds and surf, and with the fierce forms of Saints and Agonistes attaining the unattainable as only Poetry or Sainthood might attain – if the Sirens' magic voices rose in me to proclaim a different promised land, then no, never. Defeatism was childhood's trap, or else it was "horror's arrogance"; and self-punishment an artificial flower cultivated in the greenhouses of the north.

Let's be clear. I'm not against Karyotakis, who came up the ladder with skill and courage and who fell by a false assessment of the significance his fall might have. But I am certainly against the general masturbation that followed. My reaction was so strong that for a couple of years I tried to reconcile myself with Philosophy and Law which, with the arrival of the new professors, Tsatsos, Kanelopoulos and Theodorakopoulos, were enjoying favor and uncontested fascination among the young.

AT TWENTY-TWO you care less about form and perfection than about the adventure spirit can lead you to. Comprehensible or not, the theories were as so many Sirens, luring us far. Spiritual engagement hedonized me, like boarding a ship.

We're still in 1934 – our newborn ship, thrown together by some fifteen students, almost all seniors in law, was pompously christened "Ideocratic Philosophic Team of Athens University." On Saturday nights, as in a monastic commune, professors and students ate together at a long table in the student union. Then we'd go to an upstairs library to read the philosophies of Descartes or Fichte and debate them with passion. The others did, that is, because I, standing aside, felt desperately incapable of uttering a word. I noticed the facility of my colleagues' rhetoric, their artful dodges between difficult or inaccessible meanings. I often lost the thread to find myself hanging by another, at the edge of a precipice where everything, I imagined, could be saved by a single verse. With great remorse, I prepared to flee. And I'd have succeeded if one night something "unprogrammed" hadn't stopped me.

66

Someone new, an interloper, stood to speak. We'd never seen him before. He was of medium height, with thinning hair and thick myopic glasses; he more squeaked than spoke, standing on tiptoe, veins swelling his neck, his Adam's apple perched on a badly buttoned shirt. His voice, nasal and sharp, betrayed its Italian origin. George Sarantaris had just arrived from the University of Macerata for his military service. When I heard that he wrote poems characterized as "strange," something inside me squinted. How lovely, I thought, if he too – already great enough to tackle real philosophers – was a fellow traveler, and I added him to the group I had, in my impatient imagination, already envisioned forming in Greece. I went up and spoke to him. I was, for him as for the others, a friend, an admirer of new poetic ways, and nothing else.

He took a tiny book from his briefcase and gave it to me. It was *The Loves of Time*: a different way of seeing and conceiving of things, both inverted and straight, instantaneously and inseparably. We quickly became friends. His idiomatic voice, that could so well isolate a gorgeous verse to savor it at length and follow its extensions, still rings in my ears.

I have not known a purer human spiritual form than his. Inexperienced, awkward, incapable of anything practical, he lived by nothing and needed nothing but Poetry. That is, he was the exact opposite of what the bourgeois dream for their children. Therefore, he had succeeded in raising his large myopic eyes to the Platonic Essences. His presence was timely. Here was someone at last, shortchanged by nature, poor, alone, twisting the mirror away from life's curse toward its miracle. And with a faith, a confidence and strength his slight body almost could not bear. His days were filled with work. As if they were stones, he used them to build his ethical personality and so gained the courage to denounce degeneration and proudly ask the deified Kavafis, "Have you ever loved a Roxanne?" in a poem full of a meaning no one has successfully addressed to this day.

With Orthodoxy and that "other joy" as his vision, a silver ore our peasant critics took for gilt, he expected everything from the university youths whom he enthusiastically "fished" for and dreamt of flaunting, proud and erect, at Europe.

Nothing large lacks its chimera. He knew how to domesticate it. He came to my house often and besieged my timidity. We were reading French and Italian poets, especially Ungaretti, whose famous poem,

"Memoria d'Ophelia d'Alba," I had learned, I recall, by heart in the original. Anyway, in just a few minutes one fall evening, he extracted my confession as well as my first calligraphed manuscripts. I felt like a sinner before his confessor. Later, in days when leniency seemed out of place and cordiality superfluous, he did, I admit, also deal me a blow. His ethic did not allow the blessing of sensation as sensation alone, and the purely spiritual perspective from which he insisted on viewing the poetic mission forced him to censure play. "You are *hedonista*," he'd shout and I'd wonder why; much later, I saw his meaning. But back then, he was enthusiastic at my "butterflies living great adventures," my "unrepentant hand melancholy in my hair." His joy was greater than mine or so it seemed. Dizzy and shaken, as after difficult but successful surgery, I swore him to secrecy. The next day all his friends knew. First among them, accepting and curious, was Andreas Karantonis.

It must have been when we were planning *New Letters*, since it was autumn and the first issue came out in January, 1935. By the movie theater *Capitol*, just before St. Meletios Street intersected Acharnon Avenue, was a small cafe where a motley, noisy group of inspired and uncontainable students gathered, chugging ideas as easily as wine, late at night, harbored at improbable taverns. They left no subject undusted, from President Venizélos and the Greece of five seas and two continents to Psycharis or the grammatical revisions of Noumas; no view, regardless of how paradoxical, was left unchampioned between jokes and seriousness, between subtle hairsplitting and real fistfights.

There was plenty of nerve, and Greece was certainly rising. The literary generation of the thirties dawned. Returning at night from the alleys of Lycabettos, "still fresh from girls' kisses," Theotokas' *Free Spirit* in hand, we hardly knew if our heart beat so loudly for literature or eros. Taken together and gilded by youth, they formed the spirit that blossomed easily in the poor neighborhoods of prewar Athens.

Andreas Karantonis had that spirit when I met him, I remember. Loaded with pamphlets, leaning a little to one side, he'd walk through the night frost flanked by three or four friends, whispering random Greek or French verses, which he read to saturation and memorized instantly, not to mention Palamas, whom he had almost entirely by heart. With him, communication would be easier. We were much alike. Also an islander, malleable, adaptable, close to the senses but not far from ideas, he bypassed the neuroses of others – as if they didn't exist, as if they didn't touch him – wanting only the essence, the taste of the essence, which he savored wherever he found it, in good verse or good wine. I lent him all the books at my disposal, and there were many. He devoured and assimilated them all in a night. He barely noticed the dislocation they caused him. He was that ready, one could say, to receive the new. Another believer won! And 1935 was still young.

Thick, black volumes of Windscheid and Dernburg had been piling up on my little desk. One ought to get one's diploma with honors, I thought, or not at all. I laid out ideal study plans. Then, early in February, just as my spirits were lifting, I was consternated by a small notice in the paper. "The day after tomorrow, at six P.M., the poet Mr. Andreas Embeirikos will speak at the *Atelier* on: Surrealism, a new poetic school. Free entry."

I was demonized. Who was this *ex machina* on my fields? How would I convince him, meeting him the day after tomorrow, that I hadn't garnered my knowledge from his lecture but had discovered it earlier, much earlier, alone and with great effort. Childish egoism was at stake, nothing else. I felt I must hurry. My brother had mentioned that while he was at school in Lausanne, an idiosyncratic young man named Andreas Embeirikos also lived there, who read strange books and wrote even stranger poems. It had to be him. I made my brother call and secure me a meeting before the lecture by any means. So, the following evening, with the fear of God in my heart, I rang the bell of an apartment on Queen Sophia Boulevard.

A solemn housekeeper with thick glasses and a white apron like a nurse opened the door. Inside, it smelled of English cigarettes and wax. A squat mastiff disappeared down the hall. I sat on the edge of a large armchair and looked around. It wasn't the usual middle-class home. The large paintings on the walls calmed rather than bewildered me with their outrageous depictions. I recognized in the flesh what I'd only encountered before in foreign journals. Soon, I even recognized the painters: there was Max Ernst, then Yves Tanguy and then Oscar Dominguez, what miracle! I felt like a savage who, recently converted by some missionary and never having seen a real church, suddenly finds himself in a cathedral. For me, in that moment, esthetic evaluation of the work I was admiring was as insignificant as the painterly quality of the Virgin's

69

portrait would be to that new Christian, simply overwhelmed by her image. They represented revolution and new order; they *were* The Revolution beyond all revolutions, a new eon for the world of the soul.

Still sitting, I tried to guess at the books lining the walls of the small study, further back, its sliding doors drawn open. Here were all the testaments and prophets I could now rejoice in studying and touching with my own hands! I put out my cigarette in one of the large crystal ashtrays and, hands in my pockets, approached the crowded shelves feigning indifference, as if invisible police were watching. A few quick glances gave great harvest. Books I had known only by title – which I savored like candy – like *Petite Anthologie poétique du Surréalisme* edited by Georges Hugnet, all those inaccessible, fascinating titles with their disarming immediacy and plausible arbitrariness were there: Tristan Tzara's *Cinéma Calenfrier du cœur abstrait maisons*, André Breton's *Clair de terre*, Éluard's familiar *Capitale du douleur*, and Tzara again, his *Mouchoir de nuages*. There, on the spines of actual green, red and white books, were the titles in a variety of typefaces, fat, narrow, roman, italic. I had but to stretch my arm to dissolve all the mysteries.

But just then I heard steps and, turning, saw the outstretched hand of a man in his thirties, with thick plentiful hair, protruding cheekbones, clear dark skin and eyes that were simultaneously piercing and dreamy. Our conversation was a series of surprised exclamations more than it was a dialogue. In his face I saw an almost mythic creature who had eaten and drunk with my gods. He in turn saw the unexpected bounty of a young fellow-traveler in the literary desert of Athens. It was destiny. It was natural to become friends, with a friendship that, traversing as Kalvos would say "the quarter century," was never for a moment threatened. Surrealism had raised the first bridge. But could it have endured, alone, the heavy vehicles it carried from both sides, had it been unaided by the splendid coincidence of our characters that synchronized its tremors so that its girders could absorb the shock?

Embeirikos was imagination's long-distance athlete, his field the universe, Eros his stride. His work, each new work, bound by a small rainbow, was a promise to humanity, a gift that, if it still eludes the hands of some, does so only because of their inability. His Freudian studies, his psychoanalytic practice, which I would later have occasion to observe, had enabled him to regard the nucleus of life, which is Eros in its entirety, beyond any convention, development or climax. He was of apostolic stature, his only tongue the poet's tongue, and he was unprecedented in our letters, far beyond our habits of lament and guilt.

At my first shy request that historic night, just as I was leaving, he drew a shiny red notebook across his desk, opened it and read to me at random. The world overturned. What I heard, behind his deliberate monotone and warm demeanor, seemed to arrive from a great distance – even though I was familiar with foreign automatic texts – from a dimension no Greek had yet begun to localize in letters. The first phrases haunted me for days and months: "Meditation garden marine juxtaposition of texts arrayed with panpipes in cloudless springtime still forbears…"

He lectured the following day to a frowning bourgeois audience that was clearly annoyed to hear that other interesting folks besides Kondylis and Tsaldaris lived in the world and were called Freud or Breton. The young, the good conductors of ideas' heat, were absent. But the seed had fallen and soon strange names and unheard of concepts glistened in spring's gold dust: the subconscious, automatic writing, *hasard objectif*, collages, *critique paranoïaque*, *le merveilleux*, and others.

I could think of nothing else. My room had been transformed into a factory: magazine images cut and collaged in odd patterns without beginning or end, manuscripts in different inks where I had tried to ambush inspiration, anthropomorphic rocks, feathers, string and wood to construct Surrealistic "objects"… I worked morning to dusk, overtime and night shifts. Each time I visited Embeirikos, I had something to show him.

That Easter we took a trip to Lesbos. His *High Kiln* had just been published (we had with us, I remember, the first copy, still without its cover) and there, on the "island of olive coves," flanked by the two young painters Orestes Kannelis and Takis Eleutheriades, we held endless discussions or went on long expeditions to find the work of Theophilos, dead only a year.

Surrounded by a nature I had never experienced but which I felt circulating in my blood like an ancestral inheritance, I was tested again by the strange sense of two currents meeting in me from widely separated sources. One was full of Sappho's old voices: the justice inside us of short grass and the large moon, the white stone memorial fountain, something simple but of a wisdom that "stands" in the open air like the olive tree and, finally, emotion and sensation in equal measure, a kind of autarky without civilizing influence, one could say. The other current was a common desire, as if drawn from a bar anywhere in Europe, with the same wild-haired girls, the same sharp music and the same passion to unwrite and rewrite everything from scratch, to have Eros be Eros, true and free above the tangled sheets of religion and nation while the moon, poking its nose at night, illuminates a strange landscape of broken glass, trampled codices and small phosphorescent beasts.

These two intense currents vied for me and I was ready for both, born for both, so that just yielding to one I felt a traitor to the other; I had to change the shape of this small cross they made in me, feeling no attraction for the zodiac of martyrdom but for that of the infinite and flaming arrow.

C

FROM THE NEW point of view I brought to Athens on my return, I had but one field to discover: the reality of modern Greece. Where? How? What was it? Nothing was formulated. There were only recent historic events, the size of their significance as yet undefined: the ruin of Asia Minor, the Dictatorships, the remains of the Civil War, the infamous reconstruction.

The books of Dragoumis and P. Yannopoulos, to which I'd been referred by some of my best-informed nationalist colleagues, were like nearby hills that a sudden flood had rendered distant and uninhabitable islands. Their shapes didn't fit our daily life. Or so I thought then. Behind the specific political schema of Dragoumis and the hyperbole of Yannopoulos, I could not yet discern the eternal, healthy arena their views delineated, and which a "modernizing" study by some brilliant and bold contemporary fellow-thinker could have illuminated and restored to its generative power. Of course even then I was touched, briefly, by their deeper meanings and felt their beauty, but like a distant memory, a nostalgia lost among the new words and promises of a sure-footed, steadily rising generation.

Though I had barely studied the previous chapter, my mind stuck to the turning page and my interest rushed to the next one. Books sprouted every day like mushrooms. I strolled Zappeion Park with fellow students and, according to our mood, we debunked or deified the new-found authors.

Then at summer's end, if I'm not mistaken, Giorgos Katsimbales appeared. I never understood from where, nor can I remember the hour, the place or the companions. He was a typhoon and after he settled, faces and things around him were erased like insignificant details. He remained alone, enormous, twirling his cane, tugging at his hard collar with one finger and uttering a sudden curse which, before you could swallow it, he followed with the subtlest observation – a brothel incident next to a verse in *Cimetière marin*; how they cooked steak in some Paris restaurant next to some critic's view of Palamas; the role of defensive field artillery followed by the name of a little Peireas tavern featuring the world's best wine; Malakasis, Missus Anna, Karantonis, *New Letters* – laughing boisterously then stopping abruptly, gauging the reactions by side glances, then again the cane, the collar, those fine, narrow, almost womanly hands which, when I noticed them, gave me insight into the childlike, emotional soul he tried so hard to hide behind foul language and noise. I was dizzy; I was unprepared; I could not fit so many extremes in my head. His last word though, which was about *New Letters*, wedged in me. He had, if I'm not mistaken, intended it to from the beginning.

The next day I went to see Embeirikos. It was time, we agreed, for all of us to declare ourselves. Personally, I had decided to take the plunge come what may (family and friends despaired, "he will expose us irreparably"). Declare ourselves, we agreed, but not with *New Letters*, a "mixed" journal without clear editorial line. We must be fanatic, intransigent, uncompromising. We needed an aggressive, avant-garde publication that – merciless in its assault, pages wide open to a new spirit – severed all bridges with the past.

Such a plan was already in the air. Embeirikos had mentioned communicating with Randos and Demaras (who, at the time, had more than one interest) about publishing a quarterly with clear Freudian and Surreal affiliations. They already had the title, *Troupe*; the rest was a matter of time. We all knew that meant a matter of money. What to do? We agreed to insist on our line and not yield to any attacks by *New Let-*

ters no matter what, believing it wrong to embark with half measures.

But even while we were speaking, I was consumed by deep worry. I knew that the first breach had already occurred; Seferis had given poems to *New Letters*. And though Seferis was not an integral part of the revolutionary poetic schema we envisioned and sought to impose, he was, nevertheless, the poet whose second book had broken the bonds of verse and had further sought to delineate and crystallize a new arena we would have been happy to annex. Before I had time to digest this, a second blow arrived: a contribution by Sarantaris. Karantonis had extracted poems from him. The noose of *New Letters* tightened around modern poetry; I understood our turn was next.

So, half-flirting, half in defense, I accepted Katsimbales' offer, not long in coming, and one dusk I crossed the threshold of the Othon Street house where he still lived, my face pale as a traitor who, intending to withstand the tempting offers, brings the secrets in his pocket just in case. It's true: I arrived armed with a thick leather notebook of poems.

What I heard were temperate, logical views, entirely alien to a fanatic soul. "There is only one way in which the serum of the new can act upon the body of the sullen and skeptical Greek," Katsimbales maintained, "slowly and in small doses." It was important to present our texts parallel to traditional ones, just a few, not too wild, at least not at first, so that the reader, finding Seferis for instance next to Sikelianos, would grow accustomed to the idea that this was a continuum, which it was, not a reversal of Greek poetics. Besides, the only way a journal can fish for new believers is to attract the conservatives who would buck if taken by surprise; a monolithic appearance would arouse only irony and mockery, not attention and enchantment.

I beheld a temperate, calm Katsimbales, restored to human dimension. The dialogue was accessible, and somehow I was left with the impression that I had managed to rebuke him, or at least put some distance between myself and the publication of my poems. That's why in the end I found the courage to turn them over, restlessly, like a patient who, already reassured by his family doctor, turns to a specialist just in case, superficially confident of concurrence yet in agony lest, one in a million, a different diagnosis be made.

I got up to leave. Just then we heard the doorbell and Theotokas,

Seferis and Nikolareizis burst in. They were in great moods, boisterous, pushing each other around like school boys. And I, who couldn't even imagine I might meet and speak with those whose names I'd seen only in journals and bookstores until then, was dazed.

It's true that I had formally met Theotokas a few months before, when I'd gone to his home with a student committee about our club's request. He had great authority among the young. *Free Spirit* had given him a pioneer's glory. His *Argo*, which mythologized our daily life, our heartthrobs and Law School banter, our loves by the Fountain steps, our thirst for glory and poetry, was more than a novel. It was our charter and our guide. Personally, I'd been magnetized by another book, his *Idle Hours*. I liked its original, indefinite style, its carefree and risky tone that, like a game, without your knowledge, enticed you to more serious themes: Hellenism, Beauty, Inspiration and Creation. I read and reread the part on the Aegean. Here was someone attempting to make conscious a larger spirit concerning the marine physiognomy of Greece, which flooded me, nourished as it was only by authentic personal experience and demanding its expression through countless interchangeable possibilities in the tongue of contemporary sensitivity, the new poetic idiom.

The same Theotokas now nursed a cognac, threatening the Peloponnesian Katsimbales with Aegeans. We were all Aegeans, from Samos, Chios, Lesbos and Ionia. Nikolareizis was from Samos. Just one of his essays, "Hedonism in the Poetry of Kavafis," published in *New Hestia*, was enough to imprint him on our consciousness. His new tongue, new attitude, new dense original ideas, and European level of critical thought embodied something we sought and awaited. Later, we became friends. We were alike, it seemed, not only in our proclivities for a certain kind of poetry, but also for a certain kind of life. We also lived close by, which right away encouraged me to interrupt his studies (for the Foreign Ministry) to show off my latest Surrealistic achievements. He was a stern critic, but Seferis was sterner still.

That night I saw him avoid facility, saw how much he was annoyed by enthusiasm and grand words. He listened from a deep armchair, staring into space, clenching his hand before opening his mouth, speaking with clarity and weight. Each phrase was measured and full of right meaning; you understood it was indisputable. Writing was to him a burning both from afar and from deep within, a mute passion that lined his face and settled darkly in his large, warm, melancholy eyes like sand settles in a river. How many of us had "our fingers in the cookie jar," as the poet said? A perennial dysphoria made him appear ill-mannered, inaccessible and crabby, but really he only griped about the place to which conscientious work was relegated in a world of opportunists. Otherwise he loved the young, still young himself, seeking a friend, a true verse, as if by candlelight. He could be mild, too, when he thought it helpful.

A few days later he invited me to his house. It was afternoon. I remember him leafing through my manuscripts in the quiet of his study, pausing to return to one he liked. He listened attentively to my explanations and politely, gently, tenderly almost, made now and then a few suggestions. Suggestions that were, alas, not continued later, after my mind had congealed and had a chance to value and actualize their teachings. Today I understand he ventured these suggestions as though with an eye-dropper. He did not want to blunt my revolutionary mood, and though he disagreed with most of my poetic credo, he always tried, indirectly and only in reference to the texts in hand, to illuminate the part of me he judged most authentic and productive. At last he selected "Anniversary" and began to read it aloud. It was strange, unprecedented, my own words on another's lips, especially those of a successful poet. Blood rushed to my head; my heart beat loudly until he laid the page on the table, patted it and, looking straight into my eyes, said, almost in confidence, "It's a good poem."

As I came to understand, such a phrase was the greatest praise one could hear from his lips.

FROM THAT DAY to November first, when my first poems appeared in the eleventh issue of *New Letters*, many events, both humorous and serious, occurred which may be out of place here. For instance, Katsimbales, who had detected my ambivalence and sought to force my hand, went to the typographers with a selection of the poems I had entrusted to him. Page proofs arrived one morning out of the blue and of course I panicked. The funny thing is, he had used the name "Odysseas Vranas," knowing I'd need a pseudonym and thinking my mother's maiden name would do. The poor man had thought of everything, except my self-conscious quibbling. I sent him a long letter, enumerating the thousand

and one reasons why I should postpone my debut. I was not meant to overturn his conspiracy; in the end, to my benefit, he prevailed. My formal baptism took place at Barba-Yanni's taverna one night, among a pandemonium of glasses dashed to the wall, pots and pans underfoot, yelling, head thrusts, and ululations. These revelries took place regularly on Monday nights. Mondays had been especially chosen because Antoniou, the poet who was already captain of his own ship, the *Acropolis*, disembarked only one night a week, Monday. These were heroic years. Atop the checkered tablecloth, among brilliant retsinas, between clay casseroles and garlic sauce, the journal's material was spread, contributors selected, essays corrected and polemics put forth.

It took me a long time to open up and feel at ease with these gargantuans. And that first night I was completely dazed. Not only had the regulars come, Katsimbales, Karantonis, Seferis, Antoniou and Sarantaris, but, coincidentally, many others, Theotokas, Terzakis, Kastanakis and that demonic and hyper-kinetic Afthoniatis of *Voyage en Grèce*, just back from Paris, who went completely wild and finally, when we stopped a while for dessert, filled Kastanakis' historic beret with ice cream... That improbable evening – which was also, it seems, the eve of the Kondyles military coup (I remember nothing but later Kastanakis confirmed it) – ended as improbably...

None of it matters now. I returned home like a wet cat, and from that day, it was all I could do to keep that traitorous eleventh issue as inconspicuous as possible and out of the hands of my university friends. Until I warmed up to it, of course. After that...who could catch me? For the thousandth time, I put down the ill-fated *Torts*; what did I care about reactions? Now I had allies. I felt the warmth of my friends like a shield. By early 1936, a tight-knit group had already united around *New Letters*, bringing with it a pioneering conscience, a combative mood and a spirit of solidarity. Besides, Surrealism – with its mystical terminology, its secret pantheon, its Manifestoes and multilingual editions – awed the stupid reactionaries who may have had the appetite for battle but no idea where or who the enemy might be. Before long, in March of that year, we decided nothing less than to organize the first International Surrealistic Exposition of Athens, led only by our enthusiasm and the desire to pique public opinion. We even sent, I recall, a telegram to André Breton. We printed and distributed invitations. And one day, friends and reporters arrived at Embeirikos' for the finale. It was, of course, a haphazard exposition. But it was worth it and the newspapers were filled with reviews. Max Ernst, Oscar Dominquez and Victor Brauner's large pieces made up the bulk of the show. I also showed five or six photographic collages, next to some rare books, first editions of the chief Surrealists, Breton's *Manifestoes*, some photographs, as well as two Greek books, *High Kiln* and a limited edition of Paul Éluard's *Poems* in my own translation, just that moment pulled from the third issue of *New Letters'* second volume.

It was a period of great activity and thankfully my morale was high. By raising the arbitrary to dogma, Surrealism had literally untied my hands. I could do whatever I wanted. Of course this injured me, considering how it derailed my native tendency to organize and esthetically control my poems, but nevertheless, it was a benevolent force toward courage, and it opened incredibly large doors in my tyrannized psyche. What to do? With poison there is always intoxication. And when you are twenty-two... But here I want to add something.

I was sensing, as time passed, that I was not a "literary animal." I had none of the habits or manias of the previous generation. I didn't keep diaries, didn't maintain archives; I hated readings and literary soirées, couldn't stand bohemian dress and certainly didn't care whether my girl knew Eliot or not. My new friends cast a hostile eye on my detachment from the schema and my refusal to look the poet. I must be terribly "bourgeois" and a cold fish not to jump up full of flame and passion to recite my verses among them. My god, communication is so difficult for people. But in my opinion, a new poetic spirit goes side-by-side with a new stance. It was precisely because I hated the bourgeois that I didn't want the poet to give them the picturesque. A thousand times better to be isolated – I could see it coming – than suffer allergies every night.

Yet there came a day, an evening rather, when, out of the blue, as I was walking by the bakeshops of Hafteia, an unexpected fellow-traveler appeared, even more fanatical than me in this respect. It was the poet Nikos Gatsos. I don't recall who introduced us, nor if I had ever heard his name. Tall, thin and dark among the crowd, with large eyes destined to break many hearts in the following decades yet always a little blood-shot as though from permanent insomnia, he stood slightly hunched under a long beige gabardine with upraised collar, foreign film magazines under his arm, French mostly, and American. He chain-smoked and listened with a detached air; I couldn't tell if it was arrogance or plain indifference.

By the time we reached Aggelopoulou station – we had been walking that way as he lived in Kypseli – he had put me through a sieve, countering and questioning everything, methodically extracting my opinions and preferences and mentioning improbable details from obscure texts, none of which caught me off-guard. On the contrary, he spurred me to match him at every turn. This game lasted until we anchored at a cafe and took *Manifestoes* to our lips. Thank God, *this man got it* – besides Embeirikos, the only one. Even today as I write, nearly three decades later, he remains one of five or six in all of Greece (along with Randos, Engonopoulos and Valaoritis) who truly possess the secret. Of fascination, I mean, of wonder, of miracle, and not the insipid scholarship now taught by universities or encyclopedias!

Gatsos "had heard the voice"! He cared about the aleatory, its possible but inconceivable rules, not in poetry alone but also in life, eros, play, and the daily. Imagination's infinite associativeness enchanted him. He was beyond received preconceptions, even though he had created personal ones. It was natural to become friends quickly. We exchanged books, poems and secrets. We later founded our generation's first literary cafe, the *Heraion*, at the corner of St. Meletios and Patission, which was immediately reinforced by Karantonis, Sarantaris and their infamous company. When the *Heraion* closed at two A.M., we exploded onto the then virgin boulevard of Fokion Negri and launched our endless discussions under the eucalyptus. *Jeune Parque*, *Chants de Maldoror* and *The Wasteland* echoed in time to the subterranean waters of the aqueduct, while the "August Fourth" policemen glared with grim, suspicious eyes.

Antoniou lived nearby, at the beginning of Chanion Street. We saw him around, usually when his ship went to the reservoirs for cleaning. I was envious. I believed that Greece could produce only good poets and sailors. What privilege, to be both in one person! His birth in exotic lands, his expertise in rare plants and cats, his mystical poem "Indies" which we knew only in fragments, the broken line of his speech, and his swaying "nautical" walk had raised him to an idiosyncratic type and had created a myth around him, which he neither cultivated nor seemed to notice. At his home, he received you with infinite grace but would often disappear mid-sentence to reappear moments later holding a superb cat or a planter with an unprecedented plant or sometimes simply a small piece of aromatic wood from distant lands, caressing it with his hands and smelling it blissfully, refolding it in small papers with the secret joy of the fixated collector, alone in the position of appreciating the "precious." I had the chance to see some of the famous cigarette packs on which he wrote his poems during the night watch – tortured lines, crossed out, reinserted, worked like the precious stones he loved so much. Here was another prize for the *New Letters* staff.

We were six or seven young poets, along with Anastasios Drivas, who – though he held to an older tradition, humbly, without fanfare and successfully, I must say – had joined our camp. Then there was Randos; he never approached us or we didn't approach him or both. I can't remember anymore. His poems, published noncommercially in small colored notebooks, always impressed me greatly and some, for instance "Without Ruth and Valia," I loved and repeated over and over.

> *I took the night with me tonight – come too,*
> *everything is ours now, somewhere*
> *we too will find an abandoned meadow…*

He was quarrelsome and agitated; his cohabitation with the journal's conservatives would sooner or later engender fights. He wrote prolifically, with fiery libel and merciless reviews, under the pseudonym M. Spieros. One could never catch him at anything. He was the most informed, the keenest consumer of books in the international market. Long before I met him, I saw him everywhere, in the streets, the University court, the lecture halls, circulating with ease and provocation in manner and dress, tall as he was with unkempt hair, brightly colored shirts, and a small watch hanging from his buttonhole.

He wrote me regularly from Paris (where he had moved two years before the war) about Surrealism's inner workings – Breton's tempers, the heretic scandals – while he prepared his new theoretical book, *Foyers d'incendie*. After that, America swallowed him; I saw him twenty-two years later in New York. Randos too, versatile, aggressive and always prepared for any battle, could have served our team in that contentious period, as Engonopoulos did, that other irreconcilable who finally joined us at *New Letters*.

But Engonopoulos only wrote poems. He managed to combine a revolutionary line with an aristocratic one, in the best sense of the word. He was difficult to know. Nine times out of ten he'd throw you a barb, less by breaching his native politeness than by sarcasm. He endured relentless penury with the dignity of a true prince. He avoided praise as well as abuse. Red-faced, with luminous eyes and an extremely suggestive voice, he wore a thin gold chain on his neck, and on his right forefinger a thick gold ring you couldn't help but notice as he spoke, punctuating his speech with wide hieratic gestures, or silent and immobile with his finger extended, just like the figures he painted based on Byzantine prototypes. No one knew French poetry better than he. A mere hint of a text, even the rarest, most obscure from the wealth and variation of the French Middle Ages, and he would take up the quote with impeccable accent and precise phonics, noticing, behind his lenses, the reaction he caused or, more accurately, enjoying the surprise. He loved surprise tactics. He used them in almost all his first encounters. Brilliant, with a monstrous memory, he'd soon harvest the most paradoxical flower from his extensive internal plantations and throw it in the face of his unsuspecting interlocutor who had, poor fellow, no recourse but to confess ignorance or pretend to understand and be further embarrassed. All this was, I believe, a kind of payback to a crude and uninformed society that vilified his poetry. Unfortunately, he made no distinction between friends and enemies in his momentum. We were able to approach one another only during the Occupation. Still unmarried, he lived on Kypseli Street in a strange basement without heat always in danger of flooding in a downpour. Alone, amidst a panoply of great canvases of headless bodies, he was always impeccable. And he received each visitor who had secured an invitation with the ease of a gentleman who does not permit his servants to approach, so that he alone may have the joy and honor of entertaining you. And there, I remember, I heard the famous *Bolívar* for the first time from his lips.

BUT WE'VE come too far. We must return to the years before the war, the years of the Dictatorship, whose censor – I don't know why, most likely from ignorance – never considered us dangerous or caused our multiple activities much trouble. Besides the *Heraion* cafe, exclusive center of our crowd at night, other writers, primarily prose writers of the Thirties, gathered in the small bookstore, *Torch*, under the Voukou-restiou arches at noon. Another crowd hung out nearby at the bar *Apo-tsos*. At night, you could often find writers at *Askraion*, the free school founded by Mrs. Julia Ambela-Terencio. It was in these three centers that I came in contact with the rest of the literary world.

Most of them regarded us with some suspicion. In their eyes, we were more an indolent group of paradox-lovers than an intellectual team aspiring to establish a new literary regime. Kosmas Politis was an exception among them. His soul was cut to a different measure from the start. He didn't seem literary in speech or external appearance. When in Athens (he lived in Patras, I think) he'd come by *Apotsos* for an ouzo, and then, often against his will, we would extract an opinion on modern poetry. He had nothing against it. He declared that he savored the in-toxication of automatic writing the way he enjoyed the flow of grand old Romantic poems. In *Eroica* he proved that he could toast both species and create pages where prose and poetry were inseparable. Two other exceptions were the somewhat older poets Takis Papajohnis and Angelos Sikelianos, long established yet still open to all literary currents.

Papajohnis' situation seems incomprehensible to me even today. I can't imagine where he found the courage – in the exhausted years after the Asia Minor ruin, while his colleagues toyed with rhyme or mourned their fate – to remain true to the arena he had defined, faithful to his own metaphysics and esthetic perception, and to do so without com-panions or the warmth of like-minded company. Even as a student, I opened each issue of *Vanguard* (the courageous journal published be-tween 1928 and 1931 by Fotos Yophylles) with the secret anticipation of coming upon new Papajohnis poems, "Supplicants," "Tourists in the Mass," "Ships and Others," and the famous "If Only," which I knew by heart.

When I first met him, I stood amid the towering piles of books that constantly encroached upon his desk, the towers of five European lan-guages that besieged him. Then I understood why borders held so little meaning for this man, and how his characteristic humor had turned from the play of a cultivated intelligence to a defensive weapon against all half-knowledge and provincialism.

Sikelianos was something else altogether. He was the last to bear the weight of a divine role without the slightest crack. He was constantly filled with Greece and Greece with him, as if he and his land were perfect connecting vessels. His characteristics have been adequately described and do not need my presentation. I did happen to meet him a few times, whether proudly passing in black cape and silver cane, or reciting *Sybilla*, which rattled the windows, or standing in line for his ration in the Occupation, holding the tin box with the ease of a true gentleman. Another time he hosted Éluard, Seferis and me in Salamina. But what I'll never forget are the two rare, personal moments when I saw him in all his exaltation.

The first was that historic, unforgettable evening of Palamas' funeral, something intense and fleeting. I faced him across the freshly dug grave as we began to sing the National Anthem. The entire time I felt his eyes on me so insistently, I didn't know what to do. Only with great effort was I able to not avert my gaze. It was barely over before he lunged at me, embraced me with all his might and kissed me on both cheeks. He was literally outside himself. I knew, I understood, it wasn't me he had eyed or wanted to kiss but *the other*, his *nearby*, substantiated in my shape by his exaltation. This fact, rather than lessen his gesture in my eyes, gave it the scale and grandeur of symbol.

The next time was very different; it was the last image of the poet I would take with me to Europe, since his honorable form, alas, would not exist on my return. It was summer, two years after liberation. He lived in a large old house in Kifissia then, with high ceilings and airy rooms, deep in an abandoned garden of sparse, tall, ancient pines, a cistern to the side. Nothing broke the heat circling and inflaming this stone building, especially at noon. It was noon, and I had gone without warning (he had no phone) to deliver some books on Surrealistic theory he had asked for.

No one saw me open the iron garden gate. His wife was out and they had no servant. I found the front door wide open. I called a couple of times and, when no one answered, entered in my light cloth shoes that made no sound. Then an unforgettable image: Sikelianos, barefoot in a long white nightgown draped like an ancient tunic, eating a stem of grapes! Every so often, he'd raise one to the open window and admire it in the light. It was he. An authentic Greek poet who did not deny sensation, but pushed it instead until it fell and he could read in it its secret signs.

I observed him shift his naked soles on the washed planks every so often, as if taking small dance steps, savoring this primitive touch, speaking literally with the wood. I'd caught this man, whom others called theatrical, in a moment when no audience existed, and yet he was the same, exactly, as in his poems, natively magnificent and self-sufficient in his divine simplicity. Nor did he show the slightest displeasure when he finally noticed me. "Come, my dear," he boomed, and cut me a stem of grapes. Almost immediately, with the same ease, he took up his dissent with an English philologist on the interpretation of some apocryphal texts he was studying. He pointed to a pile of books on a large table. A large inkwell, a large fountain pen, and a big stack of papers filled with his large round handwriting were nearby. All big. Equal to him. How else could it be, destined as he was to endow the Greek tongue with its "Greatest Lesson." We are speaking here of two levels of largesse, neither of which his small and petty detractors were ever able to comprehend.

D

YOUTH IS NOT, as they say, always the same. Perhaps the twenty-year-olds of all centuries and civilizations unite for a moment in a lover's arms. Beyond that, however, this ideal justice does not endure. A lottery determines what portion of an era may be enchanted, and who can measure that? Invisible hands, without asking, set the stage where we dramatize our roles, and naturally it's different to wake to proclamations of war than drink your morning coffee, certain about tomorrow, even if you only collect stamps.

To keep my distance from recent events, I imagine Alexandrians and early Christians. Who will tell us what happened before the death of the weaver of wreaths for beautiful Tendera or of the one who won brothers in love? Embarrassment. Immeasurable leaps the soul.

We who lived from twenty to thirty between two dangers know only the intensity of white before the likely black, the effort to preserve the freedom of each moment and savor it – precious, expensive – to our core. And more: how to change reality? Most grabbed it by its feet, being practical. We set our sights on its head.

Poetry should express the apex, should constitute a kind of pioneering outpost in the unexplored area of life, should precede other arts in the depiction of sensitivity. It should be the word and sword intervening in the spirit, so that matter, docile, can follow. Creation, especially poetic, is above all a result. German and, especially, English letters offered a wealth of results of incomparable quality. Sometimes though, a beautiful woman and her promise of erotic fulfillment are not enough. That's when you need a bad-tempered, sinful one who'll make you check your feelings from the start. She was always represented in our eyes by Paris; she was the woman-Parnassus, the woman-symbolism, the woman-dadaism, the woman we'd fallen for, waiting with beating hearts for each issue of some French journal. She taught us real love, and how far our agitation, our neurosis even, could go. We knew that an Eliot or Lorca had greater stature than these Reverdys and Tzaras. Still, something else fueled our paroxysm, something which time can never ascribe to our emotions – since it has no heart – but which we plucked from the literal air.

It was a plunge to the seafloor where lyricism's first motives swayed – the tortuous ordeal of a martyred creation – and also a rise to the excessive sky where the all possible stars can ignite, true magic. It was poetry before and after the poem, in the streets, in love, in the heavens. It was the dream on alert. André Breton was more a "skipper of men" than a simple poet, Tristan Tzara a "spiritual activist," not at all a composer of verse, Giuseppe Ungaretti a "belated lyrical Plotinus," joining the dreamtaken crowd. Paul Éluard was a "benefactor of eyes," who made us really see where no one else could. And Pierre Reverdy was "matter's parvenu," consciously associating the unassociable. A true miracle of creation seized the front. And while, on the ground floor of life, people sadly and in ignorance counted out their days, upstairs, at windows and balconies, the bold breathed in what was perhaps the last pure oxygen.

I KNOW I am replaying a tired prewar film of outmoded acting and spasmodic, even melodramatic gestures. But if we are to see them outside their hyperbolic scale, we must accept the truth that endures to this day:

Surrealism, covering a large extent of modern poetry's adventure, was the last European mutiny to keep from fainting at life and to confess its faith, fanatical and absolute, in human spiritual powers. *"Les phénomènes de la nature sont aussi les phénomènes de l'esprit!"* Éluard proclaimed, and what gleams in that phrase is the firefly of a heart in hope, a heart devoted to hoping the world could be improved. *"Mein Feld ist die Welt,"* Breton droned beneath his magico-materialistic doctrines. And I believe that he purposely used German on the eve of the war.

Surrealism was also the first *Internationale* of the spirit. Alas it would be many years – years mediated by the works of Maurice Nadeau, Fernand Alquier and Julien Gracq – before this deeper meaning would become, even in France, the common conscience. In that time, the most serious Europeans "played dice with the past," as our Sarantaris would say. And well they did! Because our most serious Greeks, who of course had to show they were even smarter, did something else: they lifted Surrealism's definition from dictionaries ("method of automatism by which the real content of the soul is inventoried…etc.") and rushed yards of shameless, audacious articles to newspapers and journals. Even as the movement developed fully abroad, they accused us of backwardness. My heart bled, I confess. I saw an eagle reduced to a sparrow by partial knowledge. I sat down and wrote an article, "The Dangers of Partial Knowledge," which was naturally published in *New Letters*.

This mediocre text sufficed to raise a storm of protest. Napoleon Lapathiotes, feeling attacked by the new ideas, lost his sangfroid and sent an abusive letter the next day: "It has always been my joy and honor, Sir, to be considered half-learned or without breeding by the foolish, the idiotic and the audacious parvenus." At least he signed his name. Another well-known, so I heard, prose writer of the thirties emerged under the pseudonym S. Pamphylos to target my arrogance from the pages of the weekly *Modern Greek Letters*.

Modern Greek Letters, successfully managed by Dimitri Fotiades, was founded on the aspiration to entice the so-called "greater public," the one I had supposedly insulted by calling it "barbaric." This word was the root of the scandal, and not unjustly. The journal's editor, the now late G. M. Mylonoyannis, also addressed it in the pages of another weekly, *Work*: "The unjustly accused and abused Greek public has become easy victim to writers of decline, whom it ignores because they systematically ignore it...they have never tried to contact it, to taste its pains, commune with its joys, embrace it with true interest, and guide it with affection and love..." It was a tiresome article of demagogic surges and hypocritical breast-beating.

The article by the Peirean writer Levandas in *Modern Greek Literature* was punctuated by the same tone of public flattery. Karagatsis' column in *New Hestia* seemed independent and sparkling in comparison, telling us off in grand style. Even insults, it seems, must be selfless to be appreciated. Another attack, for example, by N.D. Pappas in *Kathemerene*, pulled our ears as though we were school kids but didn't bother us at all.

More seriously, no one had touched the subject's essence. How could a productive dialogue, like the one Seferis and Tsatsos would later have, begin? My first effort ended in disappointment and I published a kind of postscript in the next *New Letters* titled, "The end, period." A period that naturally never found its place. The fate of our journal was already being defined by this situation, which gave its mission a concrete content, shaping a womb with its material in which *New Letters* would assume a clearer form and find its final format. Except for work by Seferis and Sarantaris, the first year covered only traditional poetic texts and ample prose by the generation of the thirties. Antoniou pops up in 1936, and also Anastasios Drivas. Translations of Eliot and Éluard appear. And then, at the end, a brief commentary by Andreas Karantonis, "The Criticism of Contemporary Poetry," a shy harbinger of the combative spirit gestating in our camp. Only, as it turned out, it would take some time to be expressed.

FATE DISPERSED US in early 1937: Katsimbales to Paris, Seferis to Korytsa and I to the isolated fort of Officer Reserves School in Corfu, a cadet. Except for those classic Mondays, Antoniou was always aboard his ship. Karantonis and Gatsos remained in Athens to continue the journal alone; they succeeded heroically.

Risking a four-day arrest and the loss of my only Sunday pass, I read the new issues behind the covers of "Exercise Regulations of Machine-Gun Units" in study hall or on night duty. I waited impatiently for the meager passes to visit Paleokastritsa, where our then unknown friend Lawrence Durrell lived humbly with his first wife Nancy, or meet

Theodoros Stefanides, an idiosyncratic friend of Katsimbales with a reddish blond beard who was a doctor, a botanist and a translator of Palamas into English. He always received me and my friends with infinite grace. We had great need of it in that coarse, unforgiving life.

I often despaired, not of the endless exhausting marches, the mule harnessings and the oiling of weapons, but of my lack of solitude, to think for even a minute of my own problems or remember old enthusiasms. Behind the Albanian mountains, which I faced every morning as I shaved outdoors, I saw not the imaginary enemies my superiors would have liked, but another exiled poet, Seferis, trapped among "short Toskies" and "tall Geckies." He wrote me regularly, speaking of his sorrows, the eternal ones, "What a burden to have to complete someone every so often… Looking back on my life sometimes, I think, with some bitterness, that everything that could have happened to prevent me from writing always did…" And, "Each has what he has, hard or easy, and nothing else. With it, he must do something; he must justify what he feels a higher power has entrusted to him…" When I was too gloomy, he'd send Matthios Paschalis to console me, in verse no less:

> Sing, Muse, to Elytis
> playing with his bayonet
> blow your conch, muse
> wake the troop Elytis
>
> The water-clock's not dry, tell him,
> he has to turn it
> over to hear
> the rushing spring: snow melt.

Gatsos was more mysterious; immediately at home in Surreal symbology, he communicated in the lines we both loved,

> Celle qu'on appelait dans le quartier
> La petite pyramide de réséda…

and I understood. How many others did? I don't mean the specific lines, but the general spirit demanding that we communicate in them, the spirit altering something substantial in our lives:

> "*Sovegna vos a temps de ma dolor*"
> *Poi s'ascose nel foco che gli affina.*

When I returned to Athens eight months later, sunburnt, in gold epaulets and a member of the First Infantry Division, I began to understand how much still had to be traversed. By hook or by crook, amidst confusion and reaction, Surrealism was able to slowly spread roots; our more progressive writers understood it was time to seriously address it. Theotokas first approached the subject. His manner was, as usual, honorable and highly simplifying. His intent was to compromise, to walk, so to speak, over the fire without getting burned. Well, no. My own psychology was strange. Though I harbored a throng of reservations and did not consider myself a Surrealist, I could not tolerate seeing a bird scissored right in front of me just as it started to fly. I swiftly composed an "Open Letter to George Theotokas" and sent it to *Modern Greek Letters*.

His reply was brief, unjustifiably scoffing. Everything had to be taken up again from the beginning. But how? Leafing through our journal's volumes, I often thought we ourselves were responsible for the confusion. Not having clarified to others the new givens posed by our era, we'd rushed to project the *general new spirit* we felt their synthesis form. Still, someone had to explain in detail that Surrealism was one thing and so-called "Modern Poetry" another; that the "Modern Poetry" of Latin countries was totally different from what the Anglo-Saxons cultivated; and that receptivity to foreign poetic currents, common until then in Greece, differed radically from participation in their creation and development, as everything now indicated might happen. Finally, someone had to explain what Greek tradition in its core aspect meant to us, and why we didn't think we were betraying it by our stance, but rather hoped at last to value it correctly and renew it.

Unfortunately our generation had yielded no critics. Nikolareizis had devoted himself to diplomacy and Karantonis, all alone, didn't know where to turn. Still, the 1937 volume of *New Letters* seemed more cohesive, with poems by Sikelianos, Seferis, Antoniou, Sarantaris, and Embeirikos, translations of Apollinaire, Supervielle, Michaux, Jouve, and a new prose acquisition which we immediately felt, Kosmas Politis' "Eroica." By contrast, in the 1938 volume, the rope seems yanked by all sides. It contains, of course, Embeirikos, Antoniou, Éluard, and Mac-Leish, but also Giannopoulos, Psycharis' letters to Philendas, "The Dangers of Partial Knowledge," "The Poetry of Film and Walt Disney" and Seferis' "Dialogue on Poetry."

The latter would dominate. He would lend form to a fluid situation and determine the ultimate development of our country's literary affairs. Rigidities, personified by Randos and Embeirikos (Engonopoulos had yet to appear), would yield, the antithesis of tradition and new forms would ease and lead to a natural assimilation, and the exclusively international character of the movement would be replaced by a new and renewed sense of Greekness. I don't know if that was the most accurate view, but Seferis' conservative yet exceptionally strong and cohesive personality – eliminating initiative from friends and argument from enemies – had imposed it.

We had climbed an acropolis of inspired criticism and observed from there, with curiosity if not almost displeasure, the measured and sure dilation of a poet's intelligence by difficult meanings, his gradual dispersion of fog, and the sudden clarity and precision that critical thought was able to acquire in our language by what seemed like a single stroke. Though perhaps we were losing some of the crazy air that enchanted us – *critique paranoïaque* was the new siren rising from the freshly printed pages of *Minotaure* – what a relief to have someone in full possession of his faculties on guard! This has always been the meaning of *teacher* throughout generations and time. Seferis was truly the last teacher, since no one has replaced him to this day.

In the person of Kostantinos Tsatsos, he encountered a philosopher and no longer had to engage in the witticisms of *Hestia*. They held their dialogue on a high level and we reaped the benefits. The moment Seferis took the situation in hand, ours were freed. I again found time for my new poems, for translating Lautréamont, for drafting an essay on Kalvos and, further, for looking at something else: the new spirit's effect on painting.

I needed an excuse and, after poetry, painting was my greatest passion. My meager student funds disappeared in the costly art editions that came every so often from Paris. I supplemented the gaps by frequent raids on Embeirikos' library. My question was specific: what, ex-actly, was the situation in Greece? We knew the painter Parthenis only by name. Where would one even see his work? We had Gounaropou-los, Tombros, three or four contemporaries still finding their way – Tsarouchis, Hatzikyriakos Gikas, Moralis, Diamantis Diamantopoulos – and of course our friends, Kanellis and Eleutheriades, whose sensiti-vity and receptivity to the "modern spirit" we'd had immediate occasion to observe.

There had been someone who, for me, resembled no European or Greek: G. Steris. But he disappeared one day (for America I heard) and no mention was made of his work. It seems strange. His "Homeric Shores," his "Ariadnes," his "Dawns" are vividly etched in my memory. His was a mythic world, full of original poetic vision and plastic actual-ization. Otherwise, the entire Greek chapter of modern art came to this: limited, ignored by official criticism, relegated to distant, inacces-sible studios. Galleries and bourgeois "salons" were flooded by look-alike pseudo-impressionistic constructions that survive on Parnassus to this day: eternal sad dusks, little churches by the sea or peasant interiors of brass fixtures and old women by the hearth. My god, what misery! Long before I was born, Europe had resolved to face the mirror without narcissism and, years later, we still copied her thickly made-up face. We were more than ripe for the turning page, not just from one but from a thousand directions... And with such sun ahead, such tradition be-hind, making their totally different demands on anyone blessed enough to listen.

I still had fresh in mind the interviews of some of the most famous contemporary architects, who had come to Athens in 1934 for their Fourth International Conference. I admired how, with just a glance at our landscape, they had encompassed its special problems; and how they had further associated them with solutions posed by "modern art" in its effort to free itself from the tyranny of a bad Renaissance inherit-ance. From the pages of Afthoniatis' journal *Voyage en Grèce*, painters like Léger and poets like Reverdy spoke even more specifically about what could and should result by repositioning our esthetics and re-eval-uating essential Greek values.

At the end of 1939 or the beginning of 1940 (it must have been Janu-ary), the philosopher and estheticist Evangelos Papanoutsos gave two lectures on modern art to a wide and lively young audience at the House of Arts and Letters. It was, I think, the first time an authoritative speaker breached the forbidden line and took avant-garde slogans to his lips to check rather than mock them.

Though this was already a victory, a conquest, it wasn't enough for me. I wanted to hear, from third parties and official podiums, exactly what I felt: that we had entered an era in which the liberation of psychic powers could change the shape of the world. I heard instead that we were in a terrifying crisis, and that whether the shake-up would even leave anything behind was in doubt.

I immediately wrote "An Open Letter to E. Papanoutsos" and sent it to *New Greek Letters*. Its text found great resonance among the young, perhaps because it appeared at the right time. I received letters, even telegrams, with words of irrepressible enthusiasm from simple readers and unknown people.

E

SO BEGAN THE YEAR 1940, which would end among sirens and the ululations of war... No one knows how things might have turned out had we been lucky enough to escape its trial to the end.

In just five years spirits had turned. My own *Orientations*, just then published in a small but voluminous book, gave much of the old guard reason to take a stand. Papanikolaou, Paraschos, Papajohnis, Chourmouzios, Demaras, and Malanos, some more, others less, were beginning to surround us with their attention and love. In Geneva, the journal *Formes et Couleurs* published a study by Samuel Baud-Bovy, full of insight and honest admiration, on the newer Greek poetry. While from Paris Niketas Randos, who kept in touch with Breton, sent flaming letters protesting the compromising politics of *New Letters*. Even so, as time went by – and perhaps due to such politics – our camp acquired a different breadth, grew branches and outgrew the limits of a simple group of friends.

Yannis Ritsos and Nikiforos Vrettakos had long ago abandoned the old forms and etched a road parallel to ours, aspiring always to a poetry of greater social content. Two very young poets barely out of school,

Nanos Valaoritis and Andreas Kambas, expressed avid interest. Valaoritis was to play a significant role in the vanguard movement, here and in Europe. Finally but most significantly, our uncompromising wing was reinforced by Engonopoulos, whose poems instantly resonated with unusual sharpness.

He was a born orthodox, as charged by Surrealism as an electrical pole is by electricity. No one could touch him without agreeing to suffer a powerful discharge. Inaccessible, suspicious and argumentative, he refused to work with us for a long time. But even from a distance his voice reached the space we inhabited, filling it with nightmarish figures and illicit complexes that we had, until then, encountered only in our most paradoxical dreams.

We had reached the time when the Italian Fascist leadership consolidated their plan to start the war by mining the peaceful Tenos harbor. Time was cut in two, and from our half we could see the other drift off without sinking, taking with it Palamas, Drosinis, Gryparis, Lapathiotis, and Agras. So chance events acquire a symbolism no one had sought.

When we breathed again after the first phase of the maelstrom, it was spring and Athens had a Kommandatur. We had yet to learn what this meant. For the time being, we counted heads and were, unbelievably, about the same. Only different somehow, dazed...I on a cane, Antoniou shipless, Seferis among the agapanthi, Sarantaris even further... His was the only, the most unjust loss. These are not the memoirs of a life but the chronicle of a spiritual battle. So I set aside harsh Albania, so that, somewhere else and later, I might take up those days. Right now I want to openly denounce the conscription system that kept the thick-skinned Athenian pâtisserie-monsters in desk jobs but banished the purest, most defenseless creature to the front: a fragile intellectual who could barely stand yet had already conceived the most original and loving thoughts of Greece and her future. It was practically murder. An Italian university graduate – perhaps the army's only one – he might have been in great demand by services dealing with espionage or interrogation. But no. He shouldered thirty kilos of supplies and ammunition to vanish, reeling, in the snowy ravines, another poet, another innocent on the road to martyrdom.

He endured terrible hours. He lost his thick myopic glasses without which he could barely walk. "Help," he called to the other soldiers. This Christian cried "Brothers," and these brothers laughed. The most unconscionable stole his woolens, his blankets, anything of use the poor man carried. He was abandoned, a persecuted bird in the freezing cold. Without harsh word, without complaint, proud, slightest of body, his large soul kept him alive to sing a little more:

I who have walked with shepherds of Premeti

and then ascend to where "regions proclaiming sky converse with the sun as equals." So died a Greek poet, while his Western brothers cursed God and put their faith in marijuana. Now that other hardships had begun – hunger, imprisonment, executions against the wall – we should have taken this fact to heart and made it our courage and symbol. For a long time we were speechless, immobilized. "Imagine, in war, Greek poems!" was the common view of the bourgeois; it influenced us, creating in us some secret complex. Deep down we knew, we felt it, poetry was hope's ultimate refuge from general scorn, its only free stronghold against dark forces.

It was then that the figure of Angelos Sikelianos began then to acquire superhuman dimensions. His build was enough to inspire courage in a storm. His reputation for patience, endurance and high morale grew larger from one mouth to the next and reached into broader strata. He restored the myth of the spiritual which everyone suddenly, as if from self-preservation instinct, fervently sought. We made a kind of silent, unwilled truce between old and young. We needed it in order to regroup, and I still remember a conference where all generations and tendencies were represented. Our goal was to join our forces around a new journal titled, symbolically, *Antæus*. Though it was never published, its influence remained, keeping us amicable and awake. Organized political expediency had yet to turn its corrosive force on our ranks.

In early 1942, on the initiative of Katsimbales and Tsatsos, a new brotherhood, the "Palamas Circle," was formed. There one could meet writers and university professors – ranging from Amantos (the eldest) to yours truly (the youngest) – announcing new work, discussing it freely and planning varied events. It was there that I first presented my essay, "The True Physiognomy and Lyric Risk of Andreas Kalvos," one spring afternoon, unaware that it would sound paradoxical. I wanted to reintegrate this poet who, even in his time, was set apart. And now our wounded pride called him from the past with all its power. By his uncompromising life and original poetics, he was our only possible distant ancestor, and not just to my personal emotion or idiosyncrasy. The young were "discovering" him with a mania.

Invited to the University, Karantonis, Gatsos and I heard endless student discussions on the subject. The small amphitheater, still vivid in my eyes, shone with bright faces. The steps and corridors were asphyxiatingly full. The young – without stereos, transistors or film divas – discovered that it is not the deprivation of wealth that makes our misfortune so hideous. They ran – with holes in their shoes, they didn't care – to any voice promising to help them resist the devil's machines and machinations. Lectures, speeches and gatherings behind the closed doors of friends' homes abounded, their windowpanes papered over for black-outs.

The hostess of the house would always, with unvarying dignity, offer canapés, sorry sesame cakes in carob-syrup, rotten raisins. Sirens would interrupt the speaker. The throb of airplanes in the distance and the anti-aircraft torrents nearby often forced most of us to where comfort assumes the specifics of weapons. And then Katsimbales' heavy voice, in Palamas' "Gypsy's Dodecalogue," would return us to the certain endurance of Greekness, regardless of ups and downs.

All publications about Hellenism that could, of course, pass the roadblock of censorship had unprecedented success. And in their footsteps followed works speaking to their many readers of what it *is*, or rather what it *could be*, to be human. People were reading. In less than a year, new presses had been established: *Gull, Ikaros, Friends of the Book* and *Alpha Publications*. People who, you might be stunned to learn, had landed in Egypt by British submarine a few days later or fallen to an execution squad, now spoke of Federico García Lorca or of General Makriyannis' *Memoirs* as though preparing doctorals in the serene surroundings of an improbable university. Never before did the utter collapse of humanity and its highest exaltation coexist so closely, so side-by-side, in one city and one populace, often, alas, in one person. The more time passed, the more Purity lost ground. An infernal mechanism, out of control in the hands that built it, threatened everything.

Oh, bitter days, repulsive days, when the friend you spoke to might also have the mission of annihilating you. Days of secret joy and pride, days full of heartbeat, when the folded paper secretly passed under your door at night might be either your sentence or a Sikelianos poem, bright as sun. Days we prepared hope's messages for our new magazine, and days we abandoned it all, exhausted, to bear the terrible news: they executed Michael Akylas! They obliterated Kitsos Maltezos in mid-street! They murdered Karl Frieslander!

Disgrace and glory of the human race...

> *Wo aber die Gefahr ist, wächst*
> *Das Rettende auch.*

"But where danger is, salvation also blooms..." This fragment, fragrant with ancient wisdom and verified by each page of history, was written in the same tongue issuing death sentences around us! It went against logic. Was that distant brother a child of the tribe that so hedonistically now ground its heel on the human face? The moment a nation stops following the thread of its poets' voice it marches to the abyss. Friedrich Hölderlin – for whom Greece was a golden vision, a divine fleece, Christ-love enfleshed in Apollonian form – was now reduced by his descendants to a pole for raising the flag of power. How ugly, if nothing else!

> *So much is a human worth and so much is life's splendor*

he whispers, an old man, mad now for forty years, in two half-finished poems called "Greece," so profoundly did this idea follow him to the end. And he concludes:

> *Again human life is born anew*
> *Years leave silently and vanish.*

I liked, surrounded by Germans, to discover a German who showed me their image upside down, a German saner in his delirium than they, beside themselves in their iron logic. I saw in him a guarantee of the spirit's indivisibility under the arbitrary divisions imposed by its temporal rulers.

96

I had just added another victim of borders and ideological hatred to my great discoveries, Lorca. His poetry, less deep but lightning-bright, closer to our esthetic and more familiar to our Mediterranean idiosyncrasy, arrived just as we too opened our windows to demotic rhythms and traditional reverberations. Our reasons differed, but he showed us how a new, "mixed but legitimate" style could be born to that marriage of elements. Sensitivity, windlike, advances; it remains the same, but the landscape changes.

Nikos Gatsos and I were headquartered on the mezzanine of the grand cafe *Loumides* on Stadiou Street. There, literally and metaphorically, we brought our new loves – new poetry collections and new sweethearts. At nearby tables, the black market flourished; unlikely characters traded in sugar and tinned goods, signing documents and exchanging huge suitcases of moribund, inflationary millions. They were as incredulous at us as we at them, terrified that they might catch a fragment of our coded speech – so recently enriched by true-blooded Spanish – *verde te quiero verde* – and others most attractive to the tongue:

En la noche platinoche
noche, que noche nochera…

Like this and like that, Gatsos' *Amorgos* and my *Sun the First* arrived at the typographers one day. They were like a nail in the eye of the orthodox, whose fate it seems is to ignore beauty's direct communication with the ethical world. I'm not speaking of their quality, though serious battle would ensue in its name between those speaking of freedom and those enacting it. The point was that this passion for change in expression, which had first been spearheaded by liberated lyricism, should now be generalized and articulated as a catholic demand for a "new spirit," as we had originally conceived of it, and as the more awake among the young had started feeling it and had begun gathering around us.

In less than a year, the mezzanine buzzed as a motley beehive of pale poets and wild-haired girls slowly displaced the black marketeers, much to the waiters' dismay. Some are famous today and some were swept by life's conditions. During the noon hours, they all paid their dues in this informal school. Valaoritis (before he ran off to Egypt), Sachtouris, Likos, Eleni Vakalo, Korsos, Papaditsas, Aravantinos and, a little later,

Sinopoulos, Lydia Stefanidou, Fokas and Mavroidis, and also Vousvou-
nis, Xydis, Alex Solomós and Kambas who, along with Matsie Andreou,
would later form an independent group around the journal *Notebook*.

In the midst of this uproar, I recall, an unexpected prize fell from the
sky one day: a slender young man with short curly hair and large black
eyes who said he too wrote free verse but who, his manuscripts lacking
the impact he expected, was also, he said immediately, a musician. Mu-
sician? We were curious. What kind? Violinist? Pianist? No, he ex-
plained, he was a composer. This was unexpected. Did such a thing exist
in Greece? We had no idea. The last composer we knew of was Manolis
Kalomoiris. Besides, did music relate to modern poetry? Very much, he
replied. As proof, he had composed music for Gatsos' *Amorgos* and my
Variations on a Sunbeam.

We were stunned. We realized how unforgivably backward we were
in terms of music. We vaguely knew that twelve-tone music existed, and
we knew the names, and only the names, of Schoenberg and Alban
Berg. Records, hi-fi's and tape decks were as yet uninvented or at least
not in common use. Surrealism, on the other hand, did not get along
with music for some reason. Breton banished it from his *polis*, as Plato
had banished poetry from his. Perhaps it was his personality or perhaps
music's bell had not yet rung during the "Manifestoes." But now...

We looked at our young interlocutor in disbelief. If it was true, he
must prove it. We went immediately to Valaoritis' and the young com-
poser, Manos Hatzidakis, sat at the piano. What he played for us that
afternoon is no longer significant. He later confessed that he had noth-
ing specific in mind; he simply improvised. The innocent lie with which
he had approached us and piqued our interest didn't block him at all. As
soon as his fingers found the keys, he overturned the lie and made it a
magic truth. This self-made youngster, bursting with musicality, was so
close to a virgin territory of undeveloped sounds and rhythms that he
had only to nudge it with his elbow on the piano for the room, for
Greece, and then the world to fill with a different rapture.

His association with the poets of that generation helped him. Bril-
liant, immediately at home in their climate, he worked their motifs and,
in his first creations, used the same language of symbols that Greek Sur-
realists, regardless of personal experience, had made common. I men-

tion him as one example, with no wider meaning than itself, of a new spirit's development and rise, one which leaves a few shared symbols in the air that anyone is free to use without betraying himself or others. This goes beyond Hatzidakis who, with no relation to the sea, wrote music *For a small white shell*. Gatsos, too, had never lived on an island when he titled his poems *Amorgos*, and the other composer, Mikis Theodorakis, also had no such experience when he later attached the magic word *Archipelago* to his songs. Only in minor artists is Art confined to confession and observation. The first word of each step forward belongs to a power that can domesticate its epoch's sensitivity and embody, in its expression, the personal experience it guides to an objective condition.

IN THE MIDDLE of 1943, of course, we cared about none of this. We simply had youth's hurried hands, intensified by uncertain tomorrows. We wrote, rewrote, crossed out and tore; we talked all night with a sense of squandering that perhaps subconsciously replaced the unavailable wine, the forbidden journeys and the early curfew...How often didn't we dash to our front stoop with seconds to spare, while the German guards across the street yelled their harsh "*Schnell, Schnell!*" and pounded the butt of their weapon on the cobble? How equally often didn't we stay at a friend's until morning, in a frigid little room, bundled in coats and rugs, barely visible through the cigarette smoke at dawn? We'd argue about Eliot's turn to Catholicism or about Éluard and Aragon whose fame – inflated by the significance of the poetry of resistance they had begun to cultivate – had secretly crossed our borders.

By now we had another safehouse for the nocturnal hours, Embeirikos' new home on Aenianos Street. Our regular Thursday gatherings, which lasted the length of the Occupation and even, if with less vitality, after the Liberation, were legendary. Like all unplanned things, they began with a couple of friends and, by the end of the Occupation, encompassed a broad generational and stylistic circle of artists who, regardless of age and political orientation, insisted upon remaining, above all, free human beings in the deepest, most correct meaning of the term.

There, *Amorgos* was first recited, Engonopoulos' *Bolívar*, Papajohnis' *Ursa Minor*, Vousvounis' *St. Anthony*, the poems of Valaoritis, of Matsie

Andreou, of the soon-to-be-unjustly-killed Maltezou-Makriyanni, and many others. There, in the two connecting rooms, one covered with books, the other with paintings by Tanguy and Ernst, we'd crowd the sofas, armchairs, stools, whatever was around, even on the floor on pillows, and listen to our host read his new work, first *Writings*, then *Argo* or *Aerostatic Voyage* and finally, the huge, thousand-page novel *Great Anatolia*, in his warm characteristic voice that so well followed and colored the subtlest textual variations.

Thankfully, our morale was high and we didn't lack humor. Yannis Tsarouchis went from impressions of Italian and German films to full performances, disguised as a "Peloponnesian nun," a Tarantella Ballerina of New Faliron or a splendid "Traviata" in low-cut gown and fan, singing in the impeccable formality of old translations:

> *In eternal pleasures*
> *I want to fly freely*
> *and eros can't give me*
> *that bliss…*

Let the moralists, I should say the narrow-minded, call it shameful to have fun while others went hungry or were killed. But this was the whole point. Among those "having fun," most were hungry or were killed secretly at night without ever having made it an issue.

Tsarouchis had, like me, been harshly tested in Albania; Karantonis sold carob syrup door-to-door to survive; Valaoritis was to follow the secret caravans to the Middle East; and one young poet, Loes, would soon mount the gallows. As for our host, that good-hearted and noble poet, Andreas Embeirikos, who endangered his life by hiding a resistance fighter in a room of his house, would swell from lack of vitamins and later, as his reward, would join the martyred march to Krora, returning barefoot, bleeding and near death. Not letting life drag you down in its undertow was, we believed, the most difficult achievement.

Unfortunately it's hard for people to agree, even about how to face misfortune. It depends on how far each can see and how much reality one can take on one's visual field. Was tragedy *manifest*, a bayonetted body and two upturned eyes, or *latent*, a heart that beats in secret because it believes life's essence to be immortal?

It was our poems, not just our life, that bothered the well-meaning so much. But then, what emotion corresponds precisely to the act of people who, rather than weep and bemoan their fate, machinate through the night, battle openly in the streets and take to the mountains in armed resistance?

Consider the mechanism of danger. It fills the foreigner, the spectator, the outside witness with despair; but never those who live it, who are its subjects. The dying never consider the vanity of life, unlike the relatives gathered at the pillow. Their mind is, on the contrary, on life's invaluable, irrepeatable taste about to be lost forever. A casual noon swimmer reveres the sun less intensely than the prisoner does from a dark cell. Likewise, when danger threatens something with annihilation it raises it to consciousness and spotlights its value and brilliance.

In the years of Buchenwald and Auschwitz, Matisse painted the juiciest, rawest, most enchanting flowers and fruit ever made, as if the miracle of life itself discovered it could compress itself inside them forever. Today, they speak more eloquently than any macabre necrology. Because their creator refused to "bet" – forgive the word – on so-called "emotion" and its homeopathic properties but, instead, obeyed not phenomena themselves but the response these phenomena elicited from his consciousness.

An entire contemporary literature made the mistake of competing with events and succumbing to horror instead of balancing it, as it should have done. But when artistic speech merely and only rivals action, it's like it tries to walk with someone else's crutches and to appear crippled simply by disowning its legs.

It's strange, what happens to people! They find it difficult, impossible even, to believe that what they imagine is the same as what they see. They find it difficult to accept that physical phenomena are also spiritual phenomena. They prefer to endure their misery twice – once for their sake, once again for their art's – rather than transform it into a different reality, kneading one potential duration from two sure decays. Primitive people, poets before poems, not having mirrors, literally and metaphorically, in which to preen, overcame evil by reciting terrible, incomprehensible words, just as our island nannies chased demons from our cradles by pronouncing meaningless words with utter seriousness, holding the leaf of a humble weed that assumed, by the very innocence of its nature, who knows what unknown powers. This little basil leaf surrounded by the unknown powers of innocence, the strange words, *is* Poetry, precisely.

THOUGH I AM hardly brave, I have stood two or three times closer to death than life – in war, of course. It was entirely different from what I expected. I, who was so easily confused in Athens, so easily reduced by a minor toothache, felt, near death, a stunning clarity, an unmediated power ruling both forward and back, and a celestial serenity before which worldly turbulence stopped. *It* was disgraced, not I. This, I sometimes think, is what saved me.

I had been, I remember, a good distance from the nearest trench or even the slightest irregularity of terrain that might protect me from attack, when Italian batteries began shelling us with the frequency of automatic fire. In a few minutes the place reeked of smoke and the stench of gunpowder. Thick columns of earth rose in the air, raining stones and sticks on my back. I knew this would last, as it did, at least a couple of hours. There was no possibility of movement. I was alone and nailed to the ground, clutching the earth, one with it. I heard my short breaths produce a kind of panting, not from running, of course, but from my reaction to the attack.

It remained my only reaction. Because soon I began to realize with great surprise something I refused to accept: my train of thought from the previous sleepless night, on Kalvos' poetry, was still going on. I saw that, on returning to Athens, I must complete my essay on the influence of his wholly prescient, *iconoplastic* imagination on modern Greek expression. That smoke, "saddening the blue dimension of winds," the virgin's face, "damp with misery's cloud," that "night breath in thick-treed forests," that "rested brow of the universe" – how did he do it? – that "hopes of mortals vanishing like buckshot in infinite pelagic depths." What risk, what boldness for his time! That's what I should call the essay, "The Lyric Risk of Andreas Kalvos."

It's hard to believe, perhaps I exaggerate a little. But I could, I repeat, clearly see the madness of being about to be blown up or lose a leg and, at the same time, recalling another poet, Kavafis, and nearly cracking up at his ability – in thought? in poetry? – to adapt to all circumstance. *That* was his *passe-partout*. "Still, insistently, in all his turbulence and trouble, the poetic idea comes and goes." I had truly become a Fernazis. Poetic ideas came and went. The nearest explosions blasted me with their gaseous pressure but frightened me less than that soldier, a few meters away, annoyed me by constantly yelling "Cuckolds! Cuckolds!" and interrupting my thoughts.

Still, it is notable – though this is a thought I have today – that I was less attracted by Kalvos the patriot, as one might suppose, than by his successful expression and, especially, his idea that Greece already possessed spiritual and intellectual achievements that made it invincible. I think that my paradoxical response to danger is better explained along these lines. The comfort I sought was beyond guns or individual fate. I found it in a different power, one that knew how to turn to light in the dark, consciousness in madness and endurance in the misery of half-baked human creations, a sense of faith in life born of Art's capacity to create it anew on a higher level and convince us that everything is achievable beyond some point. Unfortunately, here too analysis betrays emotion. It's not just some tendency toward Good, some insistence on the vision of a Paradise we so unjustly let fall from our hands and which some voice constantly calls us to restore. What the idea of Art dictates on death's eve is more than that. It is a true readiness of all our organic powers to leap for the source of life, which is the only source of miracle.

I felt this truth even more clearly than in the scene I just described when, two months later, I woke up in a hospital bed in Ioannina, with all scientific indications that I would never rise again. Before antibiotics, all you had against typhoid was your organism's resistance. By necessity immobile, with ice on your belly and a few spoonfuls of milk or orange juice for food, you had to endure all the interminable days the fever stayed above 104. God help you! My worst crisis coincided with the first German attack. My bed was by the window and each time the sirens sounded the other patients – it was a pathology hospital, I was the only wounded – fled to the shelter with the doctors and nurses.

Playing tough with the Germans was not wise. Before leaving the ward, the staff opened the windows lest they break, pelting me. I was left alone in the empty ward suddenly boundless with its unmade beds, balled-up sheets, newspapers, duffels, and rudely arrested life – a kind of Pompeii of enclosure from which I emerged like Aphrodite, suspended and immersed in a strange serenity. And soon the explosions became thicker and closer. This was no longer war; it was *monomachia*. There were no troops, weapons, services or headquarters. Nothing. Only that invisible monster thundering from above. I was motionless, with a bleeding back and a piece of sky in the open window. A sensation I had never felt among my soldiers rose in me now; it multiplied and called with a thousand voices: you must, you must, you must live, prevail.

In solitude and unequal battle, the whole human comes awake. Also the poet. The idea of a book held me as icons held others. I saw it and turned its pages. The poems I had not written but wanted to write filled its pages with their external shape; I had but to "fill it" as you fill a row of empty glasses and, immediately, what power, what freedom, what disdain toward bombs and death it gave me. To extract your true self from the daily one, to see it before you invincible, imperishable, approaching the future in which you will no longer partake, what relief! But nothing like that had happened. And it had to, it had to happen. I hooked my nails into the sheet. I was delirious. Then, it seems, I lost my speech for days; the only thing I remember is a tiny light above my eyes, which they would move around to determine if I was still able to follow.

I regained consciousness one night as they came to take me to the little room next door, a few square meters with only two beds, where, I'd heard on entering the hospital, those about to die were isolated. Oh, no. Never. My tongue was suddenly loosened. I found the strength to protest, to refuse, to yell, even to hit a nurse who had become fond of me and who, in tears, tried to convince me it was for my own good. No! I didn't sleep all night. I guarded my place among the living like a dog. The next day, seeing a priest approach, communion cup in hand, I nearly barked. He ran away and I think the other patients were laughing. I couldn't take it anymore and broke into tears. I cried for the first time in my life. The doctors gathered around me, spoke among themselves and finally one of them gave me a shot. I sank into sleep for many hours. And the next day, incredibly, I woke almost without a fever. I had passed the crisis. The book I'd been dreaming of might yet be made.

Writing now after all these years, that ideal book has not been made. So what? Its hope kept me alive, both then in my ignorance and now that I know ideal books are never made. "Ithaki gave you good journey." Kavafis' *passe-partout* again. And another:

What you've achieved is not so small,
Far as you've come sufficient glory.

F

AND YET, one might say that Victory, in art, is always on the side of Defeat. Perhaps because the strong don't feel the need to read, while the rest try to find themselves in what they read. If it's true that humanity wallows in this kind of snowdrift, it's a shame. A shame because peace and well-being become like hard-to-find drugs: when you find them, time has run out. Many survivors, as useless as cafe chair legs, grow nostalgic for illness. And we, seeing them, fill endless pages on life's contradictory nature. Marxists, in turn, laugh at us. Each of us is a schema and all together a ball so tangled you can't find an end.

How much simpler things seemed while danger loomed and Heroism had the only word. Our folly was to leave it behind the door as soon as the peace bells rang; or else it was to turn it, as the other half did, victor against victor and remain, again and always, at war. It didn't occur to us to change its face, its breastplate, the cut of its sword and to transport it – I'm speaking still of Heroism – directly to the world of peaceful works ahead, immaculate in courage and vigilance of soul, inclined toward change and sacrifice. And yet, societies expected from it not only an economic and governing reorganization but, above all, ethical reform and biological revolution. Eros, the senses, dreams expired daily from a malnutrition unprecedented in the chronicles of human imagination. What else could a poet do but furnish oxygen? How else could he feel he had fulfilled his destiny if not by setting an example through his poems, rightfully taking the place vacated by Robber or Pirate, Guide or Conqueror – it makes no difference – and continuing their active intervention, amassment of bounty, discovery of unknown treasure, and their annexation of unexplored distant regions?

This was the meaning of the verbal debacle we took up, and if it can be blamed for something, it is that it unfortunately didn't always reach the intensity and focus the moment required. Still, it was enough for both sides to fire on us, trying to develop and pervade all the available space until they crushed us. Politicized revolutionaries, steadfast in their principles, pressed from one side while a chaotic bourgeoisie, without a single criterion, loomed from the other; fear was their only motive, their double and triple buttoning up, to say nothing of their stupidity.

We reacted immediately. We must do something; above all, we needed an instrument again. Why not reissue *New Letters*? It would be a sin, now that most of the young were with us, to leave them in ambivalence and confusion. *Gull*, a press founded a year before by open-spirited and radically inclined people, would help us.

Barely a month after our first negotiations we reached a common decision. It was the fall of 1943; by New Year's, we would reissue *New Letters* in the same shape and form but now, with renewed staff, as a bimonthly. Engonopoulos, another red flag for the critic bulls, would join us, as would the significant young writers Miltos Sachtouris, Giorgos Likos, D. Korsos, Eleni Vakalo, and Matsie Andreou. Kosmas Politis would give us his new novella, *The Circle*. Katsimbalis offered us two unpublished poems, one by Palamas, the other by Seferis. Not a bad way to start. I made the final corrections on my essay, "Art-Luck-Risk, 1935," and turned it in. We would all flesh out the issue with commentary, notes, reviews, and not leave it all to Karantonis as before. I chose what had most recently enraged me, a trivial piece, I see now, by Michael Rodas on Gatsos' *Amorgos*. I worked up a column called "Poetic Intelligence."

It's amusing what great demands I had then of a simple and aging journalist when, twenty years later, we are still being nourished by straw – and not only by amateurs and "anthology buffs" as then, but by those supposedly dedicating their life to this aim, daring to publish whole theoretical books on recent poetry. What should we admire first: their discourse on nonexistent works with nonexistent criteria, or their complete inability to discern whether or not a verse, old or new, intersects poetry's current.

I'm not speaking of the self-serving. Throughout history, many have pursued base goals while also preserving – they at least had the intelligence to preserve – the external appearance of straightforward judgment. Their contemporaries cannot even do that.

How else could poor Rodas react when he, having never encountered a *Revolver à cheveux blancs*, was suddenly struck headlong by "the

underwear of bears in the frozen valley" and "bats eating birds and piss-
ing sperm"? He tried to explain these images, to understand their rela-
tion to the general title *Amorgos*, and naturally he failed. His problem
was fundamentally the same as that exhibited today by most of the new-
er generation's representatives. They insist on judging gold by color not
by weight, oblivious to how easily everything can be painted gold, as
easily as writing a book of poems a week, in which you paint everything
black – do words cost anything? – and have the world admire.

Passons. The reactions my little column provoked proved that some
margin of productive intellectual discourse did remain, despite the in-
evitable relocation of interests that follow political fanaticisms.

Further proof was that my essay on Surrealism in that same issue,
though garrulous and tiresome, nevertheless became, with its three
magic words – Art-Luck-Risk – an instant password to an entire young
circle. Tsatsos sent me a letter, "Meaning and Coherence in our New
Poetry," which was published in the next issue along with my reply. Un-
der the same title, it was later included in Tsatsos' *Essays on Esthetics and
Education* (Difros, 1960). In it he notes: "I believe [this text] somehow
completes, to the extent that this can be done, the 'Dialogue on Poetry,'
clarifying the subtle distinction between *logical* and *sensible*, between
meaning under formal logic and *sensible coherence of meaning*, between *in-
tellect* and *logos*."

My perplexity is understandable; I was abruptly faced with a termi-
nology and methodology common to scientific thought but alien to a
Surrealist's education and upbringing. Idealistic philosophy energetical-
ly opposed a poetic theory that, more than any other and without
shame, appeared to twist in the magic of aleatory combinations and
self-rule. I was suddenly thrust into a sea ruled by different laws of dis-
placement, where my own art of swimming had no currency. Of neces-
sity, I must pretend to float and yet not drift too far. Today, this can
easily be seen in my reply.

The truth is that, despite all my disagreements with my interlocutor,
I was also grateful to him for the serious tone he had lent this matter. It
helped me bypass the cheap attacks from other quarters and never again
give them attention. Anyway, I had to face the problems of poetic ex-
pression more concretely and through action. Freedom of form was no
longer enough, nor was the revolution, symbolized by over-bold images

compressed by violent association and marriage of elements usually distant in the real world. The sense of the poem, not as a part of a perpetual confession, but as an autonomous unit of discrete parts bound by duty to converge towards some center, gained more ground in me every day. Not only did we have to preserve what we had gained from the adventure, but we also had to place these gains in service to a goal, lest they vanish in the void or simply constitute a more or less abstract poetic state.

My reaction was, of course, enormous. Instinct pulled my rope from one end and orthodox theory, with all the strength of its enchantment, claimed the other. Today's young can't understand or put themselves in my place. How could they? Revolution creates a strange psychology for its duration, which those who follow find hard to comprehend. This is why they don't, as a rule, do justice to its works, regardless of how objective we agree that they try to be.

During the writing of my first two books, to give a quick example, my entire effort was in avoiding the *subject*. I wanted only the "faceless meaning of Poetry" to take its place. In hindsight, this hurt me, and what poems survive – "Anniversary," "Marina of Boulders," "Bioteian Form" – are precisely those in which, almost by mistake, the pattern of a central inspirational motif also survives. Still, the contemporary reader – not obliged to know what overturning the very foundation of the poem meant then to a young poet, nor how he understood his gesture as infinitely more poetic than its result – judges him only by the latter and cannot do otherwise. So he enacts the oxymoron of judging by what was achieved against the poet's will. What can we do? The demonic averaging machine, balancing conquests and losses, always prevails.

The question remains: what is preferable? Stormy seas threatening to flood the boat or fair weather's certainty and boredom? Would you rather be expression's freeshooter or its future pensioner? Because you can't be both. "The beauty of folly," a particular sensation of youth, more "grace" than ability, is never offered along with the securities of wisdom.

Without Surrealism a youth of some talent might, in principle, remain truer to Art's deeper sense, but he would also be cast out of a Paradise that welcomes only some generations or eras. What else would Paradise be to a young poet but the locus where the constriction he experiences from his difficulty in adjusting to reality, the chief evil that made him a poet, is suddenly transformed to a force projecting him thousands of miles past the blocks of the Undeclared, loosening his tongue and empowering him to enact the spirit's courage while remaining the magician who mesmerizes and the nightingale that sings?

I recall once in Paris, a little after the war, Paul Éluard and I spoke about this. We were alone in his new apartment on Rue Marx Dormoy, and our conversation, during our meal of two *biftecks* that he had cooked with his own trembling hands, had tired him, I think. It hurt to see him so unhappy (he had just lost his second wife, the most beautiful Nush), yet forced to perform the duties of the Poet Laureate *de la Résistance*. Twice, while I was there, they called from the Party, once asking him to host a committee, once to write four verses suitable for enlargement and application to a banner for the "working woman celebration."

—Don't smile so ironically, he said, observing my transparent expression. This is exactly how your ancient poets worked. Pindar was commissioned to praise an Olympic winner. And Sappho took commissions for weddings, our familiar "Epithalamia."

—Except that their societies were different, I risked.

—So? That's what we're fighting for, for different societies, he replied, somewhat angrily.

But after lunch, during coffee and cigarettes, our talk turned elsewhere and I had occasion to remind him of some episode of Surrealism's "heroic" period, under the pretext of wanting more details. His eyes lit up; his facial muscles enlivened; he rose to get cognac. He had, in a few moments, "gotten high just from the memory," as we would say in Greece.

—You don't know, he raved, you have no idea; no one can ever imagine those years. They were something else, something strange, a sense of omnipotence perhaps...not even that...a divine condition from the antipodes of the divine...I don't mean the "demonic"...an experience like that of Saints, Magicians, Explorers, Pioneers... It can't be explained, I told you from the start, though I could tell you what we were feeling; *voilà*...we felt the world, all of it, was ours, at our disposal – do you understand? – when I say at our disposal I mean *to make as we wanted*, is that too little? *As we wanted!*

—As all pioneers must have felt, I said, to say something.

—I don't believe it, he replied steadily, as if he had thought a great deal on the subject. Anyway what pioneers? As far as we know, we have only isolated acts by individuals who were, often if not always, unaware of themselves as pioneers and were only tormented by an internal spasm. That's all. They were left with a pain that their terrifying isolation turned to madness, or else to denial of everything, including themselves or even their art. Lautréamont, for example, was not in touch with his future. Or Rimbaud? The last thing on his mind was that his poems would one day create an entire philology.

He was the first to endure going beyond esthetics. He had that magnanimity. Yet he shared it with no one and did not taste the wild joy of seeing it reverberate through the circles of mediocrity that choked him. He ended up on some Marseilles hospital bed like a dead dog.

—That was his grandeur.

—His grandeur and his grief. Because there is, in all of this, a grief and a human toll still paid to our romantic side – to be the victim your neighbor pities. What an unjust and unacceptable role, don't you think?

—But Surrealism was romanticism to the limit.

—To the limit, exactly. That's why it overturned it. Set foot on the opposite shore. When the subject is stretched to dissolution, only the object remains.

—Many would call this mere sophistry, a word game.

—It's not that easy to see ahead of and behind us. We are still hostages of our Christian upbringing. Our most sensitive young people suck on the dry bone Kafka threw them, under the blissful impression of moving forward. They are going backward, I declare, I who no longer give the time of day to Breton and his old friends. But they saw, at least for a moment, what no one else has seen again, and humanity will remember it much later, when the study of Surrealism is resumed outside the spirit of scandal-mongering.

—*Nous de l'avenir*

Pour un petit moment pensons au passé.

—Yes, only after I became a communist could I speak like that. Only a communist can speak on behalf of the future.

—As soon as communism enters the picture, everything becomes simple.

—Everything takes on the color of hope again, perhaps this is what you mean. I take pride in the fact that I never deigned to stand where the possibility of transforming matter for the better did not exist.

—So you admit that about Surrealism?

—I admit it was the last healthy lung of bourgeois society. It could react; this signifies health. Only recently have the young been reduced to bragging about their illness. I am revolted by this phenomenon, how to say, I am enraged.

—I'm afraid you're unjust to the young.

—Because I love them, don't you see? he asked. He seemed truly worried and anguished that I might have misunderstood his words.

His hands were trembling again, beating in space.

—Those who came with us were saved, he murmured...But the others? We faced greater difficult moments in our youth than they do now...I pity them...I truly pity them...they have nothing, nothing, nothing, do you hear me? *Rien, rien, rien!* he shouted, and with each *rien* slammed his palm on the armchair. It wasn't the posture of grief or even rage. It was hate. The kind of hate, I imagine, that any blessed man must feel who spent his life envisioning Paradise and now hears his holies blasphemed and cursed.

His outburst, slanted though it was, heartened me, and just when Paris seemed incapable of connecting me to its glorious past. I was in the throes of a crisis whose first symptoms had appeared four years earlier, at the end of the Occupation, as the Greek in me awoke, not with his senses – *he* was always awake, I believe – but the one who sought Synthesis and Myth.

LIBERATION was close! All the signs were there. The Germans would last at most another year. And then...then everyone must have his say. In mountains and cities, organized political factions intensified their activities. On the intellectual plane, the left influenced a weekly journal, *Art News,* whose literary dress was so transparent it was a miracle it passed by the censors. I thought my efforts would find greater favor there, especially since the faction's most significant and well-meaning theoretician, Markos Augeris, was a regular contributor and was always open to conversation.

The editor, my old friend and fellow student K. A. Zaimis, and I put our minds to it and quickly agreed that the best way to stir the waters was by organizing a broad inquiry on "contemporary poetic and artistic problems." I undertook to formulate its questions and compose the first reply, which would of course be the longest, since it would detail the history of modern movements and define the targets for the ensuing discussion. The journal's leadership would, for its part, try to provoke and collect as many replies as possible and select only those by the most significant poets and critics, regardless of esthetic or social beliefs. In the event of interesting results – that is, should the champions of modern art provide enough arguments to warrant a second comment – it would be my privilege to make it, summarizing their positions and drawing the necessary conclusions.

By Christmas of 1943, the readers of *Art News* had the first of five installments that comprised my reply. I ended it with a proud appeal to the young, as if to say I no longer belonged to their ranks though I still marched under their flag. I was closing the chapter on a story that had lasted almost ten years and which, despite the enmities of war and social upheaval, had achieved, I'm not exaggerating, the transformation of the national intellectual physiognomy. But not in the sense of turning the page on the futile game of euphonistic constructivism once and for all, nor of annexing a previously unexplored psychic arena. One way or another, that would, one day, occur.

For me, at least, its greatest achievement was that it had gradually created a climate in which our tongue's ethos could reclaim its rights to expression: something of the masculine in emotion and the lofty in aspiration, not favored by the half-light and chiaroscuro of Western Art. We resumed trying ourselves by the outdoors, not in a *physiolatric* sense but in endurance of the sun's metaphysical power – meaning, we had reentered Tradition by the back door. It seemed oxymoronic then, if not inexplicable, that we ourselves turned to the Solomós of "Zakynthos Woman," or to Kalvos, Makriyannis and Theophilos. Yet nothing was more natural. Even if we had latched onto some Latinate chariot again, as most accused us, we had at last, thanks to the madmen driving it, truly broken our bonds. Immediately we felt our joints become loose and free, our limbs ready for their natural gallop.

You not only gain the future with a successful revolution; you also gain the past.

The inquiry *Art News* had instigated vanished in the confusion of the transition only to reappear, after the liberation, in *New Letters*. Some, like Demaras, Vrettakos, Pappas, Sfakianakis and Augeris, had replied in the former. Others, like Sikelianos and Papajohnis, in the latter. Their two contributions, in fact, were proper studies which, reread today, must be appreciated for their open spirit and adaptability to sensitive times. They also, in some respects, proved how difficult it was to both want to change and also be able to, especially after having become a well-known personality.

"The sanctuary of the subconscious," writes Sikelianos, "is the Oracle, the central fold, where only a *creative* psyche, prepared by enormous and lengthy exercise and practice, descends to illuminate the endless field of our rationalistic Lethe, a field whose inertia includes incalculable and ancient dynamic regions of soul, body and world, from which it siphons all the memory, strength, flame and momentum it needs to illuminate, by a *steady and responsible* torch of inspiration, yesterday and today, the eternal and the future.

"No one can deny that this was indeed Surrealism's *intention*, but only its intention, from the first hour that it appeared. This is evidenced by its origins in the German Romantics, who sought to deepen cosmic vision: by conquering the 'dream' within them; by its fervent search for the most secret strata of the human psyche, 'where a *prima mater* of the intellect exists, different from thought which is only one particular occurrence of it'; by its sudden reversal from the password '*Volonté inopérante*' to a 'practical' confrontation of the era's problems and on to the study of the 'profound causes of contemporary disgust'; and finally, by its vigorously proclaimed insistence on '*réhabilitation de l'étude du moi, pour pouvoir l'intégrer à celle de l'être collectif.*' All these and more serve as proof of a large and authentic uprising by a few young psyches at a specific historical hour, although it was, as a whole, an intellectually undisciplined uprising that could not present the theoretical terms of the *new foundations of a more general human sensorium, as it had proclaimed it would,* nor its *achievements of catholic value* in terms of a clearly creative application.

"Of course this doesn't necessarily mean that Surrealism's general orientation, especially as crystallized in its final conclusions after so many unstable peregrinations, doesn't persist as a living indicator of a truth that was fundamentally the most urgent and significant at the time of its revelation: '*la précarité artificielle de la condition sociale de l'homme ne doit point lui voiler la précarité réelle de sa condition humaine*'."

And Takis Papajohnis: "I stand before an event I must accept as I accept day as day and night as night, whether I want to or not. It is, however, a different matter altogether whether I place this event among those that can be solved and proceed to do everything in my power to solve it, or whether I place it in the category of mystery, that is, of themes surpassing the power of human organs, themes that cannot be elucidated by paltry logical association, be it positive or negative. But what theme are we discussing? The Surrealistic sermon, its theory, was transmitted to us by beings like us, human beings of whom we cannot accept that they are capable of posing – creating – problems that by their nature are outside the scope of the powers and possibilities of human judgment.

"This is why I must accept the existence of a *dilation*: that the subject, the core essence that constitutes the unsolved problem, has always preexisted and had merely not yet been made conscious or, in this case, subconscious, and that this unsolved subject became the subject of the Surrealistists' proclamation. Accepting this dilation, I can explain my logically inexplicable assent to that core, as well as my resignation from an effort to solve a phenomenon, a force, an urge that has no final solution, and I can also explain my right to criticize the use of this core and fateful essence as soon as it became, under developmental and historical laws, the object of a specific proclamation and the material of theoretical formulation.

"Criticism can easily determine whether this theory, in the specific and necessarily finite form of the Manifesto, corresponds absolutely to the revealed essence – impossible, as the practical application of any essence always stumbles – or whether, since Surrealism presents itself as a theory of both esthetics and life, its enactment and application in both of those spheres is appropriate and indeed satisfies its underlying demand for radical revolutionary deposal of the established criteria of esthetics and intellectual elegance. Let's not forget that its very revelation and main demand was for instinctual immediacy toward life's pulse, an immediacy that – wasted by time, misunderstandings, fate and habit – had lapsed into a stupor or, worse, marasmus and death. This imperative was nothing less than a miracle, a resurrection from the dead. It is

Surrealism's honor and glory that it not only made this imperative sensate but also exemplified possible applications – the first symptoms of new life breathing into dead bodies.

"Having assented psychically to this imperative's core essence, I also let critical energy do its work: I began to separate its sermon, as a practice of apostolic propaganda, from the fruit it bore. I praise only the latter. I neither bemoan fate nor ask the impossible. I cannot say that the first fruits were abundant, that the harvest occurred in a new Paradise, or that its quality was wholly perfect. Still, it is more than enough to have tasted splendid, truly paradisaic fruit, and I acknowledge that the miracle was actualized truly and beyond expectation..." (*New Letters*, p. 340)

To summarize the results of this literary poll in the last issue of *New Letters* was somehow symbolic. War was finally over, a pioneering journal had folded and a discussion that would no longer have any meaning was closed. We now had other problems to face; we needed a different beginning. Even the title of my synopsis, "Apologia and New Beginnings," reveals my hurry to end a chapter along with its decade and open a new one.

HUMAN UNITS are like chemical elements. Their union produces unforeseen forces that can alter or corrode what had, until then, passed for invincible. This is so frequent we might even hope that an ethical progress, like the scientific one in evidence today, would someday solve the cosmic problem. Alas! Despite deterministic theories, the great Chemist remains invisible, ill-tempered and unaccountable on the subject. Just when you think he's about to uncover the secret explosive of the soul, he upends the sensitive instruments, shatters the glass tubes and confuses the formulas so no one can continue his work. He begins, all over again, "the game for the sake of the game." Let the poor individual await redemption. It's over, finished. Hydrogen remains hydrogen; oxygen, oxygen. They don't turn into water.

Such unions and fissions, such refutations, write our history. Still, I want to believe that something remains each time, and that these remains ultimately constitute – if it exists at all – the slow, imperceptible human spiritual progress. It might even be proved one day that it achieved its greatest victory by these endless, minuscule defeats.

In any case, two or three good books composed in as many hermitages do not add up to what we call a spiritual life. We also need the average, the bad and, above all, the ideas behind them – themes, counter-themes, currents, the playing fields and struggles. As if by signal, the very day after the war, they stopped or continued only through temporary momentum. A repositioned sensitivity had erased poetry's spearheading privilege, a common phenomenon after revolutions that, as if by divine economy, allows its creators to concentrate on their main oeuvre: the exploitation and valorization of their conquests. Besides, a revolution can never be considered justified unless it proves capable of evolving its dawn to its high noon. In my humble opinion, it was hardly time to silence the "lyricism on alert" as some who were eager to don the black of mourning insisted on, but instead it was time to guide it by the lessons of so many years' experience to its – let's not fear the word – classical period.

Very soon, in France, René Char and St. John Perse would prove that they were already working in this direction, as had Dylan Thomas in England, Pablo Neruda in Chile and Octavio Paz in Mexico. They came to "synthesis" and "counterpoint," and to the wise use of the bounty of *iconoplastic* or verbal freedom. It was there that they tested their inventiveness and imagination, and no one ever suggested that they had betrayed their virtue or risked devolving into academics. Only Greeks considered this a retreat. We have the habit of nostalgia for what only yesterday we battled, without a single intervening day to simply notice and accept.

Anyway, after the December coup, things seemed to proceed by chance. Presses were demolished, publishing houses dissolved, the economy was in turmoil. One could hardly give serious thought to a journal. Thankfully, when *New Letters* started sinking, a small corps of younger contributors detached from the wreck in a different vessel, the quarterly *Notebook*. With a more youthful air and no compass, it would stay the course for a couple of years. Vousvounis, Alex Solomós, Kambas, Matsie Andreou and Xydis were headquartered in Apotsos' bar; they were the successors to, as well as the carriers of, a new spirit that would definitely fruit if its social context lent a hand. But how could a branch bloom when all signs augured tragedy ahead? We ourselves, before the others and against our will, were swept by the centrifuge.

116

Seferis, who was just back from Africa after years abroad, seemed to gaze at us between the agapanthi and jacarandas. He was content just by contact with the physical Greece he had been so deprived of. It soon would cause him to write the poem "Thrush" and his "Erotokritos" essay. Embeirikos had yet to recover from the terrifying trials of captivity. Antoniou, who had been disembarked for years, restlessly eyed the open sea. Gatsos turned to the theater. And Katsimbales, who had taken over the *Anglo-Hellenic Review* (at first because he needed work, later with actual zeal) had gradually managed to transform it from a propaganda flyer to a literary instrument, though its creative content was limited to articles and studies.

I sent them some texts. A little later, encouraged by Seferis, I agreed to be Program Director of the newly established "National Radio Institute." I also tried to keep up a regular column in the newspaper *Eleutheria*. Anyone who could handle a pen felt called upon, in the aftermath of the war, to approach, enlighten and address the public's pressing concerns. I set out to fulfill this obligation full of good will but, in five or six weeks, I felt hemmed in. I turned to literary themes and realized that, there too, commercialism isn't for everyone. In short, I understood I wasn't made for any of this. I resigned from radio. I didn't think it unprincipled to undertake the critique of painting in a newspaper as large as *Kathemerene*. Baudelaire and Apollinaire's precedent was enough to overcome my slight doubts. I failed there too, according to my friends. Most of the artists looked at me askance, either because they believed that a poet would revert to "literature," even unwittingly, or else because the conservative among them feared I would condemn anything outside modern art's framework and, on that account, they were right. I carefully declared myself in the very first article, which served as an introduction to the style of my critical effort. But that style required that the exhibiting painters show strong positive or negative positions that justified my enthusiasm or condemnation. Unfortunately, most exhibits didn't rise above mediocrity. I continued this column until February 1948, when I moved to Paris.

I had thought of it as a voyage closer to the sources of modern art. I didn't think I'd also approach my old loves: the early Surrealist centers, the cafes of the Manifestoes, the Rue de l'Odéon and Place Blanche, Montparnasse and Saint-Germain-des-Prés. I ran through the streets with the ineffable sensation of searching for an unfaithful lover. Soon, I understood I was to find a new one, younger and more beautiful, whose name would be the same. It would always be Poetry.

G

POETRY – I must admit, after a brief false blooming during those scheming days after World War II – lay in its cradle, seriously ill. Its few practitioners, having borne the weight of its responsibility through difficult times, reminded me of sleepless, agitated doctors who circled its pillow and worried about its symptoms. One by one, I unearthed each poet in his solitude – where else could the true pillow of poetry be? – and each one beheld me with a strange mien, something between profound perplexity and shame. Reverdy, in his brief excursions from the hermitage of Solesmes, cast a jaundiced eye at the large weeklies in my hand which were full of columns about the star of the day, Prévert. *C'est une honte!* he'd shout through clenched jaws, and would proceed to empty two or three bottles of Chianti, in despair, at the small Italian restaurant we'd frequent.

Pierre Jean Jouve – no longer at the majestic apartment on Rue de Tournon, which was now, I'd heard, a real museum, but at the tiny house of Rue d'Alésia near Denfert-Rochereau – awaited me, flawlessly dressed as always and on tiptoe, as though not to disturb the great Patient. Great order reigned in his ascetic basement study with its few chosen pieces from the old collection: a wooden Gothic relief of the Virgin, two Spanish chests, a painting by Balthus and, of course, his sumptuous books. "*C'est grave,*" he barely whispered, and added after a pause, "*et c'est triste, triste.*" He spread his arms as if to say, What can we do? We have endured a great wrath of God.

As for André Breton, the only time I was alone in the house with him he was all fire and brimstone. He had Éluard's last collection on his desk, open to a very bad poem dedicated to our own Markos, leader of the insurgents. Clearly, he was prepared for me. "What are these things?" he screamed, slamming his hands on the sinning pages, "What are these things? For this we fought all those years? For this we struggled? For the writing of these childish simplicities?" His stare was insistent, as if he wanted an accounting just because I was Greek. What could I say? To me, Éluard was the poet of *Capitale de la Douleur* and of *L'Amour La Poésie*. The present, with its problems, remained open for him as it did for us, but how much more so for my glorious interlocutor and his large leadership ambitions. After his return from America, he faced an exceptionally difficult dilemma: either produce a startling theoretical expansion that equaled the new reality and proved his argument for Surrealism's eternal currency, or else shut up and be relegated to history, along with his sealed baggage, even before his death. He did neither.

He might – and I believe this demand besieged him all around – have fought the "poetic" fight on every level, with his singular, indisputable capacity for argument and his magnetic style, without ever betraying the old positions but simply broadening their base, at a time when Existentialism, an exceptionally serious philosophical movement, made its imprint on the young as a more general view of life, that, unfortunately, also imbued it with a supremely anti-poetic spirit. Yet he chose, or was unable to exceed, the status quo, meaning his eternal circle of students that he liked to dominate, his eternal quarrels and polemics that, naturally, found almost no resonance. Still, to his credit, he was not inclined to trade his integrity for the coin of a broader audience like so many others. In a time of unbridled intercourse, this was more than enough. What else could the holy relic of Poetry's cross be, if not a small permanent "no" worn brilliant and proud as a jewel of sky?

Others wore it: Tristan Tzara, even though he'd identified with a political faction, Philippe Soupault, though he'd withdrawn from active literature years ago, Julien Gracq and Benjamin Péret, to mention only those I happened to meet. They more closed a door than opened one, at least for me, who hungered for any opening. For me, the Paris of those years is irrevocably identified with that hunger, that palpating search for a way out. I literally "boiled in my juices" for three and a half years along the cross made by the bookstores of Hune and Adrienne Monnier Streets and the cafes Deux Magots, Mabillon and Capoulade on the Luxembourg gardens. I went up and down the studios of poet or painter friends, listening a lot and speaking little, making huge but futile attempts to be reconciled with the new "universal" spirit, always about to be born, whose only carriers were, as far as I could see, the barefoot,

bearded throng on its nightly promenade through the springtime side-
walks, holding an unread book underarm.

The throng had launched a costume I detested. A thousand times
better to be nude! I shut myself up in my little room and began to read
Plato, with a hedonism only the parched can feel when reaching clear
water! It hardly made sense that Greek tradition would find a way to
stretch a hand to nudge my shoulder among those Gothic churches,
rococo salons and howling *boîtes de nuit*. Deep down I think I wanted to
hear Greek. The phenomenon of language assumed unsuspected di-
mensions. The mystery of birth by baptism in the sweet exaltation of
the soul that is a phoneme fascinated me, as did the word, made smooth
by human lips as a pebble is smoothed by sea. Lips, teeth, specifics that
insist you fight or fall in love *in this way and no other*. You and your com-
rade. All of you. Faithful, willingly or not, to these trees, these ways,
this light, this history.

Oh yes, ultimately, language was *ethos*. And the Greek ethos I felt
free itself from the Platonic core to reach, unhindered and imperish-
able, to Solomós and beyond, made short shrift of the many missiles
shrieking across the European skies. Who cares about theories? Grant-
ed, Kafka's work could never have been written in Greek, nor, for that
matter, in any other language.

"To each his own," as they say. I felt like a citizen of the sky. Just be-
yond the idea of poetry as simple confession, I saw the horizon and
landscape transform, wholly, as in our country. Suddenly, from an island
peak, familiar landforms are transformed and unimagined coves, capes
and distant ridges reveal a world that is new, broader, richer in formal
variation. The sieve of conscience sorts and refines, sorts and refines ev-
erything until, one day, you feel as clean and transparent as your secret
tendencies had always meant you to and not as your circumstances had
conspired to alter. It is so difficult, so difficult to let your era mark but
not counterfeit you.

The war had already condensed, sharpened, accelerated and multi-
plied all my endogenous flirtations with Evil. By making madness and
impasse palpable, it had, for me, proclaimed their dissolution. An entire
literature, headed by Baudelaire, had sought for half a century to domi-
nate the undeveloped and unexploited psychic regions, and does so by
esthetic instinct alone, by giving more weight to "human exception"

than to "the human," and by combining its idolatry of Evil with other pathologies of beauty: pleasure in the forbidden and in guilt, remorse, pain as Virtue, the Artificial and Natural juxtaposed, and Hell's glory replacing an impoverished Paradise. These might have attracted a young person before the two world wars. But today, the blood overflowing the ink has shown that, alas, truth can't be found against your soul's native movement. Blood was everywhere; it soaked the walls of the perfumed rooms with their paper flowers and devil-worshiping incense. These walls were not too solid anyway, considering the pounding Freud and Psychoanalysis had recently given them.

If there really is a message sent to us secretly by the part of life we know nothing of, it has never appeared to me as a prowling midnight spectre. I saw it, I felt it I mean, at moments when no hand could have yanked the trickster's sheet to expose deceit. The first time was in Olympia: high noon, mid-spring, chamomile and poppy claiming the holy ground and its fallen marble. No soul in sight, foreign or Greek. Only I, lost by the river, near a rectangular site defined by the foundations of a temple I didn't recognize, being disinclined to archaeology. Heartened, enraptured, I should say, by the total quiet, a little lizard left her hiding place and ran towards the center. At my slightest motion she would stop and wait, full of suspicion, for some seconds, and only when I managed to hold even my breath did she slither, with inconceivable speed, to the symmetrical square stone set higher than the others at the temple's center, as if it were an altar, where the only quiver of sunrays fell through the dense foliage above us, as by a momentary coincidence. I lost sight of her briefly, then saw her climb it and begin to raise her face and stretch her breast to the sun: a sequence of unbelievably small gestures, a balletic system of endless shivers, a palindromic rhythm of barely visible turns, joy and awe became one as in a prayer that touches its destination! I understood that invisible threads were tightening inside me. I felt balanced on a moment of a different duration. God present, as we would say, and who gets it, gets it.

The second time, I was in Spetses. Only my window overlooked the "small back terrace," as we called it. High noon. A small sound drew me to look between the slats of the shutter. Young Irene, the girl of the house, was coming up from the beach, drying herself with a large, bright towel. Drops of sea fell from her hair to her brow, iridesced for a moment in her lashes and, finally, rolled down her cheeks. She found a corner in the sun and in one quick movement spread her towel on the flagstone and lay back, legs half open. Soon, she rose to her elbow, turned her head to make sure no one could see, paused for some time at my closed shutter (inside I held my breath) and then, reassured, loosened her top and lay back down, her disproportionately large white breasts to the sun. A miracle! I faced the crown of a large lemon tree. Below, the low whitewashed wall of the terrace. Next to it, the nude body pulsing in an apotheosis of light. And all in a sonorous background of plashing waves and the cicadas' ji-ji-ji rising invisible, almighty from the garden, the other gardens, the neighboring olive grove, the entire island. I thought I could stand there for hours, an angel in a bizarre photosynthesis.

Just then a brilliantly colored butterfly arrived, drawing large contours in the air. Its wing almost touched my window, I remember seeing its symmetrical black circles. Then without hesitation and in one swoop, it alighted on the young woman's hair. In two leaps it reached one of the beautiful breasts now rising and falling to sleep's rhythm. In the infinitesimal duration of its landing – before it soared off never to be seen again, a butterfly like all the others, soon not to exist, as I would not, nor young Irene – I felt again the sensation of immortality that the parts of life we either hide or allow to be hidden from us can synthesize and provide: the other kind of writing, the second and third Greek, which, when I can read them, cause me to totally distrust all past and present Ecclesiastes.

The miracle returned only once more, in summer, midday, midpelago, July, aboard a small vessel sailing from Paros to Naxos. Shouts of "Dolphins! Dolphins!" rang out from the crew, and I saw the gold flashes and the arcs in light, like the sheerest net cast and raised, cast and raised, in rhythm, one, two, three, four, until the shapes enlarged, clarified and leapt from the water scattering a myriad drops, a fringe of foam around them, then finally their pointed heads diving straight down at our side, tails broad for a moment in the air, embroidering the blue, a ceaseless embroidery until the needle and the pelagic tablecloth both vanished, leaving the soul alone in the victorious procession – weightless, unwrinkled, the soul free in the light, the sharp interminable brilliance.

"Clean earth rests in clean sky, where stars exist, and which most call ether...because if one should approach its center from its edge, or like a bird fly over and look down, one will see, as fish see in the sea, by leaping; and if one *could* see there, if nature itself could rise and see, one would then know this as the true sky, true light and the as-real earth..." In my small room on the Rue Monsieur-le-Prince, never forgetting the nearby small room where Arthur Rimbaud endured terrorizing insomnias, I read, I repeat, Plato.

"Ah! le con!" as Jean Genet would yell in Athens ten years later – and this on Holy Friday! – as we walked the narrow Plaka streets wondering if the philosopher himself had walked here eons ago... *"Ah! le con!"* How else could he speak? Even at its best, its most revolutionary, the West has remained Aristotelian. Not that its sense of "superlative" was dysfunctional, *au contraire*, but always and exclusively on *this*, never *that* side of "The Curse." Perhaps because an incredibly misinterpreted Christianity was interposed between it and Greece from the beginning. I tried my best to isolate the exceptions, the handful of European heretics on whom I lavished my overfed admiration. In short, I had become a fanatic. I faulted the Gothic churches, the formal gardens of Versailles, the remnants of the Napoleon and Louis eras. I even faulted the language though, how strange, I had been raised in it more than I had in my own. Not to mention the Renaissance! It was the great enemy, the great counterfeiting of a Spirit which I felt, at that hour, entrust its defense to my meager powers.

This is why I so favored Cubism. It was, in my eyes, the most beneficent movement ever in visual arts. It cast them from a bed of sin; it restored geometry's clean base to expression and the Spirit's supreme order to matter. That the meaning of this "order" aroused, without being red, all kinds of bull-defenders of *l'esprit du temps*, bumbling idiots incapable of grasping that whatever good our days had produced – Matisse, Braque, Mondrian, Proust, Joyce, Schoenberg, Stravinsky, electronic music, St. John Perse – was secured by the Cubist lines depicting the meaning of this cleanliness. The essays of Albert Camus and the poems of René Char, transparent and sharp as pale blue panes against our suffocating horizons, appealed to me from just such a perspective.

Poor Greece, scorned not only by foreigners but also by Greeks! And not even Greeks in general but our intimates, our "intellectuals"!

They regarded our land with the same condescension they reserved for any small Middle Eastern country, just because our universities lacked modern laboratories and our urinals lacked electronic eyes. Well then! I confess, with a truthfulness above any irony, I felt as an aristocrat, the only one, privileged to call the sky "sky" and the sea "sea," indistinguishable from Sappho and Romanos thousands of years ago. *Only so* could I truly see the pale blue ether or hear the pelago roar... Pericles Yannopoulos had not exaggerated. I have already confessed I was a fanatic. In a crowd of such *laryngisms* I was, I repeat, the only one so privileged.

CHAR WAS SOMEONE who understood and even envied my Greek identity. He and Camus had decided to publish the journal *Empedocles*, under the austere principle of defending light and the Mediterranean sensation. Already these two elements were being inscribed with rare energy in the poems of the former, and with adamantine lucidity in the essays of the latter. But such a journal – fundamentally a "wager" on difficult ideas condemned by their nature to lack resonance among the young, who seemed avid only for downhill slopes, or else caged in by their sense of failure – was founded under bad omens. When they asked me to record more or less what I'd been telling them for their journal, I considered it an honor and threw myself at the work. Before I had even outlined my topic, *Empedocles* had shipwrecked. My grandiose title, "For a Poetry of Architectural Inventions and Solar Metaphysics" (in French: "*Pour un lyricisme d'inventions architecturales et de métaphysique solaire*"), would have required a strength I doubt I had. I felt that the sinking *Empedocles* rescued me from rough ground, if not from a definite impasse.

The things I wanted to say were still so fluid, so inseparable, it's fair to say I felt more than thought them. I was in the condition I imagine a composer to be in, enchanted by internal musical phrases but not yet ready to collect and subject them to notation. I was concerned with two arenas that the then-current mentality insisted were separate and irreconcilable: one was the poem's morphology, the other its ideological content. I wanted to link them in a way that showed that the elements of each were a mutual, natural and inevitable consequence of the other.

The gradual belief that technique was meaningless unless it achieved the lofty goal of *becoming part of the content* began to form in me then, and was precisely why I felt *it must be a personal invention and not a received method*. Architecture was not, to me, an *a priori* scaffold. Furthermore, it bore no relation to the ambitions of the schematic idioms fondly cultivated by declining cultures. Nor was it a nostalgic return to the old *morpholatry*. I meant exactly the opposite when I asked the ideal poem to stand as a full-fledged miniature solar system, with the same serenity, the same eternal mien throughout, and the same ceaseless motion in each of its elements. This is how I still perceive the nuclear formation of the poem: as a sealed unit and also as its final, self-powered explosion. And always in terms of the concrete specifics by which, each time, imagination localizes, isolates and spotlights it. The difference is that, if this meaning is to acquire body and effectively pretend to be both the sun *and* the sun's ulterior mission in the system of images and concepts it drags along, the meaning itself has to develop constantly and in tandem with a symbolic transcription of itself, into rhythmic and strophic features analogous to those that render time sensible to human cognition.

Forgive me such a complicated sentence. I will try to say it another way. The process of formulating a calendar of celebrations or the mutual transubstantiation of physical and imaginary elements into mythology should once again resume working from the collective to the individual scale, and by a single means: *lyric energy*. The singular, specific development and distribution of meanings must each time dictate a specific development and distribution of parts, and this latter development and distribution must, simultaneously, be the sine qua non of a fulfilled result.

I speak theoretically and so am forgiven for approaching the Absolute. Besides, instinct instantaneously actualizes in practice what analysis, of necessity, interprets. Still, I can't understand why we think it self-evident that, in the realm of monumental art, a Doric temple (which despite everything can be reduced to a shape) expresses the deeper spirit of an idolatrous religion almost exclusively, or that the quintessence of Orthodox Christianity can be rendered, in a limited manner, by the shape of a dome. Yet, in the realm of lyric art, we ignore such correspondences and consider it natural, for example, that the Greek sensation of the sea, which is a singularity, can be rendered by a sonnet, or the corresponding sense of sky by a length of free verse, both of which are as alien and irreconcilable to a blue dome as the spires of Chartres raised in Aegina's air. Pity, but the contemporary poet seems unable to find his Hagia Sophia, much less his nearby chapel! I mean the hues of sensitivity by which even a folk technician apprehends the meaning of "fountain" on a mountain completely differently from how he comprehends "fountain" by the sea. How can I even speak of solar metaphysics after all this? In the "common market" of emotions everyone is struggling, unwittingly, to shape an Esperanto. They've made such progress that my concerns, my tone and my impulses begin to seem as distant and incomprehensible as Chinese.

I have always been impressed by how imagination escalates, in the mythologies of different peoples, according to their geographic longitude and latitude, a theory which many find outdated. It begins, from both North and South, with the *fiercest teratological disfigurements*, which soften as they rise or fall to the Mediterranean until they finally assume the *human shape*, with all the naturally possible combinative freedoms, exactly on their arrival there. It is no accident that lyric art was born *exactly* there, that there the meaning of Democracy was first created, that there a Socrates and a Jesus were empowered to teach. Perhaps I exaggerate. I know it's been said before, but I want to repeat it from the vantage of our time which has, after all, been changed by the perspective of human events. This Mediterranean zone is a *precise moment* in which all conditions and all factors empower one to *stand integrated*, just as, in the solar system, an analogous precise moment grants planet earth, and only planet earth, human life.

Beyond this, we can say that the sun's position in the ethical world is the same as in the natural one. The poet is an intersection of the ethical and natural worlds. The portion of darkness neutralized in the poet by conscience can be measured in light, a light that returns again, constantly clarifying the image, the human image. If a humanistic view of art's mission exists, only so can it be understood: as an invisible function identical to the mechanism we call Justice, and not, of course, the Justice of the courts, but the one formed equally slowly and painfully in the teachings of humanity's great mentors, in political struggles for social liberation, and in the highest poetic achievements. From such large effort, drops of light fall in the soul's large night, slowly, like drops of lemon on polluted water.

The sun's antiseptic quality, whose "materiality" we can feel in the whitewash with which island women anoint their houses, is another way to conceptualize the correspondence between "physical" and "imaginary," between the human body and its extensions. That correspondence is, on the one hand, a Repudiation of the Monstrous, and on the other, Nature with a human personality. Greek nature, in this sense, will always contribute, like an invisible scale, not exactly the "measure," as we like to say, or, even less, an "averaging," but a help, a support, a judgment, so that, in the last analysis, the miracle that humans constitute is not inhuman; it is, rather, God's apotheosis, not his downfall.

From that blasphemy, which is the pre-Socratic Hubris itself, the current underlying *absolutomania* begins, our century's new evil that Camus never tired of cauterizing to his final breath. As I've said before, his effort didn't survive. I was left with its impetus. I sought opportunities, left and right, to speak and hear these same things, perhaps to convince myself.

THEORETICAL THOUGHT was everything to me then. I would be satisfied just to conclude how the ideal poem must be written, what its esthetics and its meaning must be, even if I never wrote it. My notes flooded my drawers, my shelves and my suitcase. At Royamont, at the large abbey where I had stayed a few days in the company of some French students (and had, in conversation, occasions to realize more consciously the deeper chasm between us), I had conceived of giving this surfeit of thoughts the clearer and more intimate form of epistles to a young Greek colleague.

The epistles would tell of the discord between Western and Eastern spirits and of foreigners' misinterpretation of the deeper Greek spirit, a discord that hindered communication and for which we ourselves were responsible. They would talk of poetry's mission in our time, of the metaphysical need beyond the formalities of any given religion, of the significance of language and its analogy to other natural or spiritual phenomena, of the re-appearance of formal problems in the arena of modern poetry, and of the example of the plastic arts: all these would become the nuclei for an equal number of epistles and, in a way, the codification of my conclusions. "Seven Epistles From Royamont" was finished in the summer of 1951; that same summer I chanced to live near Picasso for the second time, and, because of him, to add an eighth text I called, "Postscript From Villa Natacha," the St. Jean-Cap-Ferrat villa of E. Terriade, whose guest I was.

Picasso rid me of these complexes by his example. He was almost an ancient Greek next to me. Half-naked, robust and blackened by sun, he lived, in defiance of his millions, in a small humble house in Vallauris, remarkably like our own island houses. Wearing only a pair of pants he painted, went swimming down in Golfe Juan, ate with enormous gusto, and on all fours played the little horse for Paloma, his little girl. He enacted the very sensation the Greeks had disowned – eros and sun in their first, primordial essense – like an ancient mythic king whose majesty abides not in law and might, but in simple and comfortable gestures. I understood all of his current work as an extension of that sensation. Terriade had catalogued most of it under the title ANTIPOLIS, the Greek name of Antibes, in a recent issue of *Verve*.

With lines clean as if traced from pebbles and free as the imagination guiding them, he unfurled before our eyes, the very day after the war, a vista of small children, centaurs and women, suns and tridents, a dancing equivalence of nude bodies and the objects of forest and shore, with a robustness and nerve raised to the highest degree of grace, lightness and nobility. His ceramics, their colors clean, raw and potent, also animated this world, a world that "restored the sun through objects," as another great colleague of his, Matisse, had told me a painter must do. He had told me this when I'd mustered the courage to speak to him one day about the dissolution of everything by the blinding Greek sun.

In the large wooden shed that was Picasso's sculpture studio a few meters away, were even more treasures extracted from mythic Mediterranean depths: owl archetypes in all sizes and shapes, goat archetypes in which he managed to embody bottles, tin cans, broken baskets – flotsam of a deserted shoreline, with the fresh burn of noon and the taste of salt still raw on their surface – and then the other small animals, birds, fish, roosters and doves. "Dream at night, at dawn open your window," he used to say, "the things of this world have a right to light." And once, as I bemoaned the Greek situation, he turned his large black eyes to me and said sternly, "You must see things also from the other side. If governments weren't conservative, how could the likes of us be revolutionaries?" And he exploded in such forceful laughter, I couldn't tell if he was serious or joking.

Another time, he took my arm and we walked the entire shoreline. Midday. "Look, look," he'd exclaim, pointing at the sundark blondes in their cork-soled sandals, huge straw hats and almost nothing else... "Is Greece like this too?...the minxes!...the devil's in them." He seemed a rascal of seventeen, not a personage in his seventies. Only my native timidity kept me from exclaiming, in turn, how much I celebrated him, just as he was, and how the integrity of his daily idiosyncrasies and the idiosyncrasies of his art were a great lesson for the somber, especially Greek ones.

That afternoon he asked me to lunch. This part of the Côte d'Azur was like an endless carnival. I had subdued the crushing contrast between it and my ravaged Greece by subsuming its schema into the schema of the *Axion Esti*, if only, at the time, abstractly. That is another story. But here, everything I saw made me consider just how much humans had to overcome in order to "endure peace," so much more demanding than war. Carefree, lighthearted, satisfied people were everywhere. As we got in the car to return to Vallauris, a group of waiting tourists and naval officers started photographing him like maniacs, while the local boys, who saw him every day and were expecting him, leapt in the air screaming "Picasso! Picasso!"

We crowded around the kitchen table – Picasso, his two children, his friend Françoise, Terriade and I – and ate simply, without change of service. I cannot lie. I was terribly flattered to share the most private moments of a man for whose handshake so many would strive for months. But my sensation of being tonified, aided perhaps by the splendid red wine, was different, belonging to more fundamental causes. It was as if I had suddenly, and when I least expected to, found corroboration of my ideas, and done so by a route I had despaired of yet which an actual contemporary now traversed. Some healthy cell, some root bequeathed to me long ago perhaps, leapt now and pulsed in recognition of the signal sent out by its myriad *semblables*. What a deep clear breath after four years! Four years of feeling that life could be sustained only by the oxygen tanks of the huge hospital that Europe had become, only to come to find a literary realm of bibliographers whose single *hedoné* was derived from lexicons and footnotes (even in the case of poor Poetry), whose single creative joy was diagnosing illness and whose only spiritual currency and title of value was the certificate of the Void. What a deep breath!

Picasso's work seemed to cleave through this macabre reality like Great Alexander's sword. His analogies to life, to how we love or hate, danced before my eyes. I returned to Villa Natacha and wrote the essay *"Equivalences chez Picasso"* (published in the 1951 issue that *Verve* dedicated to the painter) in one draft, in a few hours, in a euphoria that allowed me, for the first and perhaps last time in my life, to use French with such ease.

The essay was also a kind of farewell to the world I was leaving. It was time to return to Greece. A few days later, I loaded my belongings on a ship at Marseilles; three more boxes of books than I'd come with and one small cheap suitcase less: the suitcase with the manuscripts. Let it be. *The poet must be generous. Trying not to lose even a moment of your supposed talent is like trying not to lose a cent of the interest on the small principal given you.* Poetry is not a bank. It is the antithesis, precisely. If a written text can be shared, so much the better. If not, it's all right. What must be practiced – assiduously, infinitely and without the slightest pause – is anti-servitude, non-compliance, and independence. Poetry is the other face of Pride.

For Good Measure

A SUIVRE de près la manière dont s'élabore la mise en valeur des éléments plastiques chez un artiste, on est souvent amené à y reconnaître un certain "système de gestes." Ce système, tout en représentant les réactions du créateur envers le monde qui l'entoure, est susceptible par sa transposition même sur une échelle de valeurs spirituelles, de nous fournir par analogie, une table d'équivalences multiples. En plein air comme dans les ateliers, il s'agit du même drame que l'homme est appelé à jouer, toujours face à son destin, et par grands gestes allant du triomphe au désespoir.

Tel peintre est un persécuté qui s'abrite derrière un morceau de nature toute faite. Tel autre, pour sa défense, propose les tons purs qu'il a pu, à force de calcul, soustraire à un ensemble qui, d'autre part, ne cesse de lui échapper. On en voit qui s'attaquent violemment à leur propre idole, et qui font mine de vainqueurs manqués rentrant les mains pleines d'un butin dérisoire. D'autres, enfin, y mettent de la patience, et de leurs doigts attentifs guettent le moment favorable qui leur permettra de dénouer le fameux nœud Gordien de la Réalité.

Parmi tous ces acteurs involontaires apparaît soudain Picasso, l'allure d'Alexandre le Grand: dans sa main droite le pinceau tient lieu d'épée, et c'est en tranchant à grands coups dans le réel qu'il fraye son chemin et qu'il avance. Car il sait que l'essentiel est d'avancer. À tout prix et par n'importe quel moyen, sauf la soumission, le compromis ou l'obéissance aveugle.

Un secret lui résiste, il l'attaque au moyen d'un autre. Un obstacle lui paraît-il insurmontable, il va tout transformer autour de cet obstacle, de sorte qu'il ne paraisse plus comme tel. Cette vitesse n'est pas pour lui nuire. Elle est pour lui l'état normal, où il peut développer librement toutes ses facultés et entreprendre ces virages fameux, au terme desquels tant d'aspects insoupçonnables de la Réalité se trouvent être à jamais fixés. Elle lui permet aussi de plier ses façons d'agir à la mesure d'un temps minimum, celui que l'œil et le cœur exigent pour aller ensemble, au-delà du calcul, à la découverte des rapports poétiques du monde.

De cette manière, Picasso arrive, pour ainsi dire, à DÉCONCERTER *la nature des choses. Comme si un objet, familiarisé avec les procédés dont on l'approchait pendant des siècles, prenait toutes ses dispositions pour persévérer dans son entêtement à ne livrer qu'une part de lui-même; et que soudain, encerclé, attaqué de toutes parts, ne sachant où fuir (ou peut-être comme défaillant devant un amoureux possible) il se voyait contraint à se rendre.*

Ainsi a-t-il fallu l'enfant le plus désobéissant de notre ère, pour forcer le concret à lui obéir dans sa totalité. C'est en proportion de cette désobéissance, qu'il nous offre une nouvelle notion du Réel. C'est en cela qu'il devient le premier Réaliste des temps nouveaux.

REMONTONS *maintenant la pente de ces lignes sûres et audacieuses, reprenons à notre propre compte l'ordonnance de ces formes, d'où tout acte d'imiter est exclu, et où pourtant les ressemblances du monde rejaillissent encore plus vivantes: un certain comportement humain y est impliqué.*

En effet, le peintre qui agit ainsi, n'est-ce pas un homme qui au lieu d'admettre par exemple l'aumône, affirme au contraire la fierté de sa condition et PREND *ce qu'il a le droit de prendre? N'est-ce pas le généreux qui dédaigne les intérêts qu'il pourrait tirer de ses biens? Dans son domaine, l'acte de produire a d'ailleurs depuis longtemps remplacé l'or; c'est une richesse qu'il s'empresse de nous faire partager, en homme qui ne ménage point ses forces. Il ne se* SOIGNE *pas. Savoir d'autre part, comme lui, s'éloigner de la ligne droite pour mieux encore l'atteindre, c'est aussi être amoureux, c'est s'y prendre avec la femme aimée de la seule façon dont elle puisse être conquise. Affirmer comme l'affirme l'ensemble de son œuvre, que le champ le plus propice à l'imagination ne se trouve point aux cieux mais dans les choses les plus humbles qui nous entourent, c'est avoir confiance dans la vie et dans ses innombrables possibilités.*

De même que les lignes sévères d'une montagne nue, du seul fait qu'elles suggèrent la simplicité et la netteté, ordonnent des actes équivalents sur le plan moral, les lignes de Picasso, telles qu'elles se développent à travers l'étonnante trajectoire de son œuvre, nous enseignent l'aventure et la découverte enchantée du monde, nous demandent d'aboutir à la mise au jour de son potentiel poétique, en dehors de tout préjugé.

Il se peut donc qu'en dépit de ce qu'on a pu inlassablement répéter à son sujet, Picasso n'ait jamais été soucieux d'illustrer son époque. Il a, certes, vécu en étroits rapports avec elle, mais non pas pour traduire en langage plastique les préoccupations dont elle s'est fait gloire. L'appel trop avantageux à la séduction de la douleur, l'idolâtrie du maladif, l'exhibitionisme du désespoir, et, d'autre part, les mysticismes-panacées et les philosophies à quatre sous, procèdent d'un esprit diamétralement opposé à celui que sous-entend sa manière même de dessiner et de peindre. À étudier ses inspirations récentes on est beaucoup plus porté à croire que Picasso a voulu OPPOSER *aux égarements de ses contemporains quelque chose de solide, une sorte de santé physique et morale que son attachement passionné à la recherche de la vérité a su lui procurer et qu'il doit considérer probablement comme l'ultime sagesse acquise au cours de sa longue carrière. Il n'avait jamais cherché la Grèce, mais la Grèce l'a trouvé. Depuis ce jour, c'est la mer de Golfe-Juan et le soleil de Vallauris qui guident ses pas. Il nous parle de l'Univers à travers la femme qu'il aime et ses propres enfants. Debout, la face brûlée au soleil, il avance, suivi des deux archétypes qui représentent le mieux son message: de la femme enceinte et de la célèbre chèvre.*

À PEINE *engagé dans l'ombre fraîche des ateliers de Vallauris, on se sent saisi du même coup de vent qui, comme souvent en Méditerranée, sous un soleil furieux, soulève les eaux et remplit les rivages déserts de toutes sortes d'objets significatifs: un vieux panier crevé, quelques bouts de branches, une boîte à conserve vide, deux cruches à demi-brisées. Je ne fus nullement étonné de les rencontrer là, ces trouvailles d'un moment d'insouciance, incorporées solidement dans l'œuvre, faisant chair et os avec les volumes que les mains de l'artiste venaient de bâtir. Ce geste qui aurait pu n'avoir que la valeur d'un jeu, atteignait chez Picasso la gravité mystérieuse d'un acte rituel qui semblait lui être imposé par une religion inconnue. Cette religion, je n'avais jamais pu moi-même la définir, mais elle m'était familière.*

Et soudain, je me suis senti jaloux, que ces grands symboles du Midi, ces archétypes qui descendaient du haut d'un âge immémorial, n'aient pas été réalisés sur une des îles de l'Égée, là où les doigts de l'homme avec cette maladresse qui ne ment jamais, osèrent jadis modeler la matière. N'importe, la leçon reste la même: il suffit de dire ce qu'on aime, et cela seulement, avec le très peu de moyens dont on dispose, mais par la voie la plus directe, celle de la poésie.

Instinct poétique, instinct bâtisseur par excellence, celui qu'on retrouve dans la joie humble avec laquelle les pêcheurs construisent leur barque ou les gens des villages leur maison. Et voilà qu'apparaissent les œuvres de ce grand homme du peuple, UTILES *comme les barques, comme les maisons. Nous pouvons habiter leur chaleur humaine et nous laisser porter par leurs proues pointées vers l'Avenir. Peu à peu à les contempler, un domaine pour nous se constitue, où*

*règne l'idée de la fécondité, où la chèvre appelle les rocs durs et les buissons et la
mer, un monde tout simple où l'on voit les grands yeux des hiboux la nuit, et le
jour cette rangée de poteries et de tuiles peintes aux mille visages, qui nous
ramènent de la multiplicité du monde à son essence unique. Qu'il s'appelle
"Vallauris" ou "dignité humaine" ce domaine est là, offert à nous une fois pour
toutes, comme un canton de l'âme, où la ruse est inconcevable, le double jeu im-
possible, et la flatterie découragée. Il représente enfin le merveilleux équivalent
des moyens dont Picasso se sert pour faire face à son epoque et ce point extrème
où – disons-le – la lumière du soleil et la sang de l'homme ne font qu'un.*
  1951.

EQUIVALENCES IN PICASSO

BY CLOSELY FOLLOWING the system of values that an artist's plastic ele-
ments elaborate, we are often led to the recognition of a certain "system
of gestures." This system, representing its creator's reactions to his sur-
rounding world, can also, by its transposition to the level of spiritual
values, furnish us, by analogy, a table of multiple equivalents. After all,
one is called to enact the same drama in the open air as one is in the stu-
dio, face to face with one's destiny and proceeding with grand gestures
from triumph to despair.

One painter assumes the posture of a refugee sheltering behind some
ready-made morsel of nature. Another proposes, for his defense, the
pure tones he has been able, through his calculations, to subtract from a
unity that, for its part, continues to elude him. It becomes clear who
violently attack their idols and who make a show of returning as victors,
a laughable bounty in their hands. Others, finally, give it patience, and
with their long, attentive fingers anticipate that favorable moment that
will allow them to undo Reality's famous Gordian knot.

Among these involuntary actors, Picasso suddnely appears with the
allure of Alexander the Great, paintbrush in hand instead of sword, and,
dealing with it great blows to the real, he carves out the road by which
he advances. Because he knows it is imperative to advance, at any price
and by any means, save submission, compromise or blind obedience.

A secret resists him; he attacks it with another. An obstacle appears
to him insurmountable; he will transform everything around the obsta-
cle until it no longer appears so. This speed does not harm him. It is, for

him, the normal state, where he can develop all his faculties and undertake those famous turns at the end of which so many unsuspected aspects of reality are found to be forever fixed. It also permits him great plasticity of method in arousing the minimum measure of time, that interval exacted by the eye and heart for their united, incalculable journey to uncover the poetic rapports of the world.

This is how Picasso *disconcerts* the nature of things. As if an object, well-accustomed to the ways it's been approached through the centuries, employs all the means at its disposal, stubbornly refusing to yield more than a part of itself, a part which suddenly – encircled, attacked on all fronts, not knowing where to flee (or, perhaps, faint like a lover before a possible beloved) – sees itself obliged to yield.

This is how the most disobedient child of our era forced the concrete to obey him completely. In direct proportion to his disobedience, he offers us a new notion of the Real and so becomes the first Realist of modern time.

LET US NOW climb the incline of those sure, audacious lines and properly reconsider the organization of those forms from which any imitative act is excluded but from where the world's resemblances spring forth ever more vivid: a certain human posture is implicated.

In effect, isn't the painter who acts this way a man who, rather than take charity, affirms instead the pride of his condition and *takes* what he has a right to take? Doesn't he generously disdain the profits he might have gained from his goods? In his domain, the act of producing has long ago eclipsed gold; it is a wealth he hastens to share with us – this from a man who no longer manages his strengths. He doesn't *care* for them. On the other hand, knowing, as he does, how to distance oneself from the straight line in order to reach it better – this also means being in love, it means applying to the beloved the only means to which she might yield. And the affirmation, which is the affirmation of his entire work, that the field most favorable to the imagination no longer exists in heaven but in the humblest objects around us, proclaims confidence in life and its innumerable possibilities.

Just as the severe lines of a nude mountain, by the sole fact of suggesting simplicity and cleanliness, ordain equivalent acts on the moral plane, Picasso's lines, as they develop along the stunning trajectory of his work, teach us adventure and the enchanted unveiling of the world; they demand that we complete updating its poetic potential, beyond any notion of prejudgment.

So it is possible that, despite what has been tirelessly repeated on the subject, Picasso never sought to illustrate his epoch. Certainly, he lived intimately with it, but with no intention of translating into plastic language the preoccupations by which it glorified itself: the profitable call to pain's seduction, the idolatry of the morbid, the exhibitionism of despair, as well as the cheap philosophies and the panaceas of mysticism – all these proceed from a spirit diametrically opposed to the one implicit in his manner of drawing and painting. Studying his recent inspirations, we are much more likely to believe that Picasso intended to oppose the vacuities of his contemporaries with something solid, a sort of physical and moral health, procured for him by his passionate attachment to the search for truth, which must be considered as probably the ultimate wisdom acquired through his long career. He never sought Greece, but Greece found him! Ever since, the Golfe-Juan sea and the Vallauris sun have guided his steps. He speaks to us of the Universe through the woman he loves and his own children. Upright, face sunburnt, he advances, followed by two archetypes that represent his message best: the pregnant woman, the celebrated goat.

BARELY under the cool shade of the Vallauris studios, one feels seized by the same gust of wind that, as happens often in the Mediterranean under a furious sun, roils the waters and fills the deserted shores with a wealth of significant objects: an old burst basket, some branches, an empty can, two partial carafes. I wasn't the least surprised to find them there, these trophies of an insouciant moment, solidly incorporated in the work, making flesh and bone of the volumes the artist's hands have just finished building. This gesture, which might have had no more value than a game, attains in Picasso the mysterious gravity of a ritual act imposed on him by an unknown religion. I myself have never been able to define this religion, but it is my familiar.

And I am suddenly jealous that these grand *symboles du Midi*, these archetypes descending from the heights of immemorial time, were not realized on an Aegean island, where human fingers whose awkwardness never lies have dared already to model matter. Never mind; the lesson remains the same: it suffices to say what one loves and only that, with the meager means available but by the most direct route: poetry.

Poetic instinct, instinct *par excellence* constructive, the kind we find in the humble joy of fishermen constructing boats or villages their homes. And look how the works of his great man of the people appear *useful*, like boats and homes. We inhabit their human warmth and are carried by their pointed prows toward the Future. Little by little, as we contemplate them, they form a domain ruled by the concept of the Fecund, where the goat names the boulders, the bushes and the seas, an utterly simple world with the owl's great eyes visible by night, and by day that range of pottery and tiles painted a thousand faces, leading us from the world's multiplicity to its unique essence. Whether it's called "Vallauris" or "human dignity," this domain exists, offered to us once and for all like a province of the soul where deceit is inconceivable, double-cross impossible, and flattery discouraged. Finally, it represents the miraculous equivalent of the means Picasso appropriated to face both his era and that extreme point where, let's say it, sunlight and human blood are one.

1951.

ARTHUR RIMBAUD

To SPEAK of Rimbaud today is shameless. I will do so without blushing. You don't have to be wise to lay flowers on the grave of the wise. Especially when you also feel the need for some anemones among the profuse gladioli and dahlias. Beauty-smitten similes have, in Rimbaud's case, a homeopathic property.

Even at nineteen I was reading, if not understanding, Jacques Rivière's famous book. Yet when I closed it and turned off the light, its mysterious phrases pursued me: *À ma sœur Louise Vanaen de Voringhem: Sa cornette bleue tournée à la mer du Nord. Pour les naufragés.* And immediately after: *À ma sœur Léonie Aubois d'Ashby, Baou!*

—No kidding. And when? 1872.

—Lord have mercy!

WHOEVER did not run the double gauntlet of such a sensuality from that moment on remained deaf and dumb. The dissension between

137

Anglo-Saxon and Latinate poetry – despite the Briticisms of Rimbaud himself and Eliot's erotic tropics toward Laforgue and Co. – lies here, I'm afraid, in the nineteenth century's last quarter. A bare few then, and later all, learned the spoken alchemy of logos from "one ignorant of his genius." Despite the fact that he himself gave it to us, the word today incenses the narrow minds of the orthodox like the word "God" stops short before the myopia of old-style revolutionaries.

We need to clear our heads of the distorted meanings of our times to see life again, panoramically and stereoscopically, to its farthest depths and its farthest summits.

I mean to say that the transparence necessary for this "multidimensional vision" is the one graciously given us by the young graduate of the Charleville Lyceum, before he turned his back on the tribe of scribes to go live like a monk, in his way, in arid Harrar.

Who spoke to us of this transparence, of the virtue of seeing in one verse, at once, all our composing strata, since we are, for better or worse, complex? They called him crazy and that's the least of it; they called him mystic, neochristian, atheist, rebel, rabid, communist, even before the terms existed; they called him demon or angel.

If we could replace the disjunctive "or" with a simple "and" we would begin to approach the truth.

—But that's a contradiction.

—Ah, exactly.

THE LAND of Innocence is as borderless and as unexplored as the land of Evil. They are superimposed, or better yet *intra*posed, inside us at the exact point where expedience stops and the concept of commerce becomes useless to the human soul; so they must, of necessity, at some ultimate frontier, share a border. If we had soul-topographers – we do not trust the poets – they could prove just as well, and by linear symbols, that the cost of turning something black to white is *the same* as white to black and always to our spiritual "deficit."

One day, unexpectedly, a child saw the Omikron as blue and the Epsilon as white through the haze of *Oise* and of Catholic Latin, meaning that he was able to identify the "Time of Assassins" a whole century before we were forced to live it. Centuries after people demystified the anonymous Goddess's other-worldly signs, the child, skillfully and lightly, removed her veils.

The signs are still difficult to read, and this difficulty misleads us into thinking poetry is difficult, just as myopics doubt the clear water when what they should doubt is their eyes.

Having reached, no one knows how, the common border, Rimbaud appropriated as many demonic powers as he could, and unleashed them in the land of Innocence. Paradise began to acknowledge its wilderness, the audience to reject prayer-as-grunt: *De profundis, Domine, suis-je bête!*

Of course, we are the idiots. We classify hate and articulate slander in a ceaseless rehearsal of death, eager to renounce our existence instantly, so that even if the unplanned (a love-affair, a verse) were to distract us for a moment, our likeness would continue drinking whiskey, watching television and sending flowers to the Ambassador's wife.

Rimbaud wanted to abort this calligraphic lie transported into syntax, he wanted to restore adjective, verb and noun to their first nature: flower, leaf, hand, and in the field.

How does this relate to Poetry and its mission?

Singularly. Fully. *Quelquefois je vois au ciel des plages sans fin, couvertes de blanches nations en joie. Un grand vaisseau d'or, audessus de moi, agite ses pavillons multicolores sous les brises du matin.* From the concrete to the visionary, to benediction from curse! This poet, who without pursuing it anticipated all the world's religious by simply unsystematizing his senses, raised his head as no other except Hölderlin had.

He raised what was below above: spiritual creation's most difficult achievement. The ship that sinks here opens its sails there; the skin that bruises on earth is gilded in the sky; the monster we invent to enslave us today returns to its natural state tomorrow.

Rimbaud's innocence becomes frighteningly *au courant* in this light. He is both Accused Innocent and Unappointed Prosecutor, Presiding Judge and Enforcing Officer. His every verse is a synopsis of the process we endure, slowly, tyranically, the length of our lives, only to abandon it one day, inconsolable and sad.

Because the "beyond" is out of reach. The speaker of *Illuminations* and *Saison en Enfer* has, *au contraire*, transformed the future straw into present straw, so quickly that he still had the time, the ability, to walk beyond Necessity's grounds. Defying our epoch's denials, he makes these grounds extant. Nine out of ten times, Rimbaud's despair swells and explodes, phantasmagoric. A tenderness we can call by no other name turns steel to grass, flame to stalactite and wrath to sea breeze. The most we can bear is the least we acknowledge in him, as if the soul's world had been traversed equally with the so-called real one, and the poet were returning just as we set out.

—That's difficult.

—Not at all. *C'est aussi simple qu'une phrase musicale.*

1972.

LAUTRÉAMONT

THIS TEENAGER frightens me still, with his forever unknown shape, embarking one day from the shores of Montevideo to travel seas as large as his dreams and fill his inborn greedy soul with ocean air only to finish his brief life in Paris between the cheap walls of a room, where he was destined to face eternity eye-to-eye. What passerby, even one endowed with splendid imagination, could suspect that in that old and creaky attic, between a perennially unmade bed and an ancient piano, lives a tall, hunched and fragile youth, saturated by the myriad visions he pours onto paper in a feverish bacchanal, enduring terrible insomnias? Who could imagine that one of the most paradoxical achievements of the human spirit suddenly saw the light in that tiny attic of Montmartre, a spirit that would clearly define the start of a new esthetic era?

I think of young Isidore Ducasse, a mediocre student at the Lycée du Pau, standing alone before his cheap mirror, on one of those melancholy evenings that flare and inexplicably inflate the restless chests of youth, titling himself a Count. Yes, a Count. But one unlike any other, unlike any human. He was an aristocrat of a different persuasion, one who would from then on resolutely confront statures greater than his without hesitation or fear, itself a blasphemy that on his lips assumed the value of a great winged benediction. When did experience have time to saturate that child and prepare that unexpected explosion? When did sarcasm, hate and satanic laughter, usually fruits of lifelong ordeals, ripen in the tropical climate of his thought? I receive the *Chants de Maldoror* only as one can receive natural phenomena: as the lightning rod receives lightning. I remember the year: 1868.

Anything bold, new or revolutionary to occur in international letters for the next sixty or eighty years originated in him who, graced by a rebel hand, witnessed imagination's gates flung open, and the fabulous treasure of the spirit placed in the service of life, the only life that some of us (few today but more tomorrow) acknowledge as real.

I'm not exaggerating: an apocalyptic light floods these unrestrained confessions, in which everything assumes the force of a flash flood from some internal afterlife, to formulate, even against their author's will, an intractable fanaticism that disarms all resistance. Modern life, with its knowledge of danger and seductions of freedom, begins in the *Chants de Maldoror*. A modern life suspended, as a dewdrop is, from terrible truth and naked beauty, prismed by the golden radials above the endless ravines of muck and night.

Lautréamont is the first who, without affectation, teaches opposition to traditional belief, destruction of bourgeois methods of thought, and psychic exercise in the wider parameters of spirit. He is the first to not only teach but exemplify a *lack of compromise* with the ossified values and petty concerns within current literature. He also finds the poetic logic that is faithful to the order of emotion and dream, not the exterior world. He renews tone – inaugurating poetic metaphor and reconciling two or more of reality's distanced elements – to substantiate *sur*reality. It takes the lightest breath across time's dust to reveal the achievements that followed: revision of values, nonconformity, iconolatry, oneiric climate, automatic writing, *critique paranoïaque*, magic, and surrealism.

Aragon was not wrong when he wrote in a similar magic tone, "1868! I mark with a transparent jewel, which is an unparalleled sight, the origins of contemporary lyricism."

You do not enter the hellish kingdoms of Maldoror's mythology without emotion, a trembling throat, a vague bitter taste. Look out! Ideas perish here, truths quake and a merciless wind blows, rousing titanic terrors. Vertigo waits nearby; the atmosphere stinks of blood. You wake to a doggish welcome, "My reader, perhaps you want me to invoke hatred at the beginning of this work! Who says that you won't nuzzle it, bathed to satiety in unnameable pleasures, your boasting nostrils flared and your body upturned like a shark in the beautiful black air... Have no fear, the gorgeous nostrils of your disgusting snout will enjoy the smell, o monster!"

Insecurity seizes you. You try to take one more step, to advance again with the force of your first resistance, but you don't know what's ahead; will you fall into the arms of endless hatred or endless love, will you face a monster's or an angel's soul?

In a world expressing itself by unexamined truths, this poet allowed his thought its wildest gallop, as Rolland de Renéville has said, and conceived with amazing agility the relations and correspondences of the things that reveal unity to our eyes, a unity that human consciousness has always pursued, in every era and by every means. The forest of imagination undergoes a monstrous explosion of growth with Lautréamont, and the romantic dimensions we once knew no longer contain the incessant multiplication of images that leap from his teenage fevers.

No one can dispute the fact that we stand before a purely romantic creation which, arriving forty years after that familiar label first lulled dreamers, impales the paper figures of those poetic fantasies by taking them to extremes. Lautréamont violates his imagination almost sadistically, unleashing the forces that a good (that is, an ordinary) upbringing has for eons struggled to keep imprisoned in us. In such moments he erupts upon matter, transforming it by his inspiration. It is true that sometimes his titanic fantasies risk the naïve or quixotic. Still, the soul's simple presence is enough to keep you engaged with the unpleasant truth. An unpleasant force inconceivable to your senses compels you to grovel a million times, bewildered by an unprecedented firmament of stars, your hard-won civility unpeeling piece by piece as your heart races. But are you not *obliged* to recognize yourself among a series of counterfeit likenesses?

THE *Chants de Maldoror* were written with the intensity of an athletic heroism or a heinous crime, good or bad yet always poised where life first tests its dangerous power. I close the thick volume and attempt, as he says, "to return to people," though I am still pursued by the deep rumble of a world constantly transforming its liquid essence as if just being born, full of blood, dew and flame. What could the purpose of ethics be, or the necessity of beauty, or the meaning of truth to a being who simultaneously flew high above common concerns and took the consequences of his madness like a chest wound?

The paradoxical thread Maldoror trailed in his wanderings pulls me.

Here is that silver candelabra he addressed in pyretic tones, "*O Lampe au bec d'argent*," here the lament of a hair fallen from the Almighty – come down to spend a night on hedonic beds – and here one of those terrible insects *smaller even than cows* that stick to his neck and drink his blood. Whose blood? The one who tried to take on the Creator and win. Leman! Lohengrin! Lombano! Holzer! All you who reentered chaos... Wait up, I almost lost my way... What wastelands are these?

Endless wastelands, the length of an implacable moon, devoured by the howling dogs that terrorize infinity! Stunned people, their passions exploded, tremble in the Creator's eyes as though under the scalpel of some horrific *dissectory*... No, I can not bear such an *experience of evil* one more time, but you, Ducasse Isidore, who cared enough to send a greeting to your future friends, cannot dislodge my eyes from your image, perforated by pain, seeking the innocent worlds you deserve with an unhypocritical caress that would, at last, erase your brow's agony and nullify the quantities of revenge you prepared for your fellow humans... I don't want to betray you with my words, Lautréamont, I want to feel more of you. You are a Count, this world's first true Count; I recognize you by your grandeur, so courageously equalling the Ocean, by the Ocean, so harshly equalling your soul, and by your soul, so grandly matching infinity!

1939.

PAUL ÉLUARD

IN 1917, when Éluard published his first book at twenty-two, cannon fire was still audible, and intellectual Europe, shocked and exhausted, dove into an adventure ruled by acute anxiety and nihilistic anarchy. A year earlier, in Zürich, a group of young rebels had founded Dadaism: a school that meant nothing, had no positive content and intended only to overturn and trample. Through a series of spasmodic events, this movement made Paris its center, developed, had a few days of glory, only to negate itself in 1921. The perspective of time allows a cooler view of these explosive postwar expressions, and Dadaism, despite its sterility and noise, retains historical justification. It *had* to appear when it did, to excavate literature's saturated soil, eradicate academic spider webs and make way for something totally new and creative. Surrealism was born. And, more broadly, poetry, prose and painting took a giant step forward, a step whose significance we failed to even feel or notice, surrendered as we were to an unforgivable spiritual sloth.

PAUL ÉLUARD, exceptionally sensitive and restless, could not abstain from such revolutionary orgasm, especially one occurring in the heart of Paris, which was and is the global capital of artistic avant-garde. He first joined the small group "Littérature" (which briefly collaborated with Dada), participated in some of its events, published, and threw himself into action. He was the first to lay Surrealism's foundations, along with André Breton and Louis Aragon. He studied Freud, admired Rimbaud and Lautréamont. He devoted his spiritual and intellectual powers to this movement of succinct principles, this creative program based on a theory that unveiled unprecedented horizons to the world of art. His career continued to rise, and his seventeen books to date, containing an unimaginable wealth of poems, texts and dreams – as he himself distinguishes them – have enjoyed amazing circulation and resonance.

That's why his stature is so important, not only in the Surrealistic context but also beyond. Everyone, even Surrealism's fiercest opponents, came to recognize and admire Éluard. "Not since Baudelaire," wrote Benjamin Crémieux in his critique of *Annales*, "has erotic verse been heard in such lavish and potent tones." And Bernard Fay declared, "Paul Éluard is revealed to us as one of Modern Europe's greatest poets." I don't have the space here to include his most important characterizations by critics like Gabriel Bounoure, Jean Cassou, A. Rolland de Renéville, Raymond Cogniat, Louis Laloy, Francis de Miomandre...

A SPECIFIC critique of Éluard's work requires a deep knowledge of Surrealism and a parallel analysis of all the currents of today's European poetry; it would derail me from the purpose of this documentary piece. I think the following are the necessary things to say about his work:

a) One's surprise on first reading Éluard's poetry comes from the plethoric simultaneity of prototypes (idiosyncracies, some say) in his expression and craft: anti-rhetorical fanaticism, fragmentation, abolition of punctuation, extremely bold use of adjective, and usually brief yet extremely comprehensive verse. One never encounters a straightforward, descriptive evolution of the poem. The poet leaps from meaning to meaning and from image to image with the greatest ease and artistry. By this mental and spiritual agility, he is able to avoid entire syllogistic maneuvers which, if unavoidable in prose, must be omitted from poetry so that its enchanting, magical and hyper-logical atmosphere can best be rendered. This assists what is perhaps the greatest secret of modern poetry: to couple meanings most foreign to common logic, and elements most distanced by daily use, on a superior and – relative to the violation of reality it allows – specifically poetic level. This coupling ensures an unexpected and radiant presence, making poetry immediate and self-sufficient, endowed with infinite grounds of freedom, originality and imagistic wealth.

b) One could call each of Éluard's poems a small kingdom of images. But what images! These are no longer simply a masterful description of external landscapes or of elements photographically absorbed by a psychic surface – superficial impressions demanding crystallization in logos. For Éluard, the entire world has first been decomposed into its archetypal elements and then recomposed by an entirely new mentality, responsive to authentic contemporary sensitivity. Rimbaud's proclamation of a *dérèglement de tous les sens* finds its triumphant application in Éluard.

His work is an unviolated externalization of the subconscious through imagistic waterfalls that challenge a mind limited to the everyday and the prosaic. At first they are startling, but later they slowly enchant, transport and conquer. The thought that they could perhaps be made more comprehensible and accessible doesn't exist, unless by adulterating the pure poetic tone and losing the magical atmosphere everything is immersed in. His intimacy with his interior world and his journey to the depths of his being are achieved solely by images, and by image-emotions, vibrating at their secret roots and regaling the reader with a resonance equally deep.

Consequently none of his poems has a specific theme. Titled or not, none transact an *a priori* concept. Their poet's offering emerges from the totality of these spontaneous visions as a broad, diffuse mood. Cycles of varying moods are then formed and, studying them, we grasp Éluard's huge form in its diversity.

c) According to Benjamin Crémieux, the essential difference between new poetry and old poetry is how each seeks to act on the emotional human. In the past, the poem first moved the mind to comprehend it, and then provoked emotionality through comprehension. Today it seeks to shock our psychic and physical being by provoking an *unmediated emotion completely independent of comprehension*. It's the first time the mysteries of two psychic worlds are so close, the first time the distance between Poetry and humans so little. The road is now open and free.

It is the road of a poet like Éluard. His writing instantly reaches our heart, striking our breast like the wave of another life, extracted from the sum of our dreams.

1939.

PIERRE JEAN JOUVE

THE ROAD where you encounter the roots that feed Pierre Jean Jouve's bitter and rare beauty is hard. Dense, almost adamantine expressions, achieved by thick layers of wise combinations, armor his work and repel every attempt at dissection, transforming its transparence into unbreakable crystal. But, if you overcome these first disappointments and insist on penetrating deeper, you will one day be surprised to find the same always vivid and eternal roots that nourish large authentic poetry in every epoch. Still, these eternal roots offer their original and apocalyptic properties only to those who will, by painful concentration, discover and domesticate them in their innermost soul, who will unite with them, by a heroic and singular gesture, to live the incremental synthesis of a new reality like a superb adventure.

Many years of intimacy are required for these poems to assume their final form by a sequential transformation which is less a technical acrobatics than an ability to *speak in unison* with the climate and terms of a new emotional landscape. It is because Jouve trained with such astounding persistence in the anasynthesis of archetypal elements that he fulfilled his poetic duty by transforming to permanence what the rest of us only feel as a fleeting, incomprehensible circumstance. This alone explains the intimacy of his motion within his terrible universe and reveals to us his dark starting point. One of the most unheard of emotional *junctures* occurred one day at the extreme geography where the first sobs stir. Religious mysticism, the fact of death, erotic frenzy, primitive physiolatry, and perpetual desire for ultimate liberation conjoined in polymorphous struggle and interpenetration, paying in precious blood for their irreparable but awesome collaboration. This is how he created the constituents of a power ceaselessly channeled through the arteries of his new symphony.

From this natural event, all else flows. The poet is obliged to abandon his old private ideogram, to destroy and renounce his first books. They agree too much with a world that is suddenly cursed and incomprehensible in his eyes. He has to abandon the illusion of his previous external position, to look only *from within*, working the internal fire with an art of worship and cynicism, compassion and roughness, a true but almost inhuman art.

Western mysticism? Metaphysical inclination? Inverted theology? None and maybe all, replies Cassou, who discerns in Jouve a *sui generis* mysticism. Mystical poets in the East as well as the West, he writes, vacillate between total negation and partial acceptance of this world. The contradictory fate of a soul caught between desire for self-immolation and salvation is deeply moving.

The work of Pierre Jean Jouve, from *Weddings* to *Celestial Matter*, is a rising and falling arc that inscribes his struggles of conscience. At first, the initiates of Jouve's wise art find breath difficult in the alpine atmosphere of abandoned, suffering and self-destructing landscapes. Later, they taste the possibilities of reconciliation between the sensate world and the true body, in poems of sensual weight and confessed worship where the world's presence majestically erupts.

OTHER SCHOLARS of contemporary poetry, like Marcel Raymond, find Jouve's key in the concept of original sin, and discover in his verse the reactions that the archetype of Cosmogony left in his consciousness. The sense of original sin does spread at first like an invisible stain in the atmosphere of these poems, and then like a threatening, heavy, ink-dark cloud; its drama provokes its creator's escape to abysmal territories of virginity and innocence, in which the soul might be baptized, reenacting its historical drama from the beginning, and differently. This is how the paradoxical and highly synthetic poem *The Lost Paradise* was born, a religious and philosophical poem in which a contemporary Frenchman dares measure himself against the most galvanizing Scriptural passages for the first time.

His smaller poems were also created this way, like emotional pauses between the present moment and eternity, through death and beyond, attesting to the belated *recovery of an invalid of time* whose inner world was worked over by the torturous presence of matter, the inexorable tyranny of erotocentric flesh. The presence of temptation in Good is incarnated on a new plane, this time by the Freudian concept of libido which translates the poet's Christian conflicts into the language of contemporary sensitivity. "We are only," he prefaces one of his books, "masses of unconscious, our surface lightly cleansed by sun…" And a little later, "We now know that a human is only an aching abyss filled with feral powers that stir in resistance and defense like blind octopi…"

After Rimbaud, the poets working to emancipate poetry from rationalism were well aware that they had found in the subconscious *the ancient and the new fountain* and, through it, had revealed a cosmic purpose. Metapsychology offers a new and immeasurable increase of the tragic.

PIERRE JEAN JOUVE became a poet of the new tragic. In his poems the soul discovers the punishment of flesh, its bloodied dress, which it will never be able to cast off. So he turns to death, accepts its ruinous power in order to overcome it, and actualizes himself outside its terror.

The poet persuades even Nature to this fate. In fact, Nature, always present in these inventions as a poetic element, becomes a constituting idiom, equal to its analogy with the poet's deeper and original motives. It is neither a decorative requirement nor an evocative accompaniment of many breaths, nor is it a spousal shadow of life's joy overflowing some Dionysian vortex. Nature participates in the drama intact, acting within the fate humans give it. Now we see it in the depths of some merciless battle, now we see it reach with innocent thirst for the peaks of the most eagerly sought purification. It is always in motion and in concert with mystery and action. It always lends its substance to the fermentation and formation of symbols that, by their recombinant wealth, help the poet through the difficulties of newer expression.

Jouve penetrated the very roots and fibers of this Nature, the tears of its clouds and the harshness of its boulders. Using its mouth, he pronounced his vision of a Cosmic Unity lost on its way to ultimate Healing and drenched in the blood of erotic despair. This Healing is only the search for the ideal it can project beyond death, like a reconstitution of secret elements so virgin – though condemned before death to co-habit with Evil's infinite manifestations – that they will reign in the garment of the true and perfecting Soul beyond time.

His is a startling idealism derived from the dark labyrinths of the worldly, a painful idealism devoted to constant battle on the ramparts of the unattainable. This intermediate stage of his lyric journey, rejecting self-delusion and marching to its goal full of knowledge and desperate grandeur, is clearly visible in passages from *Helen*.

1938.

FEDERICO GARCÍA LORCA

NO ONE teases the cunning powers of this world with impunity. The shadow of an angel's wing will always mark the gaze of the lost who flirt with the abyss. There comes a day when everything – night, blood, moon, fate, earth's secret cries, eros, a pure human heart, the infinite charm of matter that the wise sought to betray (by the least seductive chimera) and to erect pure beauty's abstract form somewhere else (the Void, of course) – everything returns so simply to the lips of a dark Andalusian galloping *bronce y sueño* through the moon-bathed olive groves of his country. And then, the earth's identity amazingly resembles a masculine song disappearing behind distant mountains. In the name of thirsty grasses, in the name of those who paid in blood for every handful of a newly-conquered freedom, drop by drop, Poetry rises to spotlight a fragment of "the eternal holy cross."

Not even the most perfect literature is related to it. The crucial thing is not to leaf through a book looking for more or less stylish phrases, but to unite with a power that propels you all the way to the roots of trees, where you may caress the faces most in pain and circulate through the veins of your fellows like blood. The crucial thing is to be able to travel with the poet through an infinite, raw, enigmatic world – among knifed fruit, mutilated statues and designs of cosmography – with the sensation you felt as a child. It is to be suddenly perfectly freed from the seat you happened to occupy, perfectly forgotten in the streets of a city like old Granada, hands in your pockets, shirt open, whistling and meditating there, my God, upon the circumstance of a man killed by the bullets of his ideological enemies, a thirty-seven-year-old man, a gypsy, musician, actor and rebel, who bowed respectfully one day to hear, and heard, earth speak. May nothing more be heard. Earth's speech is bitter and pierces bones.

ONE SHOULD perhaps contemplate for a moment contemporary Spain's spiritual and intellectual physiognomy and tighten the invisible threads that bind the forms, landscapes and characters embedded in its history, if one wishes to explain, I mean to more immediately comprehend, the profoundly idiosyncratic Spanish and (because of it) profoundly humane poetry of Federico García Lorca.

The study of the phenomenon of Adamism, as some critics call the drama of the isolated soul of the ancient Spaniard who seeks – by his own powers exclusively and in isolation from any similarly suffering milieu – to reach the remotest regions of the Improbable, the mania for the absolute that inhabits him with such tyranny, and his paradoxical nihilism, so closely tied to a despairing, passionate love for life, whose most characteristic expression is the word *nada*, "the most Spanish word that exists," according to Cassou – such a study would have a negative impact on a fuller comprehension of Lorca's lyric and dramatic work. On the positive side, the topical colorations – Catalonian, Castilian and Andalusian – as well as the idiosyncracies born of the long coupling between Arabic and European elements, would contribute to a more secure critical assessment of his lyricism. Works such as those of the poet of *Romancero gitano* stake their fate not on the pages of some Grammatology but on the soil and blood of a homeland.

How beautiful are the Valencian fields when spring, like an infant, opens its eyes and the hours play the sun on their mandolin with a citrus leaf! Life, sweet life, carries no grudge. Beautiful women, erotic women, dancing in colorful skirts as their eyes circle the earth before finally nailing their destination, raise a cloud of dust and swallows in the village square. Thick-shod farmers traverse the fields with their spades. The scarecrows, crooked above the fences, exorcise the carefree sky. Cursing and yelling, sweaty young men drive the bulls to their pens. Saturday afternoon. Old mothers lean from their windows, a secret anguish in their eyes, while in the upper neighborhoods barefoot boys raise hell throwing stones. Why do they drop everything, leap over fences and pour into the fields? What do they know?

Already in the distant dust at pasture's edge, a strange procession appears. As it approaches from afar, a message circles the village, mouth to mouth, and suddenly joyful crowds line the alleys to greet the dusty horsemen ahead of that long coach on its four wheels, the trembling sign, La Barraca, glinting in the angled rays of the sun against its roof.

La Barraca! Everyone more or less knows it is the traveling student theater coming to perform in their village. Everyone knows or has heard that the "soul" of this theatre – actor, musician, director and author – is Lorca, the poet Federico García Lorca, whose poems have always squeezed their heart with an invisible hand, no matter how often they've heard them. Soon, this crowd of beautiful girls, old farmers, sweaty men, barefoot kids and white-haired mothers will weep and shiver with joy, witnessing, on the improvised stage, the animated work of Lope de Vega or Calderón or Lorca himself, first *Yerma*, then *Rosita*, then *Speech of the Flowers*, then *Zapatera Prodigiosa* or, at last, the famous *Bodas de Sangre* that will later be so successful in Madrid, Barcelona, Paris, Buenos Aires and Mexico. They will admire the man who stages them, acts in them and composes their enchanting music, always based on popular romances, for instance his well-known "Galecianes" and "Cante Hondos." Finally, they will hear him recite his poems, the now famous *Romancero gitano*, a *Romance de la Luna, de la luna* and a *Preciosa y el Aire*; they will let their imagination move freely over the dense expressions in which reality becomes dream and dream reality so naturally, so humanly that they barely notice...

Thank God, there are no scholars from the capital at their side, no newspapers to poison their joy, whispering that it's impossible for "dawn to shake her shoulders," "stars to become bells" and "wind to twist the elbow of surprise," that this is dementia and madness.

The virgin soul receives emotion on its breast and with its help comprehends the most difficult things, as long as those things are alive. Pure thought, in its libraries and ivory towers, can phosphoresce its vain being as much as it wants to...

BENEATH the codifying walls raised by the renaissance of 1898, by the unequal works of the authors of Miguel de Unamuno's generation –

Azorín, Pio Baroja and Ramon Valle Inclán – two strong lyric currents whose source is the seventeenth century arrive to spread their delta on our agitated times. One of them, extracted from the poetics of Góngora, which concentrated strict, hermetic, subtle and aesthetic meanings (meanings that Europe will later make conscious and name Mallarmé-ian), is embodied in a poet like Jorge Guillén. The other current, full of the freshness, wealth, fertility and spontaneity of the folk song, begins with Lope de Vega and makes a beeline for the contemporary Andalusian lyricists, Rafael Alberti and, above all, Federico García Lorca. For the first time, the sense of "the popular poet" assumes its true meaning in his person.

Lorca is neither the anemic youth seeking to make literary likenesses of folk songs out of some excessive respect for national tradition nor the illiterate versifier roaming the streets to recite easy, occasional little songs. The rich poetic traditions of both his country and contemporary Europe have nourished his esthetic from early on, while the revolutionary movements of his time and their varied conquests did not leave him unmoved. It is enough to read "Ode to Salvador Dalí" to notice how he passes, alternately, from external to internal reality, how he abolishes contradictions between action and dream, and how he creates images so bold they violate the "common mind" (though they are always wise enough to hide their correlative among the objects of the large objective world) – enough to understand just what he sought to keep from the international movement of Surrealism and what to reject, transform, assimilate, condemn and acclimate to the atmosphere of his own tradition. Lorca truly manages to discourage any temptations that could derail him from the lofty goal he had promised himself.

Innovative and radical by nature, he worked for the new in art and for the revolution without ever lapsing into psuedo-intellectual soliloquy or political propaganda. Pessimistic *and* romantic at the core, he rendered both the bitterness of life and its enchantment, as well as the inevitability of fate, without lapsing into sterile lament; concomitantly, as a technician, he was able to avoid the ragged symbols and condemned technique of academic mentality. He was never orphaned from the joy of seeing his poems cast in a new personal architecture. His song is serious and masculine. Hearing it, we are already far from the typical "cursed poet" who senselessly indulges his bad instincts, seeking to project them, terrifyingly enlarged, to infinity. Our era struggles to project an entirely different human prototype which Lorca, with his acute sensorium, seems to have felt from the start:

> *Me porte como quien soy*
> *como un gitano legítimo.*

He always did behave this way, this gypsy, this impassioned lover worthy of standing fiercely by his people, before the desecrators caught up with him.

Night and the moon almost always accompany his peregrinations and create a mysterious climate full of lovers' shadows descending to the river's edge, children dreaming among gypsies, insomniac women on high green balconies, and fabulous dwarves or archangels continuing their work among us. *En la noche platinoche*, the world's secret cause, evaporating from trees, rocks and stars, coheres thought just as it coheres human skin. Earth secretly dictates its instructions by the gentlest caress across its grasses, while simultaneously holding in its belly the myriad dead. Lorca loves this earth, loves it *unto death*. The personæ he moves upon its skin are subject to their secret fate, a fate neither humble nor hostile to their joys and heroisms but proud and magnificent like the boulders of his heroes, an Ignacio Sánchez Mejías, a Walt Whitman.

The *Primer Romancero Gitan* emphatically underscores the decline of subjective poetry in Europe. The one who speaks here may well be an ephemeral – yet how conscious – member of the world, yet his purpose is not to analyze the labyrinths of his isolated soul. It is to mobilize animate and inanimate elements in objective space, so that the same experiential and savored residue is left in the souls of his audience, a residue once left, perhaps, by some scene or morsel of their own earthly adventure. From this perspective it is clear that Lorca, by balancing and assimilating the significant tendencies of contemporary lyricism, those truly dictated by the need of our times, himself becomes a rule, the *golden rule*, which will continue to help those who might want to walk his fertile path.

THE WIND rising in the evening through the improbable cities of old Castile cares for nothing else, I like to imagine, but ferrying the heartbeats of dark-haired women singing softly side-by-side in courtyards among wells and high arches, ferrying them warm to the waiting ears of poets insomniac at earth's four corners. Love of earth, human love, love of God, love of death are always one: Eros! What do the small half-naked children playing with the swallows in the street feel?

Pure azure Mediterranean, nude burnt Arabic coasts, when you inspired history to score the Iberian peninsula with blood and dream, you also defined a people's fate, the essence and form of their lyricism. While the wind little-by-little smoothes the granite the poet stands on, a compass rose in hand, *siempre la rosa, siempre norte y sur de nosotros*, life buries its nails into its bleeding heart, and the word, made flesh, gives and takes a new, eternal rigor from the commonest events along the riverbed of time.

Oh yes, poetry never lies. Pity the people who dig war trenches or rise in agony at night, groping through thick dark for joy! Which perishing is worse, do you know, can you say? What we are given down here by precious hours is irreparably kneaded with earth and grandeur. The human body continues its story in tree bark, in blushing clouds, in yielding iron and terrible volcanic groans, in the thousand forms nature assumes each time to dazzle us. A woman's breasts rise and fall in pleasure the very moment the stars bare their meaning.

The sea turns bruise-purple in the distance, and at the shoreline devours the fishing creels the very moment the awful thought seizes the mind of the scientist, the prophet, or the rebel. The correspondences of nature and eros seem infinite. Stop lashing youngsters to the mast, Eros, unblock the mariner's ears; the sirens manifest God's work better than the humblest nuns.

Life might wear her crown differently the day we all can feel that murder, betrayal, lies and all we generally call "evil" are only a bitter, most bitter defeat. Until sensation returns to matter we must keep repeating: There are no great and small poets in this world; there are only human beings who write poems as if earning money or sleeping with whores; and those who write poems as if knifed by love or as if mounting a mare to vanish in the spacious fields, eyes closed, insatiably thirsty…

Here's to you, Federico García Lorca! The shot that felled you by the stone wall of a village in your homeland achieved nothing! The strength of the people you loved resurrects your words forever; you know full well that a peasant's tear is worth more than any academic prize, that the plane leaf carried on hazy mornings by the north wind to the struggling shoulders of rebels is superior to gold as evidence of life!

1944.

GIUSEPPE UNGARETTI

THE SINGLE POEM composed by all of Ungaretti's poems simplifies life's lines and centers them in a design whose perimeter, as clear as the sea around an island, allows us to see the world of all peoples and throughout time, freed from the weight of our vanity.

I deliberately use the image of an island because I especially love the way it composes all elements of life into a unique, clean unit. And also because, by happy coincidence, I first came to read his poetry on an Aegean island. Dusk had begun as it always does in Ungaretti's landscapes, I remember. The scent of plants in the chilly dew, the stars igniting one by one, a faucet left open in the side garden, lent to this life a holiness I felt the poet strive to conceive of with his entire soul.

Each of these poems alone seemed to me sad, shaken and trembling under the weight of fate, or else like a contrition that had not become a wound but vanished, leaving a touch of jasmine whiteness in the night. But when I shut the book, how strange, I felt all of them together, drop by drop, create a sense of trust and safety in me. The sum of this inexplicable arithmetic of the soul resembled, stunningly, the dove of a deluge which had just occurred and no one had even noticed. What was its message? I didn't want, or know how, to explain it. In any case, I had never thought to demand morality of poetry, nor education, nor a meaning that thought can analyze, even if it is full of truth. I found none of these in Ungaretti. Still, I would emerge from my sojourn among his verse, feeling I had taken a step forward in my trust of human fate.

I KNOW this isn't how one should look at a work of poetry. But I am no critic and besides, I stand outside the linguistic arena of these poems. Let others prove Ungaretti's ties to tradition. From his formal reserve and the certitude of his voice, I suspect he achieved the difficult goal of reconciling modern expression with what we call "pacing" or "breath" in age-old Italian verse. Likewise, from his innovations, which neither dazzle nor deplete themselves at the rate of fireworks, I divine his prudence (a prudence part instinct, part conscience), which helped him turn a deaf ear to the thousand misleading Sirens in the years between the Wars. And I'm certain that future generations will be indebted to him for resisting the drag of the prosaic and for not stooping to the decor of modern mechanistic civilization. Instead he remained faithful to Lyricism and to the rendering of the spirit of his time with trees, clouds and stars, as Sappho and Ivykos had rendered theirs.

From this perspective, Ungaretti's poems lead me directly to the ancient Greek Lyricists just as Braque's drawings lead me to the figures on Attic vases. But from another perspective, a purely human and liberating one, my mind goes to Plotinus. It's not the meaning of his work that leads me there. Meaning in poetry, just as in metaphysics, is not the same as meaning in other forms of the written word. He extends the powers of the sensorium and creates, from their analogy to a dimension composed by our intact substance, the third dimension, which is at once sound and echo, cause and effect, dream and reality.

Visually, this process translates to posture, and this posture, among poets at least, can be easily distinguished: the poet who raises his eyes in desperation, the poet who raises his fist, the one who hides his face, the sarcastic one, the one who wails, the one who dreams. So seen, Ungaretti's posture is, I would say, the posture of an innocent with nothing to confess who regards the world – life and death – from the safety of his innocence.

Close to nature like the Greeks, but also to guilt like the Christians, Ungaretti speaks from the meta-junction of these worlds, as he speaks from the world of memory, with the familiarity of a contemporary, almost always in the present tense. His is a continuous and ceaseless elevation, by successive circles, toward perfection. His exaltation is in pure images for which the soul, from its earthly vantage point, is nostalgic. The *infanzia di cielo* he invokes, the *primavera eterna* and Olympus, his *fiore eterno di sonno*, make me imagine a contemporary and lyrical Plotinus. And I wonder now whether this is what finally graces the *one* poem all his poems form with the security and cathartic power I could not explain earlier. Unless, in reading a poet, one is basically looking for another accomplice to one's innocence.

156

I'VE OFTEN happened to experience that sense of malaise that exists in large modern cities and has no organic source, but springs instead from other, deeper causes: from the monstrosity of a number so large it cannot be reconciled with human measure, from the internal sedimentation of images irreconcilable with the notion of cleanliness we like to have about ourselves, and from the confluence of tastes so distanced from earth's virginity for which our nostalgia quests, overcoming piles of dark synthetic matter. And then a primordial and uncontrolled mechanism, either primitive exorcism or Christian communion, unconsciously guides me to simple acts and simple thoughts that seem to have the symbolic power of opposing evil by their very nature. It is enough, for instance, to drink some clear water, eat plain bread, or intensely recollect an Aegean island in summer sun and roaring surf in order to balance once again on a sensation that is not exactly metaphysical faith, esthetic self-sufficiency or pledge of material strength but something like a certainty of light sufficient to counterweigh the dark. And by helping it to the surface, and only by that, we harmonize with the being fulfilling its destiny.

The highest honor I can offer the great Italian poet is the confession that I have in such moments, by instinct, recollected his work. It is so true that light is made from ancient sacrificial blood. And only by proffering it and accepting its extinction can one neutralize that extinction.

1958.

PIERRE REVERDY

POETS ARE measured less by poems than by what their poems succeed in leaving behind. Sometimes it's nothing but gold-dust the wind scatters as merrily as death does the glorious lives of Generals and Kings. Sometimes they leave something more solid, which is nevertheless no easier to define. Strengths rarely equal the impression their results create, and very likely one day a rose will prove more durable than the densest rock. We usually then blame the wind's bad air above the April gardens, oblivious to the fact that the power necessary to perfect a rose surpasses by far the force of the fiercest wind.

These invisible currents – fulfilling their mission in the absence of people, within or without symbolic language – leave us with a pile of

faulty calculations in hand. The hardest thing in the world is to become
what in truth you are. And I would say that the least vulnerable defini-
tion of poetry is that it constitutes the path of such self-encounter. A
schooling path, sown with heroic corpses. Few are the faces we recog-
nize, who have won their features forever. The others' physiognomies
are lost; perhaps we remember their hands, clenched and withered by
effort, or their teeth, which a superhuman defiance clenched and sealed
and left luminous in death's sun.

What most impressed me when I first met Pierre Reverdy was his
clenched teeth, a sensation his poetry might have presaged but which
now intensified his sharp gaze, a gaze trained to reach across destinies.
He was, at the time, collaborating with Picasso and Terriade in publish-
ing *Chants des Morts*. Here was someone still alive, who had already re-
deemed the fate of the dead still circulating among us, who had taken us
by the arm to the small bistros of St. Germain-des-Prés, who in true
mania could down demijohns of red wine – his clenched jaw raised
above the vivid tablecloth and insignificant humans like a stubborn dog,
head high above the floods, preserving the bandana of an ideal.

I NEVER dared speak to him about Solesmes, which I didn't even know.
He, on the contrary, often spoke to me of Greece with, I must say from
the outset, a knowledge and certainty far greater than he might have
gained on a brief Mediterranean trip twenty years before. Always, a deep
regret lurked behind his words. It seemed less nostalgia for the light
than passion for clarity. Because he didn't speak about the land of Gods,
Heroes and Platonic geometry but, often, of a bitter-orange garden be-
tween two seas, and his eyes then would assume an ineffable tameness.

Suddenly the taste of citrus, the weight of fruit, the slap of wind pow-
ered by surf and wild sweet grass entered his ascetic head like a blessing.
His palm remained open as if to receive some invisible *naranja*. I studied
him carefully, thinking he had been made for purity, an abundant fra-
grant purity that sprouts from earth, rises from waters and has, as its
spiritual analog, the simplest shape used by archaic peoples to approach
the Divine. I forced myself to be convinced by this icon before its idol
should vanish. I knew that, sooner or later each time, the heavy black
abbey wall would slide between us with a *thunk* like those iron fire-
curtains in theaters, and that instead of the little Mariner of Miracles

I would then face a tired wanderer who had never been graced by a glass of water or some fire on his way.

Some might say that behind those high abbey walls another fountain flows, another invisible road to the absolute, the serene. I have no argument, though I barely understand Catholicism. I am only afraid that this poet, who so accurately discerned his journey's end, self-destructed in transit, playing at two different speeds, walking high and low *à contretemps* and shaping, without even wanting to, the unique drama of his poetry and his being.

It is not incidental that Reverdy so loved Cubism. The idyll of his youth was no chance street meeting. His soul had long been receptive to clarity, objectivity, de-sentimentalization, abstraction and new order, so much so that this large movement and its significance take on the dimensions of fate in his life.

Though not a painter, he had, ever since *Demoiselles d'Avignon*, all the qualifications to reverse the Renaissance path, and so invalidate on the spiritual plane everything that had, on the plastic plane, adulterated authentic human expression: analysis, trompe d'œil, content and chiaroscuro. He had, that is, in his pocket the best possible passport for running *sous la nuit aimantée*…for mastering the secret *de cette main posée en souveraine sur la mer*.

This hegemonic hand cast on the sea could offer him true nature's measure, could sail him endlessly on that one spot. And the last poem of *La Belle au Bond* could pioneer a magical navigation to the soul's least accessible landscapes. Reverdy knew that speaking of Greece he spoke of ideas reached only by the regal road of the senses, as well as of the metaphysics that are a basic restoration of spirit to "recombinant" matter. That was the source of his profound and impersonal respect for the Mediterranean and the luminous Juan Gris, and also the source of his somewhat inexplicable arousal at my Greekness. It was late, and nature had been transformed in his hands from a vivid pulse and mythic prototype to theatrical cardboard. He crumpled and dragged this cardboard nature with intense psychic mania, sensing he was losing the miraculous chlorophyll of May and its faithful blooming for ever:

Le ciel se coupe en deux

on accroche le ciel d'automne aux quatre coins

quelqu'un suspend au ciel quelques étoiles

la boîte des nuages s'ouvre

le clou est là – retient la pente.

Still, if you're born for the sky you'll find your way to it, even when the natural prototype of the imagined sky turns in your hands to a dry material that you can cut or puncture. Because then you make a fort with it, to crouch in and protect the little morsel that your childhood sense preserved, which now your concentration and prayer will broaden and restore to its initial dimensions.

IN NO OTHER poet do the words *door, window, lamp, roof, skylight* and *wall* occur so often. In the greater part of his work, a house is endlessly being built, demolished, rebuilt and re-demolished. We witness a horrifying insecurity:

les étoiles sont derrière le mur
dedans pointe un cœur qui voudrait sortir

then:

on ne sait plus si c'est la nuit

then:

la maison tremble

then:

mon sort était en jeu dans la pièce à côte.

This eternal room next door where our fate is being gambled had already become, by the time of Reverdy's youth, a refuge for those without imagination who were bent on "taking even the infinite captive," one of his accurate phrases. The small black opening that gaped then at the poet's feet would grow at an amazing rate to constitute the famous pelago of the void, in which the spiritually insubordinate young are nowadays so easily shipwrecked.

This too was Reverdy's kismet: to be the first of a generation losing the right to grow old along with the ideas that had nourished it. The thought first occured to me as I watched him observe the motley crew of bearded and desperate Parisian youths across the boulevard St.-Germain one evening, his teeth always clenched. A French poet literally lost among so many French. Five minutes passed without a word. Then he cried out, pointing his hand, "None of them knows me, not one!..." And we got up to leave.

YET HE WAS known to earth's four corners. He was studied and loved, at least by those who support Poetry and are the final arbiters of Literature's defining fate. Thank God that in our era delusion dissolves as quickly as it triumphs. The front page stars are the future dead. What can the isolation of true poets mean? Of course, the deeper isolation has always existed and will always continue to exist. You may not trespass on God's properties unpunished. But the exterior social isolation – what true beneficence it is! Without pale young ladies and their albums, without idiotic salons, without cafes packed with stingy failures and armchair critics, today's poet's only choice is to remain alone with his high aspirations, which he might discern better in a clear and undeluded atmosphere. *We actualize in the present the verifications once allowed only by the past.* Pierre Reverdy's verification had been accomplished by all poets worthy of the name, throughout the world.

In those very days I had occasion to speak with young people from Nicaragua, Mexico, Israel and Portugal about the two-volume publication of his collected works. The poet himself had mentioned letters he'd received from Greece. He didn't seem to care much, it's true, possibly not wanting to appear weak or because he had, in fact, like most of his colleagues, failed to grasp that the pre-war poetic centers no longer held a monopoly and that the post-war intellectual market had moved to other, smaller countries far from Europe. Only once – when I showed him some of his poems that – along with those of Breton, Éluard, Jouve,

Supervielle and Char – I thought most highly of and would, if I were able, include in an "Anthology of New French Poetry" from Apollinaire to the present – did he reveal both surprise and approbation. "There's a great idea for our publishers," he exclaimed. "It will take a foreigner to compile our ideal Anthology!" It might have been mere hyperbole or momentary politeness. But the concept of some distance or separation from the agora's racket still held true.

No ONE dreamed of contesting Reverdy's historical rights to the new expression (a relevant phrase by the Breton of the heroic epoch comes to mind), though the consumerist exploitation of his discoveries by his juniors had seriously lessened their significance. Just opening his books at random, you'd find the best Éluard before Éluard:

> Un éclair d'hirondelle...
> La mer dans les oreilles...
> Les frissons bleus de l'eau...
> La tête aux cheveux de satin...
> Un nuage passe à cheval...

and even the most recent Éluard:

> La rue est plafonnée de bleu
> Et nos projets sont sans limite...

or René Char:

> Le tonnerre aplanit le toit...
> Roux de liévre...
> Le sang bleu de la plaine...
> Les rochers serrent les dents...

and why not Breton:

> On n'a pas récolté la sombre couche de fleurs
> artificielles qui poussaient là
>   aux dernières limites

La main ramenait l'air chargé de petits poissons à peine éclos...

Il y a moi
   Et toutes les sonneries se mettent en branle à la fois dans
   la maison
Pourquoi apporte-t-on tant de cloches et de réveils
   De la tapisserie où mon corps s'aplatit de profil les mains
   en forme de plateau demandant grâce...

   La danseuse enflammée sort du porte-manteau
   Les maillots gonflés se raniment...etc.

On the technical level and below the apparent monotony there exists a wealth which I believe testifies to Reverdy's search for the precise linguistic parallel to the one Cubism established in the plastic arts. His insistence on the object, his cutting and interpenetrating of planes, his use of expression serving parallel meanings, his simultaneous projection of optical surfaces, his shift from first to third person in the sense of *en face* and *profil* – these experiments went more or less unpursued, even by him. However, their ultimate benefit to lyricism's health and agility are found in the totality of subsequent poetry. Poets of quality proffer them, even unwittingly, to this day. And the critic, after analysis, extracts from their instantaneous gesture the arrows that Reverdy shot everywhere: toward clean language, recombinant images, net of meanings, musical or plastic analogies, etc.

We have learned to place ourselves, our artistic esthetic, under emblems of decline, perhaps through a bad habit which our successors will revise. Even so, our technical experiments bear no relation, as motives, to the experiments of the Alexandrian era, to use a common example.

What was dictated once by simple mimicry or intellectual joy is now most often dictated by the dire necessity to render more vivid and accessible the sensation the poet aspires to. Grace, elegance, flexibility – all the specific attributes of the poem-song abundant in great eras – have yielded in our time to grossly serious, tonally formal, almost hieratic speech. Pierre Reverdy, perhaps the only contemporary poet to speak exclusively in the present tense, is surely singular in exclusively maintaining a poetic tone both sharp and heavy. He cannot play.

Though this is not a qualifying criterion, it does delineate his stance toward life: something too holy to make light of is in his hands. He continued to taste the same amalgam of bitterness and grandeur he had first known as a young man – observing the world through the elliptical skylight of his Paris refuge – to his dying days behind the cracks of the sealed windows of his black Solesmes cell.

Reverdy's cross was inscribed once and for all between Greece and Solesmes, between participation and denial, between the roar of surf and the harmonium echoes where God's secret words might equally well be heard. His great success was that he clung, with his defiantly clenched teeth, to a life without servitude, and that he preserved the fragment of "the honorable" that luck deals each mortal. In the meantime, the years of stone and verdure too quickly became the years of chromo-cobaltium and super-alloys.

Whether this leap, more than the poet's toward God and the unknown, brought human beings closer to what they really *are*, remains to be seen.

1961.

T.T.T.

(ART-LUCK-RISK)

[TECHNE-TYCHE-TOLME]

plus –

A

ART-LUCK-RISK: these three, no other words but these celebrated three, come to mind each time I start to open a letter and linger, gazing at the large formal seal of T.T.T. [the Greek postal acronym]. For a long time now I have been carrying my own seal, scored on my skin with un-justified pride, and I am used to reading it only according to the emotions that inspired it.

Art-Luck-Risk: these three words stubbornly standing by their con-tent became the inextinguishable satellites of my early puberty, my first perception of the world, satellites that to this day, in a surfeit of intensi-ty, have not ceased to be faithful. Still, among the even or odd years bringing us wavelike near to or far from what we love, aren't there also some, singularly decisive, piercing the surface as though the strongest light suddenly flared inside them? Graced by dense content, such years acquire an emerald brilliance and solidity and are worn like rings of creative memory on the fingers of those who wished one day to cross the common line – above or below is irrelevant – but always toward some attainable or unattainable conquest.

Writing this today, the year 1935 extinguishes and reignites for me like a lighthouse buoy in the little pelago I love to travel; it is marked by my first contact with Greek nature, my first acquaintance with and practice of Surrealism, my discovery of the painter Theophilos, the publication of two seminal books by poet friends, and the unveiling of a bold Greek journal: *New Letters*. I want to imagine that a well-meaning reader will see these insignificant events as significant, since they are not folds of a private biography but nuclei of a thoroughly objective cir-cumstance.

SOME MOMENTS in human life reveal, by a quick imperceptible blink, the surrounding world bathed in strange light, stripped of daily meaning, and recognized by another and first-seen – the real one perhaps? – physiognomy. These are moments when the events that dryly and relentlessly define your way break their orbit, gleaming with different meaning and different goals, moments you suddenly see yourself on never-chosen trails, under strange arches of trees, among people who assume the stature of your most obvious emotions to become *friends*, your friends, as you had always wished them to exist and await you, there, in some bitter corner of your life. No alien element or super-sensory presence explains the world's bizarre turn in such moments. Simple, earthly, human, they are the actions and events that occur in a *second circumstance*, more real than the first, one we would distinguish by the name hyper-real.

Why have we given the world a single tongue, a single mode of expression until now? Why only a single view, piecemeal, invalid, measured exclusively by logic and named pretty-pretty reality? And why, in the name of such reality, do we let nothing surpass it?

As often as I am forced to this conclusion, a sorrow trails my pen like a large sundial shadow.

Alone at the borders of panic and enchantment, the poet, struck by such fleeting revelation, suffers the passion of adapting his breath to the newly revealed climate; he bleeds to express this secret taste, the indefinable essence, the immortal hue the elements of his internal world swiftly assume. Differently valuating life from that moment on, he painfully measures the distance between himself and the great human plurality. He sees this plurality entrenched in convention and denying what might cause it to face its essential problems with such frenzied despair that he comes to understand it is his destiny to undertake, along with the burden of expression, yet another: the burden of empathy, if not the fate of solitude. It is always so: the poet risks, while the misled behind him insist on keeping sealed a door whose lock has long since lost its purpose. Still, though this vendetta between conservatism and change, between natural and unnatural animate development, has remained unextinguished since Heracleitos, we must recognize that it flared with the full weight of its meaning for the first time in our century, insisting that our artists place beauty's eternal element upon the *forever transforming* point of human flow, insisting, in other words, that they feel this truth as the eternal law of their being. Revolutionary flag in hand, they were led by a harsh necessity to re-examine their inheritance and undertake a radical reorganization of values. Some said it was only youth's oblivious thirst to forge its road by any means. So what? The truth is that the "moderns" enacted what their knowledge and their heart dictated them as much in the regions of first epochs or neglected territories of Art as in the forgotten (by the false modesty of later generations) pages of Literature and Poetry; and they either dredged works of substantial value from obscurity or they trampled, with justified fanaticism, on some deplorable constructs that had temporarily managed to reign.

Art-Luck-Risk, yes! *Art*: since for better or worse we long to free the Pythian spark impatient to be Logos, and lead a new evaluation of the world; *Luck*: which unifies colors and shapes, fragrances and sounds, our heart and the heart of the universe in the lyric we dream of; and *Risk*: since, in this society, every true step is destined to a trail of blood, smoke and tears.

I SPOKE of 1935. It's time now to return to its spirit and letter, to bring its glorious New Year's day to this present, leaping forward in its turn like a grasshopper, though the valley looms dark and full of danger. By God, there are times when life skips no occasion to show its impatience, whether it's by a horseshoe on the cobbles or by a beardless boy's gaze upon the forms of enigmatic women and freshly printed books.

I recall that just as the ancient Lyricists had one fine day awakened my interest in poetry from one side and Kalvos and Kavafis from another, so had two contemporary French poets – though perhaps not the greatest – Paul Éluard and Pierre Jean Jouve, compelled me to notice and accept without reservation the *potential* inherent in lyric poetry's essential free enactment. Even then I promised myself to bring them to the Greek public, and later did.

I was not yet a senior at the Gymnasium when, impelled by my disoriented bibliophilia, I'd wedged myself one afternoon into the old and dark Kaufman Bookstore, leafing through magazines and books but pointedly and scornfully avoiding poetry, whose content, asphyxiated by rhyming quatrains, exuded a binding and uniformly repetitious sentimentality that was completely opposed to my then rebel moods. I

167

recall it as if it were today. Still, tempted by the luxury, the bizarre fascination of the black and red letters of their covers, I lost my last hesitations: *Capitale de la douleur, Défense de savoir, Noces...* I leafed through them one by one...and...

Luxury was immediately displaced by the light vertigo and first-tasted rapture rising from a few chance verses that overwhelmed me, not by their evenly rhythmic sway but, most significantly, by their magic and stunning confirmation of a second world, a world existing inside or around me whose only question was how to declare its existence better. That *how* was found. The practical, contented people coming and going every day suddenly turned to lumber in my eyes, lumber no god had commanded me to mimic or serve. What devil doctor, engineer or lawyer could I be, feeling as I did that a single, solitary inspired phrase could re-inspire a myriad others, all brilliantly enduring without end? *Le poète doit être beaucoup plus celui qui inspire que celui qui est inspiré.* Hearing Éluard speak with such confidence ten years later, I remembered the moment I had stood in the bookstore reading:

> *Si tu t'en vas la porte s'ouvre sur le jour*
> *Si tu t'en vas la porte s'ouvre sur moi-même.*

I was uninformed but not mean-spirited. I never thought to take a ruler and measure the door that opened to the day or wonder if this door could ever be manufactured; for me, the door existed and I was bound to help it open with my small powers. A mistral of emotions already whistled through its crack, directly on my chest.

A true world existed there, yet was condemned to obscurity, unsuspected by most, and visible to a few only at the peak of eros or despair. A world harmonious with its most secret, most untamed and freest emotions yet nonetheless isolated behind huge trenches of loneliness! The insane will to never yield but enter instead a nearby soul and together re-right our fiercest dreams, give them flesh and blood of our flesh and blood, communication by heart: could we achieve it or not?

Could ideal communication – the briefest route between two people, a communication felt wholly, like warmth or cold, ravishingly, like eros or terror, mysteriously, like roar of forest or sea – could it become one day the very instrument and goal of Lyric poetry?

168

B

FROM THE eleventh century B.C. to our twentieth, and from the first Tibetan priests to our European Surrealists, humankind has continued to follow this paralogical phenomenon called Poetry along with its myriad other concerns. I risk saying paralogical because logic would never, not even in the most classic epoch, suffice to encompass and justify the human act that suddenly attempts to render, by rhythmic association of some word,...what? I don't know... the world, the self, the soul's least unknown. But the fact that this sacred dance of words endures the multiform waves of so many centuries' sensation must mean that it responds to a fundamental need of human existence. The light, the light that needs no sun or underworld machine to spill in us, is enough to guide our feet surely to the eternal source.

Did anyone ever ask what strength is spent, what distance neutralized and what resistance overcome for mystery to rise from root to fruit, from a plant's travail to human senses, for motive to turn into result? Future scholars of our generation's work will, I believe, not waste a moment re-erecting for their own eyes what ours saw at the moment of action. Wanting to have constant contact with the vivid rigor of the spirit, we naturally inclined toward its ample source. With the Greek legacy in our veins, and in our souls a thirst for a more catholic life, we simply had to fix our eyes wherever humans seemed the most inflamed by daily trials.

We were in fact often envious of the atmosphere created by some vigorous French and German youths through violent reversal of enshrined values, youths aspiring not to immortal works, or even works at all, but to the fist, raised wherever blood was lacking and in urgent need to flow! We often thought how much the beneficial commotion of a "Dada period" would profit the calligraphic mediocrity of new Greek letters! We knew that a periodical in the style of a *Nord-Sud*, a *Manuel Festival Presbyte* or a *Nor Cacadou* chorus would bequeath nothing of literary substance but would nonetheless unleash a life-force able to erase many wrinkles and turn, two by two and three by three, the pages of our history as by a magic breeze. But other concerns, more precise and to the point, overtook us when we came to feel mature enough for action. The practical problems of Lyricism – rhythmic perception, image-potential, word validation, formal and contextual correspondence, mythic existence and reach, mnemonic devices and the synthesis, legal or not, of poetic meaning – came to a crux which many then wanted to and tried to prove non-existent.

With Paul Valéry's imposing figure on the proscenium, Stéphane Mallarmé's suggestive one in the rear, and with L'Abbé Bremon's support in difficult theoretical moments, pure poetry rose, with superior airs, to face a Surrealism presenting in its proscenium, and with great disorder, the fanatic, possessed physiognomies of Breton, Éluard, Aragon and Tzara, while the enigmatic or fantastic figures of Rimbaud and Lautréamont stirred in the background. It seemed that the very fate of poetic speech turned on this juxtaposition. The Anglo-Saxons, islanders as well and isolated even in their innovation, forged a different effort through T.S. Eliot and Ezra Pound, whose great qualities did not appear to influence the broader European sensibility, at least not then. The other nations more or less joined the Parisian center without losing their topical colors in the least, and I will one day find occasion to describe how, in my opinion, some if not all of them took advantage of France's international fermentations with considerably more fruitful results.

The fresh and powerful voice of Vladimir Mayakovski, erect between the old futuristic clatter and the current Surrealist arrogance, was still abroad in Europe and was echoed by the protesting cry of the Turk Nazim Hikmet in the south. In Italy, Giuseppe Ungaretti, an old comrade of Breton and Aragon, lent a Mediterranean character to essentially Surrealist principles, though perhaps weakening their example. Wealthy, more wealthy than all the rest, the Spanish lyricists cultivated a poetry of warmth and vigor in the works of Pedro Salinas, Federico García Lorca, Rafael Alberti, Manuel Altolaguirre and Vicente Aleixandre, whose poems were marked by a beneficial reaction to the overworked and fragile esthetic of Jorge Guillén, their most Valéry-like contemporary poet. As for Greece, the indirect assistance of the Kavafian œuvre, which achieved such distance from traditional forms, and the post-Karyotakis era, which, by devaluing all values, came to signal the dissolution of one world and the need for the birth of another, are sufficient to describe our path – not to forget Sikelianos, who, graced by powerful idiosyncrasies, was preparing rich surprises and extensions that could align him with us.

I needed to sketch this small emotional topography in order to illustrate two things: first, that in today's world it is not possible for more than one particular view of poetics to rule at one time, and it would be wrong to repudiate it as potentially neglecting the multi-colored, multi-toned ethnic idioms, since it could in fact serve and fill them with unprecedented rigor, elevating and enabling them to be heard in the artistic, at least, concert of the human family; and second, that in most, if not all, European countries, those independent poetic circles attempting to abstain from the discipline of a given school proved incapable of working outside Surrealism's broad influence. The superiority of the latter, its imposing power among the young and its endurance through a second World War scandalizes and annoys many, as it did when it first appeared. An unbiased youth, faced with so many miracles of speech abundantly broadcast by pure poetry, might easily be misled into thinking that the road to the future originates there. Still, as it turned out, poetry was not some special and isolated esthetic yearning, nor an intellectual experiment with fixed parameters and masturbatory goals; it wasn't a private and irrelevant matter, nor, as it also turned out, was it a simple instrument in the hands of those proclaiming social, political or philosophical beliefs.

"Infinitely different from writing technique," to quote Novalis, poetry seemed the only possible thing we could be given to express the totality of our substance and not just our logical domain, to encounter our enigma and, beyond it, our destiny's now integrated demand. Poetry seemed an instrument of psychic function able to resist an evil ethic and its horrific material repercussions; it seemed the imprint of a spiritual adventure containing all the oscillations of its animate trial – pain, joy, sorrow, mystery, nostalgia, intoxication and ecstasy – intact in space and time; it seemed to be the human initiation, body and soul, into the essence of objects as well as the secret place where that essence and the Universal essence join; it seemed a radical and ceaselessly revolutionary instrument whose only duty was to lend a form to the revelation of beauty and the essential value of life, a form equal always to the demands of imagination.

Grounded here and striking both left and right, Surrealism managed to see humankind without its acquired infirmity and to address all aspects of its earthly adventure. Whether or not it also managed to remain without sin will be determined one day without reservation. In fact, a conclusive study – for which I feel, alas, most ill equipped – could absolve this revolutionary view from its misinterpretations, by the simple deployment of new criteria. Unfortunately, as I've already noted, our most well-intentioned critics arrived, always out of breath, just as the well-rested creators broke new ground, and were unable to apply the new criteria offered by the era's sensitivity to its new creative achievements.

For instance, the unrestrained subjectivism and remove from reality, so characteristic of a particular European literary period, which climaxed most ingeniously with Marcel Proust and James Joyce, had first been targeted by Surrealism, both in theory and in practice. Yet Surrealism was placed among the very principles it had so bravely and publicly denounced. Perhaps the nature of the subconscious or the dream misled those who were still somewhat unprepared for psychoanalytic concerns and their relation to Hegelian dialectics. In any case, the interpretation of the dream as part of reality (indeed, a crucial one) was instead allied with popular opinion as synonymous with daydream, as "an escape from the real." Instead of being seen as a large anonymous world intolerant of any subjective judgement, it was perceived as a private matter willfully demanding to enter Poetry. And finally, instead of hailing the subconscious as the great baptismal font where the *community* of symbols and their free interpretation is allowed outside the confines of national or stylistic bias and borders, it was presented as a mere and unnecessary descent into a single being's personal isolation.

When intellectual movements advance with a series of actions and reactions as their sole support, only comparative study can yield significant conclusions. Anamnesis of a historic epoch's pulse, revitalizing a past sorrow, the vigorous lithe wind of rebel youth resurging for a while, all arguments, even the most quixotic, brought back to the proscenium, the naïvetés, the hatreds and grand words: these are not the futile elements of some criticism, at least no criticism hoping to conceive of its subject not only by intellectual exertion but also by emotional contact, by a biological, I would say, whole-body assent. Nothing could better reveal the causes of Surrealism's success in our generation or better justify our inclusion, despite personal objections, in its movement than carefully taking the pulse of our somatic and psychic organism's slightest reaction to the despotic and lengthy imposition of a hideous order: mechanization, bourgeoisie, narcissism, counterfeiting of all ethical meaning, rationalization.

Poetry first, by its daily enactment, agreed to radiate that diffuse spirit to the entire world's emotional centers. Its every moment must be one of new reality, its every conclusion a new, riskier intervention in the world. The revolution must reveal the same transforming energy in *praxis* as in *logos*, and posit equal analogies between internal and external human reality – politics, philosophy, verbal art, daily conduct. To succeed in this, words would need a new ground of action; they must renounce the graceless and cheap fate assigned them by academics, as well as the narrow aristocratic fate of "pure poetry"; they'd need more support than sonorous composition or advantageous fellowship could provide; they must no longer serve a spiritual mathematics, no matter how exalted. They must instead embrace the magnitude and wilderness of their material root, partake in adventures worthy of instinctual urges, revel in or be calmed by the infinite couplings that liberate imagination from its ectoplasmic condition and allow it to embody trembling images in nerves and plenty of blood, images that reveal the still-damp hues of freed human emotions.

*too ethereal -
more mystic
ally.
NO - MISSION
- Is he
calling
for a
poetry of
the every
DAY?*

The two crystals that so successfully seemed to symbolize the ideals of Valéry and Breton shared nothing but the will to strike brilliant limpidity atop the painful spear of their century. Perhaps because I was in the habit of always translating my impressions *visually*, I found, in the image of the crystal, properties which, by their simple synthesis in me, represented Valéry's spirit. Later, I saw that Breton's effort likewise iridesced in such a form, and was confirmed by his statement, "A work of art, just as any part of a human life, seems to me deprived of all meaning if it does not also present, in its totality as well as its details, the internal and external brilliance, hardness and limpidity of crystal." This startling meeting of two worlds so different in substance does not confuse us but rather helps us understand the rightness of working deep below the illusory surface until we unite with our object's essential meaning.

Valéry's crystal, crafted with unimaginably patient devotion and

173

minute detail, bespoke the expenditure of an individual effort that
evened protrusions, equalized facets, balanced brilliancies and mirrored
the world with admirable splendor. Breton's crystal on the other hand
was formed under natural laws in the single moment it took to pass
from liquid to solid. Behind its lightning flash the same world is waving,
but with the beauty of its natural freedom and no sign of forced submis-
sion to laws not its own. In fact, while the first crystal's form was exclu-
sively defined by the calibrations of an intellect trained for that very
purpose, the second was defined by the force of chance in the singular
manner in which it inscribes its path through reality, using people or
natural elements as its instruments, illustrating the honest relations of
form and matter *post facto*.

Valéry isolated art and assigned it specific laws; Breton let life's laws
function *also* in art and proved that, for him and those like him, life and
art are two communicating vessels wherein the endogenous and exoge-
nous constantly flow and synthesize one and the same reality: hyper-
reality.

IT IS IN this context – what other? – that I enjoy revisiting 1935. Its first
spring days were marked by the appearance of two books of poetry that
for me are destined to remain brilliant atop the gates of a new era of
modern Greek lyricism: two books by my friends Seferis and Embeiri-
kos, reflecting the same profound desire though originating in totally
different sources, by opposite means and with separate goals, and on
whose juncture I was held by what I, almost exclusively, loved. This
juncture is not the "middle ground," nor was I ever proud to hold such
an ideal.

Between the biologically liberated human who risked becoming the
instrument of an ecumenical voice on the one hand, and the Greek who
dramatized his racial destiny in his own personality and never denied
the superiority of live and free expression on the other, I could easily
accept that no marginal or middle roads exist, but only roads that lead
nowhere and roads that lead everywhere, to all the finish lines and goals.
At the beginning of my effort then, as now, I can only remember grate-
fully the atmosphere that the close friendship of these poets created
around me. Leafing through a stack of notebooks today – green, red,
gray, full or half-full of the varied verses and strange drawings of the

174

year that so befriended them – I see the poetic gymnastics, the hyper-
boles and passionate enthusiasms of a freshly opened imagination; they
tempt me to preserve some samples, even if not one curious reader
might be found for them. As for vanity, don't even bring it up. The *coups
à l'inconnu* five or six of us friends gave then were not without result.

Now is the time to examine what has come to be known in poetic
history as "automatic writing." No definition can boast of autarky, and
practice almost always discourages punctiliousness: it deforms, aban-
dons and overflows the templates that attempt to nail it down. The un-
impeded transcription of psychic associations is theoretically possible
for all, since we are all carriers of a submerged flow of image-producing
language while awake and the officiates of the world's magnanimous ac-
tion while asleep. But the question persists: to what degree is such para-
doxical incarnation possible? And, if possible, why desirable? How does
it serve beauty and liberation, Lyricism's two goals?

The proud rebels attending Surrealism's birth providently armed it
with *dicta* that would absolutely preclude inconsistency. They said: **REread Manifesto**

—Beauty does not seem indispensable to us.
—A spiritual point exists wherein all contradictions reconcile.
—The poet does not impose his own voice but transmits the voice
that exists always and resonates for all.
—Deeper insight into the dream and its significance calls for the
world's metamorphosis.
—Esthetics are not within our criticism's scope.
—Poetry must be made by all, not one.

After these, shouldn't the defense of ideals that to others represent
nothing seem fruitless? Where should we hurl our arguments? As for
me, I know another trail and I will follow it regardless of whom I annoy.
The solitary walker doesn't always whistle in the dark for fear.

As a general outcry engulfed the first European Surrealists, I fol-
lowed their activity, alone in my poor Athens room, with a stubborn ad-
miration I never renounced nor ever intend to. I didn't see fashion,
advertisement or stylistic vanity behind the angers, hyperboles, blas-
phemies and naïvetés of those so frightful to the bourgeoisie. I left the
superficial views to many Greek and foreign critics, who thus washed
their hands of anything painfully reminiscent of deeper truths long
since uncovered with excess diligence, which they set aside with great

relief. It's true that next to figures like Breton, Éluard, Aragon, de Chirico, Picasso and Dalí, many small and large mediocrities also stirred; should I care? Was any movement ever composed only of peaks?

Rejection of self-delusion, unimpeded knowledge of and appetite for all of life's nuclei, thirst for a free ethics, emotional valuation, and faith in the spirit's absolute power were the most distant but also the most stable peaks of the Surrealistic horizon I gazed upon. When history one day confirms them, we will all see who fought a two-front war, liberating art from asphyxiating rationalism, from static and sterile idealism and from directives imposed from above. No Surrealist conceived of immobilizing life. The mouths that birthed the previous proud phrases would soon birth others aimed solely at integrating possibilities of development and re-adaptation into a theory intended by its very nature to be a continuous *praxis* independent of the existence of a group, a School or a password *du jour*.

Careful study of each Surrealistic teaching easily reveals the secret of its perennially twin meanings, just as an undefended regard of its practical applications reveals its perennially twin faces. One face – the most ephemeral but also the most convincing – is justified by the absolute expression that is a specific historical moment's combative need and which, in its intransigence, reveals another that is destined for more permanent life.

If automatic writing appeared under the flag of the unleashed subconscious actualizing itself outside volition and intolerant of esthetic critique, it also proclaimed the poet's innermost wish to force inspiration (the fusion of luck and excessive sensation) to an unhesitant and accelerated progress beyond ethical, social or esthetic impediments. Genuine spirituality abides in this intent, whose human (and only human) ethics storm their bourgeois idol. Habit, which neutralizes the poet's innate tendency to walk where no one else has walked, had been struck and fell, taking with it the dimmest and most worn, by the rust of the commonplace, part of the world. The point was to relieve the fear that caused people to stop each time before whatever they – being ill-cultivated – considered unesthetic, unethical, illogical or dangerous. Afraid, in other words, of that percentage of human experience which until then was excluded from poetry but had the same rights to expression – all those overwhelming human emotions and horrendous desires that had impatiently and for so long stamped their feet at the prohibitive signs a particular society and its art had erected by conventional and useless borders.

Logos, transmitter *and* receiver of life, now led the way. The world's bewilderment at the sensitive and hard-to-define point of metamorphosis was so intense that it forced virgin expression to vocalize its first phrase at the moment of feeling it, while automatic writing became its best instrument, repulsing calculation and returning imagination to its source.

Now, if everyone couldn't use this instrument, as the theory promised, it was because they lacked the strength to repudiate that calculation by anesthetizing the defenses of their logic, and because they lacked the same psychic overflow or quality of imagination. This is analogous to the variations of poetic wealth in texts written by different people or by the same person at different times. Still, when *some* stand out by virtue of special qualities, the concept of *poet* re-earns its meaning. The student's goodwill must seek and find, in terms of the General theory of Art now, the singular gain offered by automatic writing to Lyric poetry.

PHILOSOPHICALLY one could argue, along with Rolland de Renéville, that the astounding speed of thought's well-augured gallop through such infinite freedom apprehends all possible associations so convincingly that it reveals their unity. And even more fundamentally: that though we can cover the entire spiritual arena by expanding the center of its consciousness through intense devotion, as pure poetry maintained, we can also do so by eliminating it altogether, which is like placing it, as Surrealism had, anywhere on the spiritual circumference, at any time. Still, the motion of this self-intoxicated thought produced some other *de facto* results which, translated into our familiar noetic structure, show the role of lightning-quick thought in exposing life's perpetual becoming as manifested through the ardor of automatic writing. This ardor – basically an intensification of the will to live that caused Professor Gaston Bachelard to exclaim, *"L'ardeur est un temps, ce n'est pas une chaleur!"* – gives the concept of time a new dimension.

Poetic metaphor, by instantly transcending terrible distances, reveals the spiritual physiognomy of things at their very birth. Just as a plant about to bloom withholds from even the most patient observer the phenomenon of its "becoming" but will, if filmed and projected at high speed, unfold in seconds the compact history of its dozen hours, so also any worldly secret, inconceivable under logic's supervision, is mobilized by falling into the domain of human emotion and is visibly projected as a new poetic icon in a matter of seconds. Even unused, this instrument suffices to open our eyes to three fundamental principles: the spirit's absolute reality, the perpetual metamorphosis of life within its motion, and the existence of magnanimous associations among its elements. These principles ended an essentially *slavish* view of life and allowed lyric confession to achieve a precisely phrased and integrated expression.

In time, it entered our consciousness that a different cosmic order, one governed by emotion, ruled every sensation, and that we had the right and the obligation to pursue combinations of speech equivalent to this new order and seek images equivalent to imagination's noetic bliss, if we were to render this sensation more immediate. The experience of automatic writing birthed another psychic function. It empowered the Surrealist but also the poet to be actualized immediately and essentially through what I have elsewhere called *emotional lucidity*. I speak of the courage to attempt the least probable unions of elements, knowing – and here lies perhaps Poetry's superiority over Science – that two simple things in their humble daily role, freed of their servile orbit and brought to swift kinship, can approach the dramatic human enigma, despite our dense material weight. Henceforth, whatever young poets do or think, however they are actualized, possessing by nature now a new way of interpreting the world, they must know that they inhabit regions that Surrealism conquered and they should take the time to turn its commandments over before rejecting them, to see their permanent face and hear the eternal proclamation behind their temporal one.

They would then see that the proclamation "poetry must be made by all, not one" hides *dethronement of the theocratic concept of the poet's nature and destiny*; "beauty does not seem indispensable to us" hides *replacement of the enshrined notion of beauty by a new one*; "esthetics are not the scope of our criticism" hides *end to an era that limits art to dexterity*; "the dream must proclaim the metamorphosis of the world" hides the conviction that *the creator must impose a new order on the elements of the sensible world*; and finally, "a spiritual point exists wherein all contradictions reconcile" hides *faith in hyper-reality and, through it, the much desired unity of all things.*

I AM NOT moved to these conclusions by a conservative mood, nor do I mean to soften some harsh line or edge of Surrealism's paradoxical architecture. I do want, even if by hyperbole, to illuminate some scattered nuances that modern activity engendered in poetry's large body. Perhaps my criticism seems disproportionate to the results. Still, if you can balance in yourself a grandiloquent theory with a humble experience – all of Hegel's philosophy, for instance, with the simple sensation of some scorching sand on a Paros beach – you'll let the wise laugh and become a poet. And if the right thing for a poet is to give a personal impression gained from long service to something, then I must say that my first impression of automatic writing is similar to *expressing your gratitude for the internal and external wealth you were given to develop*, similar, that is, to the applied recognition of the world's autarky in its infinite combinations of goods and virtues.

I have elsewhere had occasion to observe how singularly some painters, like the Douanier Rousseau or the Greek-kilted Theophilos, were motivated by the passion of plastic expression, transubstantiating soul and material object into one artistic event, and how deeply they were saturated by this sacred apprehension of infinite natural wealth in their works.

Modern poets and artists, who sought to reach the psychic purity of primitive vision by opposing paths, ended up walking in tandem by systematically transposing tendencies like Rousseau's and Theophilos' into the spirit and creating works whose inferences are more or less the following:

1) By their infinite combinations, internal and external worlds constitute an actuality whose homeland is the spirit.

2) In the spiritual realm the illegal is non-existent.

3) Poetry is spirit's unmediated expression and its circumference is unimaginably larger than that of consciousness.

4) A significant part of life cannot find expression in the conscious realm.

5) The collaboration of all cosmic elements is possible, achievable and desirable.

6) Objects must be embodied in the exigencies of human desires.

7) Emotional valuation of the world gives a different content to the meaning of life; it restores, in fact, the source of human freedom to the center of our being.

In the spring of 1935 – helped by Embeirikos, who had generously opened his large library to me – I became, awkwardly at first, the amazed observer of a strange world that leapt from my very being without my comprehension. Frequently we would write a plethora of poems and texts in five or ten minutes, smoking endless cigarettes among the canvases of Ernst, Dominguez and Tanguy, either in his cozy apartment or at a family estate in Lesbos that faced the mountains and pelago of the East – poems and texts that a host of critics and literati would later claim had cost us long days of exhausting mental effort! A few days earlier, in the company of a young painter friend, I had first been visited by the aleatory in the guise of a game: we exchanged questions and answers of whose content we were mutually unaware. This game concealed the very mechanism that set the novice at ease by dissolving resistance. I remember how often the result was accurate in associative coherence and iconoplastic originality.

Q – What is the color red?
A – A slap in the face by poppies!

Q – What is glory?
A – A mountain for the centuries to gaze upon!

Q – What is the chrysanthemum?
A – A good-hearted day in a glass.

Q – What are the Pleiades?
A – Secret crypt of poets.

Q – What is Poetry?
A – Intercourse for infinity.

Q – What is the eagle?
A – That which we place much higher than our heads.

Q – What are the four seasons?
A – A peacock, a meadowlark and two large seas.

Or, in a variation of the same game:

— When the bows of the day are loosened
— Heathberries call out their names.

— When the mackerel muddies its waters
— The cat flag changes three colors.

— When a young kore catches a firefly
— The whirl of high noon shines in her head.

— If we had no small children
— Our fields would be orphaned.

— If the roar of the cherry was not enough
— The one the two the three would refresh us.

— If luck were not unloading carobs
— A thousand sailing vessels would tear the seas.

No one has the right to laugh or call these things silly; these things
are games. Aside from the fact that it's okay to play from time to time,
the truth is that these games conceal a most serious principle: they
knock on the door of the unknown; they trust the value of Luck; they
create new prospects; they loosen the poet's fingers, held back for so
many centuries from simile's wealth. Returning now to my forgotten
notebooks that contain a hundred or so poems in series, I am lost in
titles I enjoy to this day for their chromatic quality and, why not, their
unaccountability. In some, the image assumes an objective value: *Dis-
appointment under zero. The little cove and its pulse. Unhanging of a summer
hour. The neighboring lighthouse as a prolonged plunge. With the help of*

asphodels. Country arrow. In the innermost of shiver. Radiant fold structure of *woman. Replacement of destiny. Azure squandering. As foliage by her. The* *miss of April. Her augur. Master of the mistral.* Elsewhere are humorous titles, or ones of ironic or caricaturish mood: *Chiaroscuro husbands. The* R *of proverb. Leftovers of diurnal life. In the gazebo of illegal joy.* Finally, in other titles, the impromptu and the magical reign: *789* B.C. *Aerodynamics. The stones of noise. Historical crutches. In the small port of our small* *desires. Calendar of simplest noon. The two-breasted notebook. Chromatic contemplation. Smart escape wing of matter. Alsing.*

In such a garden more than a few would stop, seized by the comic or the futile. "In the gazebo of illegal joy," what a dumb title, really, for those too dumb to visit it and savor its potent potions! What foolish titles for fools lacking the courage to penetrate the innermost of shiver, to pass, masters of the mistral, from the country arrows or to escort the young miss of April so that, graced by an azure squandering, by unhanging a summer hour, they could abandon themselves to chromatic contemplation and become, with the help of asphodels, the chiaroscuro husbands letting go of historical crutches, throwing the stones of noise, keeping a calendar of simplest noon!

Fine. Those too ashamed to enter a world that replicates the mystery of their creation by a clearly poetic – that is, an animate – act may not proceed to texts whose orbit of esthetic care has been deranged and where their education, such as it is to date, will suffer and be sorely tried. My first texts recall those of Embeirikos. This is not only because of the formal *katharevousa*, which naturally filled any realm deserted by will at that time, but also because of my difficulty in resisting the incursions of external impressions and surrendering to the authentic flow of associative phrases. For example:

On the sea floor of lamentation, shorelines enlarge into perilous precipices *where acrobat virgins balance, nude from the waist up. How did we plunge into* *these azure spheres, traverse these deep-toned films, scythe the heads of celebratory movements? We don't know; nobody knows; perhaps the headache of a* *stork raised by other oceans knows. Again, after silence comes silence. Colossal* *trees shrink the vision nestling like a warm beast in the fork of their fairy tales.* *Airborne lightning and high-jumps pelting us with stars fill our palms with* *rainy olfaction.*

Out of breath the knots of joy, and from the throat of each unfolds a flaxen
lie.

THE NEIGHBORING LIGHTHOUSE
AS A PROLONGED PLUNGE

as well as some isolated phrases from other writings whose full tran-
scription here would be tiresome:

Fundamentally roses are but tears; nothing else, and the departing train's
whistle a breached promise; nothing else, and sorrow a night leaning on April.

DISAPPOINTMENT UNDER ZERO

The sun would gladly have yielded his place but is fascinated by a laugh that
curves and arcs, entertaining the foliage. It monitors his course. He melts of
immortality and takes to his cradle the vegetation turned landscape, the land-
scape turned image and likeness of his emotions.

789 B.C.

My first efforts were influenced not only by Embeirikos but also by
Niketas Randos. I think it useful to include parts of the series "*14 agile*
poems." what light does he borrow to paint his forms?

IV

Day turned its face oversized heliotrope
And instantly I stood at the feet of so many horizons
I'd like to be like it pride of light
Unyielding to the Ganymede of longing
I would desire above all insomniacs as rivals
But their alliance already disarms me
Forces me to imagine polychrome vials
In the shape of mouths of moist girls a crown
Of hostage time's conquests and defeats.

VII

In the erotic penumbra the grassy devotion of our two hands meeting
And beyond the limberness of trails that claim all footfalls
By the approachable fire the palpable sun

I christen emotion with time to make it deadly to endure
Infinity I consummate inspiration.

XII

Butterflies in inverse proportion to the colors of flowers
Kidnap my calm in asymmetrical circles
Savor it while careless time
Floats in its agile willows
In whose gymnasium I learned each time to fit the world
That answers no
When luck's eyelids finally and for good free silence. ➜

XIV

In your despairs the alarums of dovecotes
The chrysanthemum fountains in the rearing thoughts claiming
  your head
So life may be ungirdled by desire
The insects feel the earth
And the shoulders of the sky find bliss in vision
Baptized in magnanimity by silence hawk wings beat
The diffuse meaning of your old small worlds.

The second part of this period ends with poems written somewhat later, in the early part of 1936. In these a hint of esthetic care is evident: ➜

REPLACEMENT OF DESTINY

Sensitive as the knee of a young girl
Searching for her canaries
The hour stirs the courtyard geraniums
The ocean is perpetual discourse
Extracted from ivy
From the climbing dew
It enters woman
And she caresses the uncombed wind
Runs by its side to be undressed
Lest on her tender skin
Fate's finger-marks remain

Her gaze alone reclines the flower beds
Love has its hand high
Above her breast
Nurse of so many dreams
Just there her lovers die.

AZURE SQUANDERING
Among the reeds of dew living its secrets
The peacocks of our radiance open
Wheat
Long-hour dreams
The line of words crossed out
Like a dove flyway lambent in innocence.

THE CONSCIOUSNESS = ID +
EGO I SUPER EGO
e = ID + E + SE

I BELIEVE THAT my last automatic writings, smoother in linguistic expression and almost totally relieved of foreign influence, more clearly show my authentic face. The following three are the only ones I happened to save.

A QUARTER TO SIX
Just as the melancholy voice left the well
The white falcon and the willow's clear signal
Hours changed clothes in the corner garden
The deepest colored bird asked for the ethered grapes
A quarter to six carnations rejoiced
One could not bear it and vanished in the large girl's breast
Another rinsed in water became a nightingale
But the poor man holding barbed wire
No longer had hands – a large insect adorned itself
The festival passed full of fire
There was a peasant woman living on butterflies
A fat shepherd covered with snow
And a clock of rain without shadow…

The ones who loved the sky-depths still gaze on
It's enough to make you wonder about those snails
Perhaps the girls are invisible from the shore

But in the garden they open like umbrellas
The rainbow is the ease of seeing dreams
Just yesterday the little children saw them
Begonias and fruit on a neighbor's sill
How beautiful the peacocks
They call and the day unfolds from joy
You barely see the little carts beneath the sea
Even when a viola remains open in the sunset
The world fades with a creek's whimper
And once again I see the girl I loved so much…
Quiet gleams among the grasses
Only the gardener startles and whispers
"Hush kids – the clouds will notice…"

THE FIVE OF BRINE
This year too the swallows' nest grows fragrant
Told over and over in churches
Day on the doorsill standing
With its apron of berries
Even empty they sweeten you
And the sun's sea in the large rooms
Where the play of waves ripples the ceiling
There you touch your pillow hearing those who cry…

How could such large eyes not contain
The mushrooms of the sky – everyone will leave
And the hair of boulders and windmills
Will blow and flutter

A ship from far away entered the parlor
It smells of green soap and sponged floors
Where can I hide – better to shout
To call the tribe and hang its life – like this
A laundered garment in the sun with wooden pins.

OPENESS – difficult – automatic w breaks open door →
openess (confusion, acceptance)

186

THE SIROCCO'S LAST BREATH

Windowpanes gleamed the joy of a bee
The children sat around the food
And in the street innocent speech ran from the fountains
Finches rang in the higher branches
"Children what do you want so early in the world?"
Spring dresses up with more than rains
A light wind splits the iron doors
The shutters in the hills are banging
"Eah…eoh…eeh…" – and the echo: "uuh…eeh…"
Passengers across a blue peninsula
Arrive from the Pleiades asking for bread
Oh let the river run a little longer
A little longer stir the sea
Let falcons climb the god-high mountains
Carts pass outside sing the Sirocco's last breath
Cart-keepers standing ululate
"Today children today."
A carnation bursts just then into the air
Many shed tears and share words
Others spread grass on earth in silence
So the sun can sleep again
So the sun can sleep again.

Art-Luck-Risk: these three, no other words but these celebrated three (but are they words?) adorned the pages of a year, if not the unveiling of a youth, with chlorophyll's deep green ink, Eros' deep red and sea's blue deep. Its only philosophy was to elevate truth to the simple and profound stir of live organisms. In fact, the only thing I cared about in 1935 was a strong natural existence that could comfortably expand to the outermost limits of a catholic freedom. Whatever was to come, of course, came later…

But when benevolent circumstance brought me that summer to the mountains and shores of the Peloponnese, the Islands, Evoia and the mainland, when it sent me touring the deepest ravines and the frothiest coves in an old pair of pants and a short white shirt, I often reflected,

NOW
2009
same
place—
same?

The word resists the passage of time → Elytis 2009 — είναι
με τον στίχο μου — τραγουδεί

"struggling breast by breast toward the wind," on the deep unity of my love for this poetry, this earth.

The sun, erecting the marble torso of a Hygieia here, the fervent serenity of a Virgin there, was the same sun penetrating and flowing through the tissues of Art's plain leaf like chlorophyll, as I had always imagined and wanted it to represent, for me, the greatest and most magnanimous human expression.

In poetry's countryside the houses no longer have roofs! They are uncovered, and the cicadas wedged in earth's hair sing erotic songs, as do wild birds roosting in the pale blue wrinkles of deserted bays. There, a couple passes at such hours, embracing always. Eros – let us worship – engenders life through all its surfaces and depths, while heart's hands point to brilliant noon... Oh to walk by a companion's side, voicing emotions...to reunite with elements that cause us once and for all to live!

1943.

BOOK DESIGN and composition by John D. Berry, using Aldus Page-Maker 5.0 and a Macintosh IIvx. The type is Janson Text, a digital adaptation by Adrian Frutiger of the 17th-century type of Hungarian punch-cutter Nicholas Kis. Kis spent ten years working in Amsterdam, and his type is one of the sturdy old-style typefaces typical of Dutch printing of the period. In the 20th century, it was adapted for hot-metal typesetting and widely used in fine books. The revived typeface was called "Janson" because it was mistakenly attributed at first to Anton Janson, a Dutch typographer who worked in Leipzig. Janson Text maintains many of the idiosyncracies of the original design and maintains its legibility at text sizes. ¶ The new Copper Canyon Press logo is the Chinese character for poetry, and is pronounced *shi*. It is composed of two simple characters: the righthand character is the phonetic and means "temple" or "hall," while the lefthand character means "speech" or "word." The calligraphy is by Yim Tse, who teaches at the University of British Columbia. ¶ Printed by Thomson-Shore, Inc. Copper Canyon books are printed on acid-free, recycled paper, and are made to last.